Basics and Foundations of LIS

Ansaar Hussain
Tabasum Zehra

ATLANTIC
PUBLISHERS & DISTRIBUTORS (P) LTD

ATLANTIC
PUBLISHERS & DISTRIBUTORS (P) LTD

7/22, Ansari Road, Darya Ganj, New Delhi
Tel.: +91-11-4077 5252, 2327 3880
E-mail: orders@atlanticbooks.com
Web: www.atlanticbooks.com

Published by Atlantic Publishers & Distributors (P) Ltd 2024

Disclaimer

- The author and the publisher have taken every effort to the maximum of their skill, expertise and knowledge to provide correct material in the book. Even then if some mistakes persist in the content of the book, the publisher does not take responsibility for the same. The publisher shall have no liability to any person or entity with respect to any loss or damage caused, or alleged to have been caused directly or indirectly, by the information contained in this book.
- The author has fully tried to follow the copyright law. However, if any work is found to be similar, it is unintentional and the same should not be used as defamatory or to file legal suit against the author.
- If the readers find any mistakes, we shall be grateful to them for pointing out those to us so that these can be corrected in the next edition.
- All disputes are subject to the jurisdiction of Delhi courts only.

Printed & bound in India by Atlantic Print Services

Contents

Part II

INFORMATION SOURCES AND SERVICES

Preface

Library and Information Science (LIS) is an intricate field that plays a fundamental role in the dissemination, organization, and utilization of information in society. As the information landscape continues to evolve, it becomes imperative for professionals in this domain to have a strong grasp of the basics and underlying principles that govern the field. The book, *Basics and Foundations of LIS*, seeks to provide a comprehensive and insightful exploration of the core principles and essential concepts that underpin the field of Library and Information Science. It has been designed to provide BLIS/MLIS students of Indian universities with a solid understanding of the subject, aligning its content with their academic curriculum.

Divided into two distinct yet interrelated parts, this book offers a thorough exploration of the multifaceted dimensions of LIS. In Part I, titled "Library, Information and Society," the journey begins with an exploration of the intricate relationship between libraries, information, and the knowledge-based society where we inhabit. The chapters encompass a wide range of topics, including the various types of libraries that cater to diverse needs, the roles and functions of information institutions, and the laws and legislations that underpin the principles of Library Science. Also, this section delves into the crucial aspects of resource sharing, library networks and consortia, and the ethical considerations inherent to the profession. The discourse is enriched with insights into the role of professional associations and the pivotal organizations shaping the development of library and information services.

Part II of the book, entitled "Information Sources and Services," embarks on a journey through the diverse array of information sources available in our increasingly digital world. The chapters guide readers through the categorization of sources into primary, secondary, and tertiary forms. It delves into the evaluation criteria of these sources and the pivotal role that humans, institutions, and media play in acting as sources of information. The realm of information services is also meticulously examined, covering topics ranging from reference services to literature searches and database management. The importance of user education and information literacy is underscored, along with insights into user and information use studies. The book concludes with a discussion on the strategic aspect of marketing information services, a crucial component in the present-day information-driven society.

Each part and unit have been meticulously crafted to provide an in-depth exploration of the subject matter, presented in a clear and structured manner. This book stands as a testament to the importance of the principles of Library and Information Science in an increasingly interconnected and information-centric world. Its coverage of both theory and practice, coupled with its relevance to the ever-evolving information landscape, ensures that readers are equipped with a robust foundation to excel in their academic pursuits and professional endeavours.

We extend our heartfelt gratitude to educators, practitioners, and scholars in the field of Library and Information Science whose insights have greatly enriched the content of this book. May this book serve as an illuminating guide, fostering a deeper understanding of the vital role libraries and information services play in shaping our knowledge-based society. It is our sincere hope that the book will prove to be a valuable companion on the academic journey of all aspiring professionals in the field.

Ansaar Hussain
Tabasum Zehra

Acknowledgements

I gratefully acknowledge my indebtedness to all those who have extended unsparing assistance in the successful accomplishment of this book. I sincerely thank Almighty Allah (swt) who blessed me with enough courage to write on such a subject. I thank my mother who always inspires me to be a better individual at every sunrise and add a special note to my father, whose memories are too faint and too little, yet bound with strong principles. I also feel indebted to all the colleagues, friends and competitors who motivate me to keep moving forward irrespective of all the odds. Finally, I am thankful to my wife, who has been a consistent support and with whom the dream of writing and publishing a book has been fulfilled.

Ansaar Hussain

PART 1
LIBRARY, INFORMATION AND SOCIETY

Unit 1

Library, Information and Knowledge-Based Society

ROLE OF LIBRARIES IN SOCIETY

Libraries play a fundamental role in society as gateways to knowledge and culture. The resources and services they offer create opportunities for learning, support literacy and education, and help shape the new ideas and perspectives that are central to a creative and innovative society. The primary job of a library is to build up a collection (both print and non-print) and provide access to such material. It helps to develop and promote the spread of knowledge, education and culture and provides facilities for both formal and informal lifelong self-education in the community. It not only furnishes up-to-date facts and information on all subjects to all but also provides reliable information to a variety of users irrespective of their age, caste, creed, religion, sex, profession, etc. A library supports the activities as mentioned in this section, in society:

(i) **Education:** A library supports both formal and informal education by providing access to quality material and resources. Every institution of formal education, be it a school, a college or a university, has a library attached to it. It should have a collection of books relevant to its courses of study. Students should be encouraged to read books and imbibe the knowledge contained in them. In non-formal education where the help of the teacher is minimal, the library is the main resource. A library also provides facilities for lifelong education and helps in self-development in various stages of education.

(ii) **Dissemination of Information:** Libraries provide current and accurate information to the intended users according to their subject of interest. They act as information centres or referral centres for a specific source of information like information regarding employment, social programmes, public utility services, etc.

(iii) **Promotion of Culture:** The first cultural role of the library is that it preserves the cultural heritage of the human race as represented by the books and other documents it holds. Libraries act as cultural centres and promote participation and appreciation of various arts. It helps to broaden our views and develop creative abilities by reading and thinking. It also helps in cultural upliftment by organizing extension services like lectures, seminars and book exhibitions.

(iv) **Recreation:** Libraries help in utilizing leisure time properly by providing books on fiction, magazines, newspapers, etc. Audio-visual materials are also kept in the library for use.

(v) **Preservation of Knowledge:** Libraries maintain archives of old and rare documents thereby preserving the literary heritage for posterity. It stores the literary works in various formats which help researchers do their work.

(vi) **Aid to Research Work:** Libraries assist research scholars in their work by procuring research materials such as books, journals, etc. and by facilitating easy access and discovery of vital research materials. In addition, it provides information and advice regarding publishing, copyright, open access, citations, etc.

INFORMATION AND ITS IMPACT ON SOCIETY

There has been an informatisation of contemporary society. The whole information environment or info sphere is understood to be of growing importance. Even at the untutored level of experience, there is a widespread awareness that information in some ways is affecting a transformation of the social world. All three realms of society—polity, economy and culture are subject to major principles of innovation.

Information and knowledge are deemed to be social wealth. The benefits of this social wealth should be available to all the members of the society. This social wealth is available in a variety of physical forms (for example, books, periodicals, microfilms, computerised databases, etc.). Ordinary citizens require a variety of information in their daily discharge of duties. The use of information certainly affects their mental growth and brings changes in their outlook as well as lifestyles. The impact of information and knowledge may be noticed in a number of human activities. Some of these are: education, research and development (R&D), government activities and mass communications, etc. Society itself has undergone significant changes at different periods of human history and information use has been cited as one of the most important agents of this change. Three stages are generally identified in the course of societal evolution. They are: the agrarian society, the industrial society and the post-industrial society. In all these societal transformations, the use of information played a vital role. The emergence of a post-industrial society in the 20th century is based on technological developments, and the revolution and processing of information and its subsequent use.

INFORMATION SOCIETY: DEFINITION, MEANING AND EVOLUTION

An information society is a society where the usage, creation, distribution, manipulation and integration of information are significant activities. Its main drivers are information and communication technologies, which have resulted in rapid information growth in society and are somehow changing all aspects of social organization, including education, economy, health, government, warfare, and levels of democracy. The people who are able to partake in this form of society are sometimes called either computer users or even digital citizens.

According to Branscomb (1986), "It is a society where the majority of people are engaged in creating, gathering, storage, processing or distribution of information". Ronfeldt (1992) is of the opinion that "information society is one which sees the steady blurring of the boundaries, which presently separate computer hardware, communication systems and satellites, global networks and more".

The information society is seen as a successor to the industrial society. The concept emerged during the 1970s and throughout the 1980s rapidly gained popularity and currency, its proponents ranging from scholars and academic authors to popular writers. Prominent among the first group of writers were Masuda, who in the Japanese context, perceived an eventual transition of the society to the point at which the production of information values became the driving force for the development of the society. The second writer belonging to this group was Tom Stonier, who perceived the dawning of a new age for Western Society. He draws explicit parallels and contrasts between industrial and information societies. Although not very comfortable with the term information society, Daniel Bell did much to sustain it through his work on post-industrial society. Bell argued that the increased part played by science in the productive process, the rise to prominence of professional, scientific and technical groups and the introduction of computer technology, are all the evidence of a new axial principle at the core of the socio-economic system, namely the centrality of theoretical knowledge. The emerging social framework of the information society builds upon this base. Information increasingly becomes a source of added value and thus of wealth. A growing portion of workers is employed in the information sphere. The important factor, enabling discourse to shift from post-industrialism to information society is the massive growth in the economic significance of IT.

Although, in its current form, it is something of a novelty, it would be a mistake to think that the idea of information society is entirely of recent origin. Alongside the analytical strands of thought about social change, we also find another theme, "technological utopianism". In fact, the writings of Masuda,

Stonier and Naisbitt depict a new kind of society which on the one hand, points to an empirical analysis but, on the other, is full of good society imagery. The newness and attraction of these ideas and the vigour, with which they were expressed, fired the public imagination and helped to sustain the interest in the concept of the information society and its literature.

FACTORS DETERMINING THE ARRIVAL OF INFORMATION SOCIETY

The pre-requisite for an information society is a telecommunication-based information service infrastructure, which gradually builds up until at some point a critical mass of terminal users will be connected to a more or less universal network. The term refers mainly to the social structure of the post-industrial society. It describes the characteristics and the structure of the society of which the driving force will be the production of information values and not material values. In considering when it will be realised it is necessary to look at the four stages of technological development which have to be achieved before we say that an information society has arrived. These four stages are:

(i) Science-based computerisation, where computers are used extensively in national scale projects;

(ii) Management-based computerisation in both the government and in businesses;

(iii) Society-based computerisation in which computers are used for the benefit of the society as a whole;

(iv) Individual-based computerisation where each individual has access to the terminal and computer information to solve problems. As a result, creativity will flourish in this high mass knowledge creation society.

The most advanced stage of information society appears to be high mass knowledge creation society. It may also be inferred that a high degree of computerisation, large volumes of electronic data processing and employment of information technology with telecommunication-based information service structure, are the main criteria, that signify whether a society or nation has become an information society or not.

KNOWLEDGE SOCIETY: DEFINITION AND CHARATERISTICS

Knowledge society is a society that is capable enough to identify, produce, process, transform, disseminate and use information to build and apply knowledge for human development. In such a society, knowledge plays a crucial and decisive role, with its entire mechanisms and organisation giving an impetus for new knowledge, ensuring the conditions of its inception and use, which further increases new knowledge, etc. Knowledge society is, therefore, structured on knowledge. It simply penetrates into the complete functioning of society, including the entire development and progress. In a knowledge society, the traditional measures of competitiveness such as labour costs, recourse endowments and infrastructure are replaced by new dimensions such as patents, research and development (R&D) and the availability of knowledge workers. The emphasis is not on the knowledge anybody has but the knowledge one produces. Knowledge resides exclusively in people. Therefore, it is clear that the greatest wealth of any nation, any society is its people. This is a vastly underused resource, which offers the opportunity for any country to make a major breakthrough and catch up with countries that are presently more developed.

There are many components of a knowledge society. First of all, there is a huge quantity of newly created knowledge in all fields continuously expanding and exponentially growing. Statistics are known about the exponential growth of knowledge in the entire past historical period, including all kinds of publications as one of the proofs of the whole process. The situation with the total number of researchers in the world and the entire research capacity can be compared with past times. Not only the number of literate people, but also that of the educated people has increased enormously in the whole world. To this we need to add new possibilities of informing, communicating and teamwork which were incomparable and unthinkable earlier. Modern ICT has connected the world on all levels so closely, that the entire globe has become a net from which we can connect practically from any one point to another. The possibilities and the speed of communicating, the transfer of information and knowledge and the acquisition of new ideas as well as views have drastically changed. All this creates conditions for the development of new knowledge and awareness, uninterrupted progress, and development. This process is advancing with such speed and dimension that all those who are not directly or indirectly involved will ultimately stay on the fringes. Knowledge is no more connected with an individual. As far as characteristics of a perfect knowledge society are concerned, all people have:

(i) Open and timely access to information and knowledge;
(ii) The capacity to absorb and interpret information; and
(iii) Avenues and opportunities to use knowledge and decision making and for transformation to higher quality lives.

ESTABLISHMENT OF A KNOWLEDGE-BASED SOCIETY

A careful analysis of the literature available on knowledge society reveals that establishing a knowledge-based society is clearly desirable and, looking from the perspective of the imminent future, it may well be the only possible society.

> The establishment of such a society is a political process—it requires political decision making and political actions. The process of establishing a knowledge-based society would be facilitated if one would define benchmarks, indicators providing quantifiable measurements indicating whether we are going in the right direction and how far we have progressed. In fact, the essence of progress is to assure order among changes and preserve changes amid order. (Slaus, 2007)

It may be stated that the emergence of a knowledge society means an ever-increasing demand for a well-educated and skilled workforce across the entire economy. In connection to this, it is worth noting that the appointment of the National Knowledge

Commission (NKC) by the Government of India has been a step in the right direction. The NKC had been entrusted with the preparation of a blueprint for reform of our knowledge-related institutions and infrastructure. It has submitted its report which will take us a long way in a knowledge society.

KNOWLEDGE-BASED ECONOMY (KBE)

Knowledge and technology have become increasingly complex, raising the importance of links between firms and other organisations as a way to acquire specialised knowledge. A parallel economic development has been the growth of innovation in services in advanced economies. Most advanced economies have undergone significant structural changes in recent years. One of the key characteristics of the changes is the growing importance of knowledge in all sectors of economic activities. These economies have developed from an agricultural economy in which land is the key resource, then to an industrial economy in which natural resources and labour are the main resources, and now to a knowledge-based economy (KBE) in which knowledge is the key resource. In order to facilitate an economic analysis, distinctions can be made between different kinds of knowledge which are important in the knowledge-based economy: know-what, know-why, know-how and know-who. "The knowledge-based economy" is an expression coined to describe trends in advanced economies towards greater dependence on knowledge, information and high skill levels, and the increasing need for ready access to all of these by the business and public sectors.

The term KBE was first coined by the Organisation for Economic Cooperation and Development (OECD) and defined as "economies which are directly based on the production, distribution and use of knowledge and information" (OECD, 1996). The World Bank has recently developed the knowledge assessment methodology and score cards. They have formulated a set of sixty-three variables as proxies for four areas that they consider essential in the development of knowledge-based economy (KBE). They are:

(i) Economic and institutional regimes to provide incentives for the efficient use of existing and new knowledge and flourishing of entrepreneurship;

(ii) An educated and skilled population to create, share and use knowledge well;

(iii) A dynamic information infrastructure to facilitate the effective communication and processing of information; and

(iv) An effective innovation system of firms, research centres, universities and other organisations. A knowledge-based society has the following ten characteristics:

1. Institutional structures that provide incentives for entrepreneurship and the use of knowledge.
2. Availability of skilled labour and a good education system.
3. Access to Information and Communication Technologies (ICT).
4. A vibrant innovation landscape that includes the academic world, the private sector and the civil society.
5. An increased demand for workers in STEM subjects.
6. The development of "clusters" of industries in certain geographic regions.
7. A steep rise in the number of patents.
8. Global diffusion of knowledge.
9. Knowledge exchange between industries.
10. Innovation-driven producers and users (for example, open-source software and customer feedback).

Unit 2
Types of Libraries

DEFINITION OF A LIBRARY

A library is a collection of resources in a variety of formats that is organised by information professionals or other experts who provide convenient physical, digital, bibliographic or intellectual access and offer targeted services and programs with the mission of educating, informing or entertaining a variety of audiences and the goal of stimulating individual learning and advancing society as a whole. In other words, a library can be defined as a collection or group of collections of books and/or other print or non-print materials organised and maintained for use (reading, consultation, study, research, etc.). Libraries are organised to facilitate access to information, are staffed by librarians and other trained professionals to provide services and to meet the information needs of the users. A library provides access to physical (hard copies) or digital (soft copies) materials and may be a physical location or a virtual space or both. A library's collection can include printed materials and other physical resources in many formats such as DVD, CD and cassette as well music and other contents held on bibliographic databases. Libraries are broadly classified into the following three types:

ACADEMIC LIBRARIES

An academic library is a library that is attached to an educational institution like a school, college or university and serves two complementary purposes that is to support the school's curriculum and to support the research of the faculty as well as the students. The use of libraries for reading and referencing is an integral part of learning, teaching and research. Libraries in schools and colleges provide facilities for students and teachers to read books or consult them for reference, thus widening the scope of classroom learning and teaching. University libraries provide additional facilities for higher learning, research and dissemination of knowledge. The three types of academic libraries are discussed in this section:

1. School Library

In India, schools are further divided into four groups according to the levels of education they cater to. Schools can therefore be primary, middle, secondary, and senior secondary.

Objectives of School Libraries: All types of schools have a library with the objectives to awaken and foster interest in reading books, create a love for books, promote reading habits and inculcate communication skills through extra-curricular activities like storytelling, viewing and discussions on audio/visual programmes, workshops, etc.

Functions of School Libraries: In order to attract students to the library and develop their interest and curiosity, a school library should acquire a good stock of teaching and learning materials for students and teachers, display books in a classified order, provide functional physical facilities such as building, furniture and equipment and hire qualified, committed staff.

Services Offered by School Libraries: School libraries offer the following services:

(i) Lending,

(ii) Reading,

(iii) Reference services, and

(iv) Guidance and advisory services with the objective of inculcating an interest in children for reading books and other materials.

2. College Library

The support of a library at the college level is essential to broaden the minds of young students to meet new challenges. Compared to school education, college education is completely different for them. The students have to depend on the college library for their studies and develop a habit of self-learning.

Objectives of College Libraries: The chief objectives of a college library are to give the enrolled students a wider and deeper understanding of the various disciplines, provide guidance for higher studies and self-learning, prepare them for shouldering higher responsibilities in schools, government departments, civic organizations, commercial establishments, business and industrial companies, etc., train them to become more enlightened, knowledgeable and responsible citizens, and prepare them for varied professions like law, medicine, engineering, technology, etc.

Functions of College Libraries: A college library performs different functions like to assist its parent body to carry out the requirements of its teachers and students regarding reading, studying and doing research, provide infrastructural facilities such as functional building, furniture, equipment, etc., provide latest editions and multiple copies of curriculum-based textbooks and recommended books for their study, equip the library with a wide range of reference books, develop a collection of latest books in different subjects and periodicals including their back volumes, procure multi-media material and computer-aided teaching-learning material, subscribe to important newspapers and other lighter materials such as popular fiction, biographies, travelogues, art books, etc. for recreational purposes and preserve previous years' question papers to help the students.

Services Offered by College Libraries: The college library staff provides the following services:

- Provide reading, lending and textbook services;
- Guide students in the use of manual or computerised catalogues;
- Assist in locating books and reference books from the shelves;
- Train and instruct students to use library resources in an effective and efficient manner;

- Provide information, reference and referral services to all library members;
- Display new books and lists of multi-media materials;
- Procure adequate multi-media materials and equipment to render them usable; and
- Reprographic services.

3. University Library

A university library is established, administered, and maintained to assist the university in five major functions such as—teaching and learning, research and generation of new knowledge, dissemination and publication of research results, conservation of knowledge, and ideas and extension programmes. The university libraries have to play a very challenging and difficult role to satisfy the demands of a large group of students, research and post-doctoral research scholars, members of the various academic and executive bodies of the management, administrative, and professional staff of the university.

Objectives of University Libraries: A university library plays a very important role by supporting and helping the university in achieving its aims and objectives. It has to cope with the multidimensional activities of the university. Its objectives are to provide intellectual and managerial leadership among the professionals in various fields of government, industry, health, engineering, law, medicine, defence, education, agriculture and inculcate in them a sense of social purpose, guide researchers in all areas mentioned above so that the results can be harnessed to improve the quality of the life of the people and conserve knowledge and ideas for posterity.

Functions of University Libraries: The major functions of the university library are to develop collections of print and media resources in a wide variety of subjects for learning, teaching, research, publication, etc. organize and store the acquired collection/knowledge for use by the readers, provide a variety of library, documentation and information services (both responsive and anticipatory) and encourage students, researchers and teachers in using the library for pleasure, self-discovery, personal growth and sharpening of intellectual skills.

Services Offered by University Libraries: The nature and efficiency of services provided vary from library to library. With the introduction of information and communication technologies, most of the university libraries have automated their operations using Library Management Software (LMS) and are providing a variety of services which were not existent before. A university library provides the following services:

- Reading and lending service;
- Bibliographic instructions and library orientation;
- Assistance in the use of the library catalogue and locating documents;
- Reference and information services;
- Current Awareness Services (CAS);
- Selective Dissemination of Information (SDI);
- Bibliographic services;
- Inter-Library Loan (ILL) service;
- Reprographic services;
- Maintenance of newspaper clippings;
- Maintenance of vertical files containing pamphlets, prospectuses, reports and question papers of previous years' examinations;
- Preservation of documents;
- Exhibitions and special displays;
- Special lectures, demonstration of new software and services; and
- User education, user-oriented seminars and workshops.

PUBLIC LIBRARIES

A public library is a library that is accessible by the general public and is usually funded by public sources, such as taxes. It is operated by librarians and library professionals. There are five fundamental characteristics shared by public libraries:

- They are generally supported by taxes (usually local, though any level of government can and may contribute);
- They are governed by a board to serve the public interest;
- They are open to all, and every community member can access the collection;
- They are on an entirely voluntary basis that is no one is ever forced to use the services provided;
- They provide library and information services without any charges.

Public libraries have an impact on five major facets of public life. They are education, social policy, information, cultural entertainment, and economic development. UNESCO in collaboration with IFLA published a manifesto on public libraries in 1995. This manifesto emphasizes the following aspects:

- The public library, being the local gateway to knowledge, provides a basic condition for lifelong learning, independent decision-making and cultural development of the individual and social groups;
- A living force for education, culture and information, and an essential agent for the fostering of peace and spiritual welfare in the minds of men and women;
- The local centre of information, making all kinds of knowledge and information readily and freely available to its users;
- Accessible for all, regardless of age, sex, religion, nationality, language or social status;
- And lastly, the libraries which have collections and services, all types of appropriate media and modern technologies, as well as materials with high quality and have relevance to local needs and conditions. Materials must reflect current trends and the evolution of the society, as well as the memory of human endeavour and imagination.

Objectives of a Public Library

The objectives of a public library are as follows:

(i) Help the lifelong self-education of one and all;

(ii) Furnish up-to-date facts and information on all subjects to everyone;

(iii) Distribute all recorded information to the citizens in an unbiased and balanced way to help them discharge their duties towards local, national and international affairs;

(iv) Convey new knowledge to the researchers as early as possible;

(v) Preserve the cultural heritage of the country;

(vi) Provide facility for fruitful utilization of leisure time; and

(vii) Work for the continued social well-being of citizens as the in-charge of all material.

Role Played by Public Libraries in a Knowledge Society

A public library plays a crucial role in the following spheres of life:

Education: Especially self-education (non-formal) where public libraries have a long and successful history, also in lifelong learning which is an irreplaceable way of personal growth in today's world.

Information: Ensuring access to information for all has become an obligation in the realization of human rights.

Cultural Enrichment: Access to different sources of information and knowledge for all. This also includes literacy advancement, which today also means information literacy, as well as awareness about the need to read as the main process to acquiring knowledge, which means not only to see something, but to be informed and acquire knowledge about it.

Economic Development: Public libraries act as a form of local economic information service, in accordance with the main economic aspects of the areas such as tourism, agriculture, manufacturing, technologies, etc. Public libraries are also the most appropriate places to obtain the required information and statistics concerning all the above.

SPECIAL LIBRARIES

A special library is a library that provides specialised information resources on a particular subject, serves a specialised and limited clientele, and delivers specialised services to that clientele. These include corporate libraries, government libraries, law libraries, medical libraries, museum libraries and news libraries.

Objectives of a Special Library

A special library is an integral part of a parent institution and fully supports its programmes and activities. The main objectives of a special library are to develop a current as well as a retrospective collection in core subjects based on the projects and programmes of the parent organisation. Their aim is to promptly provide the latest information about significant developments in the field whenever requested by the users. It provides all types of academic, technical, and documentary support to render appropriate services to the specialists.

Functions and Services of a Special Library

A special library performs various functions and provides services as mentioned in this section.

- Performs exhaustive literature search to compile comprehensive lists;
- Selects, procures, organises, stores and retrieves current information required by the users;
- Analyses, synthesises and evaluates available information;
- Provides state-of-the-art reports, critical reviews, monographs, research reports and reprints;
- Lending and Reference Service;
- Provides indexes, abstracts and extracts;
- Prepares accession lists, bulletins, newsletters, summaries, handbooks or manuals and bibliographies;

- Issues documents including inter-library loans;
- Renders reference and referral services; and
- Provides Current Awareness Services (CAS), Selective Dissemination of Information (SDI) and Translation Services.

In addition, there are certain other types of libraries that exist. These are:

NATIONAL LIBRARY

A national library is a library established by a government as a country's pre-eminent repository of information. Unlike public libraries, these rarely allow citizens to borrow books. Often, they include numerous rare, valuable or significant works. A national library is that library which has the duty of collecting and preserving the literature of the nation within and outside the country. Thus, national libraries are those libraries whose community is the nation at large. Examples include the British Library, the Bibliothèque Nationale de France in Paris and National Library of India in Kolkata. In most countries, there is a national library maintained with national resources, usually entrusted with the responsibility of publishing a national bibliography. National libraries collect and preserve the nation's literature. Most national libraries receive, by legal right (or copyright, or deposit), one free copy of each book and periodical printed in the country.

Objectives of a National Library

The main objective of a national library is to identify, acquire, organise, store, and retrieve all print and non-print documents published within or on a particular country and by or on all the nationals of that country in other countries.

Functions of the National Library

The functions of the national library recommended in the Final Report of the Regional Seminar on the Development of National Library are to:

- Provide leadership among the nation's libraries;
- Serve as a permanent depository for all publications issued in the country;
- Acquire other types of materials;
- Provide bibliographical services;
- Serve as a coordinating centre for co-operative activities; and
- Provide services to the government.

It may be pointed out that Lor (1997), drawing on the work of Line and Line (1979) and IFLA (1992), established three dimensions to the work of the national library, identifying functions concerned with,

(i) Heritage,

(ii) Infrastructure, and

(iii) Delivery of comprehensive national library service.

Of these three dimensions, the delivery of comprehensive national library service is worth mentioning. Under it, he considers the following aspects:

- Acquisition and processing of library material for other libraries;
- Recycling and disposing of materials acquired for other libraries;
- Central support of reference, consultation, loan and document delivery services by other libraries;
- System-wide professional and technological leadership;
- Advice to other libraries;
- System-wide planning and coordination;
- Research and development related to the development of the service; and
- Literacy programmes using constituent and affiliated libraries as centres for literacy promotion.

DIGITAL LIBRARY

A digital library, also called an online library or e-library, is an online database of digital objects that can include text, still images, audio, video, digital documents, or other digital media formats or a library accessible through the Internet. Objects can consist of digitised content like print or photographs, as well as originally produced digital content like word processor files or social media posts. In addition to storing content, digital libraries provide means for organising, searching and retrieving the content contained in the collection. In addition, digital libraries are also defined as a set of electronic resources and associated technical capabilities for creating, searching and using information. In this sense, they are an extension and enhancement of information storage and retrieval systems that manipulate digital data in any medium (text, images, sounds, statistic and dynamic images) and exist in distributed networks. The content of digital libraries includes data and metadata. They describe various aspects of the data (i.e. representation, creator, owner, reproduction rights) and metadata that consists of links or relationships to other data or metadata whether internal or external to the digital library.

Characteristics of a Digital Library

Digital libraries have the following characteristics:

- These are the digital face of traditional libraries that include both digital collections and traditional, fixed media collections. So, they encompass both electronic and paper materials.
- They also include digital materials that exist outside the physical and administrative bounds of a single digital library.
- They include the processes and services that constitute the backbone and nervous system of libraries. However, such traditional processes though forming the basis of digital library work will have to be revised and extended to accommodate the differences between new digital media and traditional fixed media.
- Digital libraries provide a coherent view of all of the information contained within a library, no matter its form or format.

- They serve particular communities or constituencies, as traditional libraries do now, though those communities may be widely dispersed throughout the network.
- Digital libraries will require both the skills of librarians as well as those of computer scientists to be viable.

ISSUES AND CHALLENGES IN THE CREATION OF DIGITAL LIBRARY

The optimism and hype from the early 1990s have been replaced by the realisation that building digital libraries will be a difficult, expensive, and long-term effort (Lynch, 1995). Creating effective digital libraries poses serious challenges. The integration of digital media into traditional collections will not be easy like previous new media (such as video and audio tapes), because of the unique nature of digital information—it is less fixed, easily copied and remotely accessible by multiple users simultaneously. Some of the more serious issues facing the development of digital libraries are outlined in this section.

1. Building Digital Collections: One of the primary issues in creating digital libraries is building digital collections. Obviously, for any digital library to be viable, it must have a digital collection with critical mass to make it really useful. There are three methods of building digital collections:

- Digitisation—converting paper and other media in existing collections to digital form;
- Acquisition of original digital works created by publishers and others. For example, electronic books, journals, etc.;
- Access to external materials not held in-house by providing pointers to websites.

2. Technical Architecture: This architecture will include components such as high-speed local networks and fast connectors to the Internet, relational databases that support a variety of digital formats, full-text search engines to index and provide access to resources and electronic document management functions that will aid the overall management of digital resources. The availability and management of such a sophisticated architecture is also a challenge for the establishment of a digital library.

3. Metadata: Metadata is another issue central to the development of digital libraries. Metadata is the data that describes the content and attributes of any particular item in a digital library. It is a concept familiar to librarians because it is one of the primary tasks that librarians do. For example, they create cataloguing records that describe the documents. While there are formal library standards for metadata, namely AACR-2R, such records are very time consuming to create and require specially trained personnel to undertake such work.

4. Naming, Identifiers and Persistence: Another important issue related to metadata is the problem of naming in a digital library. Names are strings that uniquely identify digital objects and are part of any document's metadata. Names are important in a digital library just as the ISBN number is in a traditional library. They are needed to uniquely identify digital objects. Any system of naming that is developed must be permanent and be lasting indefinitely. It means the name cannot be bound up with a specific location. Both must be separate. The name must remain valid whenever documents are moved from one location to another. Three of the schemes proposed to solve this problem are: PURLs, URNs, and Digital Object Identifiers (DOIs).

5. Copyright/Rights Management: One of the barriers to digital library development is copyright. The current paper-based concept of copyright breaks down in the digital environment because the control of copies is lost. Digital objects are less fixed, easily copied and remotely accessible by multiple users simultaneously. The problem for libraries is that they do not own their information and do not hold the copyright of the material they possess. Therefore, they cannot freely digitise and provide access to copyrighted materials in their own collections. Instead they will have to develop mechanisms for managing copyright. Such mechanisms which allow them to provide information without violating copyright are called rights management.

6. Preservation: Another important issue associated with digital libraries is preservation that is keeping digital information available in perpetuity. In the preservation of digital materials, the real issue is technical obsolescence. In other words, preservation of digital information will mean constantly coming up with new technical solutions.

VIRTUAL LIBRARY

A virtual library is a selected and organised collection of units (nodes) of documentary resources that are spread everywhere (space) and are accessible always (time), where individuals and groups as authors (producers of documents), publishers (editors of documents) and readers (users of documents) are linked across the global electronic network and related in different ways to documents that are:

- Fast and easily obtainable
- Available in their full version.

In other words, it is a library with little or no physical plant of books, periodicals, reading space or support staff but one that disseminates selective information directly to distributed library customers, usually electronically. It has been a traditional library that has transformed some significant portions of its information delivery channels into electronic formats, so that many or most of its customers do not need to visit the library to obtain information.

Characteristics of a Virtual Library

A virtual library has the following important characteristics:

- There is no corresponding physical collection.
- Documents will be available in electronic formats.
- Documents are not stored in any one location.
- Documents can be accessed from any workstation.
- Documents are retrieved and delivered as and when required.
- Effective search and browse facilities are available.

Services by a Virtual Library

A virtual library offers services in the following five spheres:

Resource discovery services; Access services; Reference services; Instruction service; and Patron account service.

1. Resource discovery service: This service provides users with a variety of tools and approaches for discovering the existence of appropriate resources. Typically, a user will search one or more repositories of metadata, full-text or images to identify and select resources. Three types of searches are possible:

(i) Single Database Searching,

(ii) Broadcast Searching, and

(iii) Integrative Searching.

2. Access service: Once the user has discovered the resources, the access service addresses the concern of getting the information to the user. It depends on the users' paying capacity.

3. Reference service: Both cost and quality of service are important considerations for establishing reference service. With the limited resources made available the library must consider priority of serving various user groups.

4. Instruction service: This service focuses on appropriate training and instruction activities to assist users. Users will need to know how to use the new and emerging technologies. But, more importantly, they may need help in understanding what resources are available, their costs and their authenticity.

5. Patron (user) account service: This service area addresses user activities including accessing account information through the network, using the service to order materials or paying for the resources.

HYBRID LIBRARY

The hybrid library is a term that has entered the parlance of library and information profession recently. It is stated that the term "hybrid library" was first coined in 1998 by Chris Rusbridge in an article published in *D-Lib Magazine*. Hybrid library is a term used by librarians to describe libraries containing a mix of traditional print library resources and the growing number of electronic resources. In other words, they are a mix of traditional print materials such as books and magazines as well as electronic-based materials such as downloadable audiobooks, e-books and electronic journals, etc. The challenge associated with the management of a hybrid library is to encourage end-user resource discovery and information use, in a variety of formats and from a number of local and remote sources, in a seamlessly integrated way.

Hybrid libraries evolved in the 1990s when electronic resources became easily available for libraries to acquire for public use. In the beginning, electronic resources were typically accessed for materials distributed on media such as CD-ROM or searchers of special databases. OCLC helped to push libraries towards acquiring digital resources by providing a centralized technology resource for participating libraries. Now, with the widespread availability of digital content, it includes Internet resources and documents which are online, such as e-prints.

Issues in Hybrid Library

Some of the issues faced by the hybrid libraries are: digital divide, interoperability, collection development, ownership of electronic resources and preservation of digital media.

Digital Divide: The term "digital divide" is used to describe the gap between those with information technology knowledge and those who do not possess this knowledge. To access such libraries, both the staff and users need to have digital knowledge.

Interoperability: The concept of interoperability is focused on technical interoperability between information systems. The hybrid libraries own and subscribe to different resources in different formats. Some of the common formats are e-journals, serials, print monographs, CD and DVD. The main components of digital library framework are user interfaces, repository, handles system and search system. The handle system and search system are the major components that should be designed with interoperability features to search across different repositories owned by different vendors.

Collection Development: It is another challenge faced by hybrid libraries. The process is similar to that of a traditional library. In fact, hybrid libraries follow the same policies and procedures followed in a traditional library collection development.

Ownership of Electronic Resources: This is one of the problematic aspects faced by hybrid libraries. Ownership of electronic materials is virtual and not physical. There are no clear policies about the ownership of electronic materials once the subscription is cancelled or expired.

Preservation of Digital Media: To make the preservation of digital media cost-effective, standardization of different media formats is required. The three possible approaches to the problem are:

(i) Technology preservation,

(ii) Emulation, and

(iii) Migration.

In technology preservation method, both hardware and software related to digital information are preserved. This may not be cost-effective because changes to hardware and different versions of software need to be either maintained or constantly upgraded. In emulation, some emulator software programmes will mimic the hardware and software of the original data and display in the original format. In migration, digital information is converted to a standard media with a standard format.

Children's Library

A children's library is a place where there are books as well as committed and enthusiastic staff to assist the children to develop their reading skills. These libraries depend on financial and staffing resources and come in a variety of styles.

Reference Libraries

A reference library does not lend books and other items. The materials available in such libraries can only be read within the library itself. Typically, such libraries are used for research purposes, for example at a university. Some items at reference libraries may be historical and even unique. Many lending libraries contain a "reference section", which holds books, such as dictionaries, which are common reference books and are therefore not lent out.

Research Library

A research library is a collection of materials on one or more subjects. A research library supports scholarly or scientific research and generally includes primary as well as secondary sources. It maintains a permanent collection and attempts to provide access to all necessary materials. A research library is most often an academic or a national library, but a large special library may have a research library within its special field and a very few of the largest public libraries also serve as research libraries.

Unit 3
Information Institutions

DEFINITION OF INFORMATION INSTITUTIONS

Information institutions are organizations that are charged with the responsibility to provide information resources and services to meet the educational, informational, cultural and/or recreational needs of the citizens. Information institutions such as libraries and archival institutions are the navigators and evaluators of information. They are the gateways to knowledge and hence their resources and services are crucial to the development of information literate, creative and innovative societies. Information institutions preserve culture and heritage and hence foster continuity, promote information access, stimulate the search for knowledge and support literacy. They are important key players in the fight against disinformation, since they are uniquely placed to teach critical thinking. These institutions are critical learning spaces that could promote intercultural education if the resources they hold are leveraged. They shape their collections and activities in a manner that promote the community and their information literacy programs are designed to strengthen information literacy and to promote people's abilities to engage in learning. Such institutions give access to primary sources of information and thereby promote critical thinking and also equip one with skills that can enable its users to identify, select and use the information it contains. All such institutions employ highly trained professionals who, in addition to administering the organisation, engage in three kinds of activities:

(i) Collection development: This includes selecting, acquiring, preserving and in some cases, weeding of the collections.

(ii) Systematic organisation and classification of resources in order to ensure their effective retrieval and use.

(iii) Provision of appropriate access to the collection by the primary clientele and other designated users.

EVOLUTION OF INFORMATION INSTITUTIONS

In the literature of library and information science, we do not come across studies exclusively devoted to the evolution, development, organisational structure and functions of information institutions. However, if we examine the institutions that have come up during 20th century, especially in the latter part, we can discern a typical pattern in their growth. However, this pattern could be perceived only in the industrially advanced countries of the West. As it happens, their influence extended to the Third World countries also; as a result many Third World countries have accepted the Western Model in designing and developing their own institutions.

The report entitled "Into the Information Age: A Perspective for Federal Action on Information" prepared by Arthur D. Little Inc. describes the development of information institutions in the USA. In doing so, the report identifies three basic models of information transfer. The report contends that the process of transfer of information/knowledge comprises a chain of activities, the main links being generator, editor, publisher of primary publications, indexing and abstracting journal producers, libraries, documentation and information centres, on-line services, information companies and the end-user. The institutions that normally perform these activities can broadly be grouped into three categories indicated below:

(i) Knowledge creating institutions (under this category come: research laboratories, R&D institutions, institutions of higher education and research centres attached to universities, etc.),

(ii) Knowledge/information processing and dissemination institutions such as: publishers of books and journals/ statistical data organisations, science and technology data centres and the like, and

(iii) Institutions that collect, store, process, disseminate and service knowledge/information recorded in various forms such as libraries.

A careful analysis in this aspect reveals that over the years, there has been an increasing interaction and cooperation among all these categories of institutions. It may also be noted that with the application of modern technologies in information generation, processing, dissemination, distribution and use, many of these functions are getting blended, reducing the distinction between different link elements of the information chain. At this point in time, the different types of institutions mentioned above operate with their distinct identities.

GROWTH PATTERN OF INFORMATION INSTITUTIONS

The effort made by Arthur D. Little Inc. in the form of Vincent Giuliano's report remains the model historic perspective on growth pattern of information and institutions. The three modes considered under this model are described in this section:

1. Discipline-oriented Information Transfer (Era-I): The basic principle associated with Era-I organisations is that they are created to provide knowledge and so are to support education, research, and development. Knowledge and information are generally disseminated through journals, monographs, seminars, and meetings usually associated with academic and research institutions, learned societies, professional bodies, etc. Access to the primary information is provided through bibliographical tools like indexing and abstracting services which are made available by institutions facilitating access to documents and use, mostly the libraries and other departments attached to the parent bodies. The user community comprises academicians, scholars, research workers, and students. Financial support to the system is derived from internal budgetary provisions, grants, and subsidies provided by the government. This traditional system of free information service has been continuing since a long time, notwithstanding the difficulties encountered every now and then.

2. Mission-oriented Information Transfer (Era-II): The organising principle behind the Era-II systems is that they exist to accomplish a specific job. For example, information systems developed during 1950s and 1960s have been created to provide information support to mission-oriented agencies such as AEC, NASA and similar purpose-oriented projects. In this context, the information transfer process is characterised by a defined need for coordinating and using information and knowledge concurrently from a variety of disciplines. For example, in the case of NASA mission, inputs of information from diverse subjects like electronics, biology, medicine, aeronautics, chemistry and physics, etc. are necessary. In this context, information is disseminated through technical reports, besides conventional publications like journals. Technical information centres attached to the main agencies undertake the responsibility of developing interpretative information services meant for the user communities comprising scientists, engineers, technologists, and managers belonging to the agency. The system has a feedback mechanism, which enables it to determine the performance efficacy of the system.

3. Problem-oriented Information Transfer (Era-III): The organising principle that paved the way for the establishment of information organisations in this era is solving societal problems by exploiting appropriate information. Systems that evolved in this period reflect a context in which information is used in problem solving such as economic development, industrial planning, agricultural productivity and environmental protection, etc. The institutions that came into existence during this period had the capability to handle specific type of information and could provide new products and services. However, they could not evolve appropriate structures. The systems which were developed during this era exhibit characteristics necessary to meet the informational requirements of the times, needed further development and legitimisation. The community of users whose needs the systems were expected to fulfil was somewhat amorphous and ill-defined involving a variety of groups such as elected representatives of people, judiciary, technologists, media people and the general public. In addition to the amorphous nature of the users, the information systems had to tackle different types of information largely some of the categories being local, ill-organised, proprietary, value-added, and reflecting value judgements. Naturally, this situation augured well for the proliferation of information brokers, consultants and information intermediaries in the form of new types of institutions to offer specialised and qualitative services. Repackaged information, collected from a number of sources with validated and authentic data, in the form of new type of specific information service came into being.

TYPES OF INFORMATION INSTITUTIONS

In the literature of Library and Information Science, we come across different types of information institutions. The primary objective of all these organisations happens to be collection, processing, organisation, and dissemination of information to individuals, groups, and organisations as and when they require it. The most important type of these institutions are: libraries, documentation centres, information analysis centres, etc. Apart from these traditional institutions, which have been in existence for long, many de-institutionalised information services have sprung up lately. Some of these are discussed in the following sections:

1. Libraries: Libraries are important resources both for individuals and for communities of people who are interested in the preservation of knowledge. Their importance stems from their ability to maintain records of human endeavour within a range of different contexts using many different media. Libraries will, therefore, continue to play important social, cultural, technical, and pedagogic roles in the future. Indeed, for a majority of people libraries will act as a powerful multimedia window on the outside world, particularly through the use of computer network systems. Obviously, some changes in the library concept will be needed in order to accommodate the requirements of the new information storage and delivery technologies and what these enable people to do. It may be noted that the increasing availability of information generally and of new kinds of information more particularly will lead to a redefinition and integration of the different categories of information organisations. Traditionally, these have been created to manage different formats and media such as print and its surrogates (libraries), objects (museums) and paper records of organisational activity (archives and record repositories). Differences in organisational philosophy, function, and technique have arisen from the exigencies presented by these different formats and media. A library has to serve as an information centre or a referral centre for specialised sources of information. The employment opportunities, public utility services and social awareness programmes undertaken by various departments are considered to be essential areas of information. In the modern information society, libraries and information centres have a new role to play. This is due to the increasing use of web-based information sources and electronic services. Libraries are also being managed in a more democratic way due to flexible communication system and efficient work organisation. Their services are also user-centric.

2. Documentation Centres: Before World War II, research activity was largely an individual affair. But the situation changed rapidly and it has become a team work. Both government and private organisations came forward to fund research and development activities in a big way. Specialisation became the order. Information explosion took place in science as well as in technology. Keeping abreast of new developments in any one discipline became a problem for scientists, engineers, and technologists. Library-based information services proved inadequate to meet the specialised information needs of many research workers. To cope up with this new demand documentation centres came into existence. One of the basic functions associated with any documentation centre is that it brings to the notice of specialist users current and recent literature of value to them. However, the functions that are assigned to a documentation centre vary from one documentation centre to another. For example, a local documentation centre has the sole function of providing information services that support the activities and programmes of its parent organisation of which it is a part. It would collect and serve information concerning the actual work in progress of the parent institution. Towards fulfilling this objective, the local documentation centre may be engaged in the selection and acquisition of worth-while material and its organisation for use. Its services may be designed both to satisfy the existing and anticipated needs of users. Generally, local documentation centres are attached to individual R&D institutions, business houses, industrial enterprises and are administered by their parent institutions. The general norm recommended for financial support is that 5% of the budget spent on R&D must be diverted to meet the expenditure of a national centre.

3. Information Analysis Centres (IAC): The origin of activities pertaining to information analysis may be traced back to the nineteenth century. But the idea of a systematically organised centre for information analysis activity is relatively new. The centres not only disseminate and retrieve information; they create new information. Knowledgeable scientific interpreters who can collect relevant data, review a field and distil information in a manner that goes to the heart of a technical situation, are more helpful to the overburdened specialist than is a mere pile of relevant documents. Such knowledgeable scientific middlemen, who themselves contribute to science are the backbone of the information (analysis) centre; they make information centre a technical institute rather than a technical library. The essence of a good technical centre is that it is operated by highly competent working scientists and engineers—people who see the operation of a centre as an opportunity to advance and deepen their own personal contact with their science and technology.

The key activities of IACs are: analysis, interpretation, synthesis, evaluation and repackaging of information carried out by subject specialists, resulting in the production of new, evaluated information—in the form of critical reviews, state-of-the-art monographs, or data compilations, as well as substantive, evaluated responses to queries—for the purpose of assisting a community of users more broadly representative than the staff of the parent institutes or laboratories.

4. Data Centres: Data is an important ingredient of research. Its importance in society cannot be under estimated. The contemporary society needs data for various activities such as planning, development and decision making, etc. in every sphere of human progress. Data must be collected, processed, and organised so as to facilitate its utilisation in an effective manner. Managing scientific data has been identified as one of the most important emerging needs of the scientific community because of the sheer volume and increasing complexity of data collected. Effective generating, managing, and analysing the data requires a comprehensive approach that encompasses all the stages from the initial data acquisition to the final analysis of the data. For this purpose, an institutional mechanism is essential. Such institutional mechanisms are known as data centres.

According to UNESCO, a data centre "constitutes an organisation handling quantitative material data". Such centres take the primary function of collecting, organising, and disseminating data and also provide a measurement service and are in a position to advance relevant measurement techniques. There can be data centres at the local, national, regional, and international levels. A data centre generally includes three major components:

(i) an organised data collection (i.e. the database);

(ii) connection with data sources which feed the database; and

(iii) contact with users who are expected to interact with the data base with different types of questions.

Modern data centres are usually maintained by organisations in order to handle core operations in information services including the Internet connectivity, intranets, LANs, WANs, and extranets. The most basic data centre will have a computer network and security applications which will have very large amounts of data stored in a number of computers. Generally, larger companies will have IT infrastructure to handle the activities of a data centre. It may be stated that the activities of data centres comprise data collection; data control; data codification; data organisation and structuring into a database and information institutions; and data retrieval. For accomplishing all these functions, a data centre should be equipped with suitably trained manpower. In India, many data centres have been established under the erstwhile NISSAT programme. National Information Centre for Crystallography is an example of a data centre.

5. Referral Centres and Clearing Houses: There are a variety of organisations involved in activities related to the dissemination of information. These different organisations need to be properly coordinated by an agency for their effective functioning. A new type of establishment with a specific mandate to act as a switching mechanism among different information dissemination institutions is an essential requirement. Such an organisation is referred to as a "Referral Centre". A referral centre is an organisation for directing researchers for information and data to appropriate sources, such as libraries, information evaluation centres, documentation centres, documents, and individuals. In other words, a referral centre serves as an intermediary, directing those who have queries related to information requirements on scientific and technical subjects, to the organisations as well as to individuals who have specialised knowledge in those fields and are willing to share that knowledge with others. To carry out its functions, referral centres must be equipped with an inventory of all significant information resources in different disciplines; compile and publish directories of scientific and technical information resources and analyse the operating relationship that exists in the scientific information complex.

In scientific parlance, a "clearing house" is a relatively new concept. It represents a depository for documents with the additional objective of serving as a central agency engaged in the distribution of information. It also includes functions such as collecting and maintaining records of research and development. Sometimes, subjective questions about items in these records are referred to the source and thus a clearing house may have to perform the function of a referral centre. In India as well as UK, such clearing houses are in existence and are functioning. Most of the clearing houses have information gathering networks to acquire documents in their subject areas. They answer specific and general type of questions and may act as a central searching place for enquiries especially relating to R&D reports.

6. De-institutionalised Information Services: For a long time, information handling has been the preserve of a group of trained people called librarians or information professionals. The profession's strength stemmed from the fact that it operated as society's institutionalised information retailer. The universal non-availability of information allowed the profession to fulfil a useful role at the societal, organisational, and individual level. In many cases, access to information was, and is, via designated institutions like libraries, information centres, etc. However, technology appears capable of deinstitutionalising information and handing over access to the individual, thus cracking the mould of library. This deinstitutionalisation of information has created a lot of dissonance within the profession and the burgeoning of info-businesses. However, the information service is no longer exclusively defined in terms of activities carried out in a traditional library and information centre. During recent years, the concept of "information broker" has emerged in developed and developing world. The information broker is an individual or a firm, who, on demand seeks to answer questions using all available sources and who is in business for profit. Brokering rests on the axial principle: information for payment. In case of libraries, information is provided but costs are not charged to the user. One must understand the important distinction between information which is freely available and information which is free. The services offered by brokers comprise:

- Briefing or instant education;
- Information repackaging;
- Market research/analysis;
- Personnel recruitment;
- Press cutting service; and
- Seminars/workshops.

ROLE OF INFORMATION INSTITUTIONS IN A KNOWLEDGE-BASED ECONOMY (KBE)

The role played by information institutions in a knowledge-based economy (KBE) can be highlighted by identifying the performance indicators of various parameters. Information institutions significantly help in improving these parameters which comprise:

1. **Organisational restructuring:** These include,
   (i) Reorienting the structures according to markets, products or processes;
   (ii) Becoming flatter and more flexible;
   (iii) Relying more on informal communication; and
   (iv) Creating flexible work groups.
2. **Expansion in roles and functions of:**
   (i) IT specialists
   (ii) Trainees/educators
   (iii) Negotiators
   (iv) Filters
   (v) Navigators
   (vi) Knowledge managers.
3. **New initiatives in products and services:**
   (i) Development and/or involvement in the intranet
   (ii) Customisation and development of databases
   (iii) Design of websites, web pages and interfaces
   (iv) Introduction of push-technology-based services
   (v) Creating and launching of knowledge products.
4. **Strategic alliances and networking:**
   (i) Enhancing internal communication
   (ii) Strengthening networking
   (iii) Building new partnerships
   (iv) Expanding external relations.

5. **Effective user liaison mechanisms:**
   (i) Redefining user groups
   (ii) User consultation and defining information needs
   (iii) Refocusing newsletters
   (iv) Initiating, briefing and online delivery of hot news.
6. **Creative use of outsourcing of operations:**
   (i) Procurement of information materials
   (ii) Processing operations and services
   (iii) Automated delivery of documents
   (iv) Portals.

Unit 4
Laws of Library Science

THE FIVE LAWS OF LIBRARY SCIENCE

Dr. Shiyali Ramamrita Ranganathan (1892-1972) was an inventor, educator, philosopher, mathematician, and a universal librarian. He made several significant contributions to the library profession. A fundamental contribution made by him is the Five Laws of Library Science. He formulated the Five Laws of Library Science in 1928 and published these in his famous book entitled, *Five Laws of Library Science* in 1931. Many librarians from around the world accept the laws as the foundations of their philosophy and consider them as the basic principles of operating a library system.

These laws, as presented in Ranganathan's *Five Laws of Library Science*, are:

1. Books are for use.
2. Every person his or her book.
3. Every book its reader.
4. Save the time of the reader.
5. A library is a growing organism.

These laws provide scientific basis and general principles which serve as guidelines to librarians in organising and managing information products and services. These laws convey the fundamental philosophy of library science and convey a deep understanding of libraries. The basic tenet of these laws is to unite users with their desired information. These have been discussed in detail in this section.

FIRST LAW: BOOKS ARE FOR USE

The First Law of Library Science is simple and states a self-evident truth. In ancient and medieval periods, the use of books was limited and the emphasis was on storage and preservation rather than on use. The libraries were regarded as institutions for preserving the books. With the onset of post-industrial society, the concept of modern library came into being. The library is now regarded as a service institution to serve the social information needs of its users. Ranganathan did not reject the notion, that preservation and storage were important. But he asserted that the purpose of such activities was to promote the use of books. By emphasising the use of books, he focused his attention on access related issues such as location, building, library hours, book selection, library staff, etc. Ranganathan suggests the following methods (implications of this law as well) for maximizing the use of books.

Implications of the First Law

(a) **Library Location:** A library must be located in the midst of its users. If it is a public library, it should be located in the heart of the city. If it is an academic library, it would be wise to locate it centrally to enable accessibility to all the students. The surroundings must be free from noise and other disturbances which impede the use of library resources.

(b) **Library Hours:** The timings of the library depend upon the community it serves. The law implies that the library be kept open for as long as it is possible. Opening and closing hours of the library should be adjusted to ensure maximum utilisation of library resources.

(c) **Library Furniture:** Library furniture should be comfortable, functional, and easy to use. The stack rooms should be made vermin proof, theft proof, and air proof. The law states that the best reading facilities should be provided, like sufficient lights, fans, and sound proof floor. It may vary from library to library, depending upon the nature of clientele to be served, like children or adults. This law enforces that the height of the book racks should be short enough, so that books in the topmost shelf can easily be picked by a person of normal height standing on the floor. Tables and chairs should be comfortable to the user.

(d) **Book Selection:** Book selection should meet the needs of the present and potential users. The selection should also consider physical appearance of the books and ease of handling. The books should be kept clean and in good condition. Worn out and obsolete books should be weeded out from the library collection from time to time.

(e) **Library Staff:** The law states that to disseminate knowledge and to put the books to maximum use, the libraries must have highly qualified and professionally trained staff. The First Law has the most vital effect on the library staff. Assisting the users to find and use library resources is the responsibility of the library staff, as most of the users do not know how to use the resources. To know the needs of the users, and teaching them the uses of library resources, is an essential task of library staff. In order to put library material to maximum use, qualified staff in proper numbers with suitable status and emoluments is required. The staff should cultivate a service attitude towards the readers.

SECOND LAW: EVERY READER HIS/HER BOOK

According to Ranganathan, if the First Law replaced the concept that, "books are for preservation", the Second Law widens the concept that "books for the chosen few." If the approach of the First Law is from 'books' point of view, the approach of the Second Law is from 'users' point of view. It emphasises the availability of library services to every kind of reader, irrespective of age, sex, vocation, the capacity for self help, and the ability to read.

Implications of the Second Law

It imposes a number of obligations on:

- The State,
- The Library Authority,
- The library staff, and
- The readers.

These obligations are discussed in this section:

(a) **Obligations of the State:** The establishment and maintenance of library systems and their development along proper lines is the State's responsibility. To meet this responsibility, the State has certain obligations. The first and the foremost is the library legislation. Through library legislation, the State can create the public library system in different areas by its policies and decisions, which makes adequate provisions regarding library cess, percentage of the cess to be collected from the people and grants to be given by the government for library system. Legislation leads to cooperation between libraries in a State and integrates them with State Central Library at the apex. This type of coordination strengthens their resources through interlibrary loan, which enhances the efficiency and standard of service for the readers. It also recommends making a provision for

- Union Library Act;
- National Central Library Law; and
- Finance.

(b) **Obligation of Library Authority:** The choice of the books and the choice of staff are the two necessary obligations of library authority.

(i) **Choice of Books:** Selection of books is determined by the demands of the users. Demand refers to the selection of reading material for a given library. It is the duty of the library authority to make necessary provisions to build a collection for the community to be served. A comprehensive user survey of different groups of people can be done in this respect. This will help to build a collection according to the tastes and interest of the readers.

(ii) **Choice of Staff:** Careful selection of books is not the ultimate aim of the library. To exploit these resources, competent library staff is needed. Only a competent staff can satisfy the user's requirements and be able to locate the books and other materials that they want. To implement the Second Law, the library authorities should make all possible efforts to recruit well qualified library staff at the stage of planning.

(c) **Obligation of the Library Staff:** The objectives of the Second Law cannot be achieved unless the library staff discharge their obligations in an efficient manner. To perform their duties, the library staff has to adopt certain attitudes and practices to realize the word "His". Providing reading material is not the only duty of the library staff. The staff must ensure that the readers get the material of their interest before leaving the library. Besides this, the staff should try to know the readers, possess adequate knowledge of books and other collections of the library, to provide reference services and help readers in all possible ways. The Second Law puts another obligation on the library staff, i.e., to provide bibliographical, indexing, abstracting and other services to the users as per their requirements. Catalogue is another facility that the Second Law demands. The catalogue is such a tool which reveals the hidden contents of such documents by cross reference entries and subject analytical entries. Otherwise, the reader may not get this material in spite of their best efforts. Besides, other implications, the open access system will satisfy the expectations of this law, which enables the reader to decide what he should read. In an open access system, books are kept on the shelves and are easily accessible to the reader. If a reader is not satisfied with a particular book, she/he can choose another suitable book. Thus, it will increase the chances for every reader to get the book of his/her choice.

(d) **Obligation of the Reader:** The Second Law imposes certain obligations on the reader towards the library. It is the duty of the reader to follow the rules and regulations of the library in order to use and utilise library resources in an effective and efficient manner. Thus, by fulfilling the above-listed four obligations, it becomes possible to provide every reader his/her book. The Second Law recommends that all the libraries of a country/region cooperate with each other and work as a single system. The entire documentary resources of a country should be regarded as a single pool of knowledge. Every book lying idle on the shelf of any library should be made available to the readers.

THIRD LAW: EVERY BOOK ITS READER

The Third Law stresses the maximum use of books by their readers. It urges that an appropriate reader should be found for every book. It is closely related to the Second Law, but it focuses on the book itself suggesting that each book in a library has an individual or a number of readers who would find that book useful. It is the duty of the library staff to bring the readers in contact with the books. The law advocates an open access system, classified shelf arrangement, subject analytical entries, provision of reference services, publicity methods, extension services and a book selection policy.

Implications of the Third Law

(a) **Open Access:** In an open access system, the reader is allowed to select books/items on the shelves on his/her own. It increases the use of the books. Open access thus helps in achieving the Third Law.

(b) **Shelf Arrangement:** The law emphasises the need to arrange the books on shelves in a classified sequence based on their thought content. This arrangement brings books on the same subject together for easy browsing. If the shelf is provided with well-devised guides and labels, the use of each item increases.

(c) **Easy Access:** Another important factor helping every book to get its reader is that the books may be placed within the easy reach of the readers. The Third Law emphasizes that the height of the racks should not be more than the average height of the reader, i.e. the topmost shelf of a book rack should be within the easy reach of a person of average height. The shelf should not have more breadth than what is required.

(d) **Catalogue:** The Third Law also advocates that the library catalogue should play an important role to provide every book to its reader. Subject analytical entries help in finding readers for a suitable book. There are series entries and subject cross reference entries. The series entries provide information about the whole set of books to the reader. In the alphabetical part of the catalogue, all the entries having the same series as the heading are brought together.

(e) **Publicity:** Publicity through annual reports, library bulletins and magazines, printed catalogues, subject book lists, list of latest additions, etc. is a powerful technique to attract the attention of the readers.

(f) **Display of Books:** The newly added books to the library should be displayed as it enhances the chances of every book finding its reader.

FOURTH LAW: SAVE THE TIME OF THE READER

This law requires that there should be no time lag between the demand received from the user and the document supplied. This law makes its approach from the point of view of the user. It almost completely centres on the user from the moment he/she enters the library to the moment he/she leaves it. The objective of this law is to save the time of the reader. To provide better services, it is required that, the latest technologies in library operations be adopted and the users be trained to use them independently.

Implications of the Fourth Law

(a) Classified Arrangement

The classified arrangement of books in the stack room saves the time of the reader, as it is easy for a reader to find all the books on the same subject arranged at one place for browsing. The arrangement of entries in the catalogue cabinet in a classified manner, aids the reader to select the books easily from the respective shelves. The Fourth Law, therefore, calls for the classified arrangement of books in the stack room.

(b) Catalogue Entry

In case of composite books, classified arrangement is sufficient to save the objective time of the reader. The various facets of composite books can be brought to the notice of the reader by making cross references and subject analytical entries. Therefore, the Fourth Law calls for (i) classified arrangement of cards in the catalogue cabinet, and (ii) analytical entries for composite books.

In order to save the valuable time of the reader, the Fourth Law also recommends a bipartite classified catalogue for this purpose, because readers have diverse approaches to find books, i.e. author, title, collaborator, or series approach.

(c) Open Access

The Fourth Law strongly opposes the process of the closed access system. It supports open access system for saving the time of the reader.

(d) Reference Services

The law supports that the library staff should provide adequate personal help to their readers. Such help is known as "reference service". A reference library staff should have adequate professional knowledge and be active to serve their reader in an efficient and effective manner. The message "save the time of the reader" makes all necessary efforts to meet the demands of the reader in the least possible time with the help of reference-cum-guidance services.

(e) Issue-Return Method

Adopting an efficient circulation system is another step towards saving the time of the reader. This enables maximum books being issued and returned in the minimum possible time.

(f) Centralised/Pre-natal Cataloguing

To save the time of the staff, Ranganathan has advocated a pre-natal centralised cataloguing and classification. The law urges the library to evolve a uniform cataloguing code to make way for international cooperative cataloguing.

(g) Stack Room Guides

To save the time of the reader, the library should provide an efficient system of guides in the stack room. The guides, along with placing tags, should enable the readers to find books easily.

(h) Library Location

The Fourth Law also deals with the time taken by the readers to reach the library. It should be located in such a way so as to save the time of the readers. But the location of urban area libraries is not always equally accessible from all parts of the city due to geographical constraints. The law demands setting up of branches of the libraries and delivery stations for the same. In rural areas, the branch of a library can be as useful as it is in the town. The rural population can also be served by the mobile vans which serve the small libraries and delivery stations. All these libraries should be connected to and operated along with the district central library.

Thus, this law deals with different aspects of library policy and administration for reducing the time factor in all the library activities. The devices proposed in the law are the best classification and cataloguing system, open access, shelf arrangement, stack room guides, reference service and central location of the library. The basic objective of all such measures is to save the time of the reader.

FIFTH LAW: LIBRARY IS A GROWING ORGANISM

The Fifth Law states, "library is a growing organism". It is an accepted idea that a library along with its services is a growing organism. This law maintains that the library as an institution, has all the attributes of a growing organism, which takes in new matter, casts off old matter, changes in size and takes new shapes and forms like human beings. Since a library is a trinity of books, readers, and staff, it is bound to grow in all three respects. Therefore, library authorities should plan the library building in such a way so as to make it easy to keep pace with the necessary growth in terms of the size of its collection, number of readers and the members of staff.

Implications of the Fifth Law

(a) **Growth in Size:** As the body of a child grows steadily in size and weight, similarly a newly started library grows steadily in size in terms of its reading materials. The growth and size of reading materials help users to acquire up to date information in different fields.

(b) **Growth in Infrastructure:** This includes growth in stack area, circulation area and reading room area, etc.

(c) **Growth of the Reader:** The growth of a library is dependent upon the growth of its readers. The growth of readers affects the size of the reading room, the issuing method, and certain safeguards (in case of an open access system).

(d) **Growth of Staff:** With the growth in size of its reading materials and the readers, increase in the number of staff is also inevitable. The book selection activity, cataloguing section, binding section, periodical section, and the reference section have to grow as the library grows. The Fifth Law advocates that the library authorities make all necessary provisions for growth of the library staff in these sections.

The Fifth Law urges the library authorities to provide an adequate, well-qualified and trained staff to serve its readers. It also supports the development and enhancement of the working environment in accordance with the latest tools and techniques in the working area.

NEW INTERPRETATION OF LAWS

1. Document/Information/Web resources/Software are for use.
2. Every person his or her Document/Information/Web resource/Software.

(c) Every Document/Information/Web resource/Software its reader.

(d) Save the time of the Document/Information/Web resources/Software user.

(e) A Document/Information/Web resource/Software library is a growing organism.

EXERCISES: UNIT 1 – UNIT 4

1. Define "information society" and trace its evolution.
2. Write down the role played by a library in an information society.
3. Explain in detail the factors that influence the arrival of an information society.
4. Define a "knowledge society".

5. What are the characteristics of a knowledge-based society?
6. What do you understand by the term “KBE”?
7. What do you understand by the term “library” in the context of a knowledge-based society?
8. Explain the different types of libraries along with their major objectives and functions.
9. How are the objectives of a school library different from that of a college library?
10. Enumerate the different services offered by a university library.
11. Explain the functions of a public library in a society.
12. Explain the role of a research library in a modern ICT-based society.
13. What is a national library? Explain its objectives and functions.
14. How can you define the characteristics of a digital library?
15. Highlight the challenges associated with and faced by the establishment of a digital library.
16. Define a “hybrid library”.
17. Trace the evolution of information institutions.
18. Explain the growth pattern of information institutions.
19. What do you understand by mission-oriented information transfer?
20. Explain and illustrate the library as an information institution.
21. What are the different types of information institutions?
22. Explain the role played by information institutions in a knowledge-based economy.
23. Explain the five laws of library science.
24. What are the major implications of the five laws of library science?
25. Write down the modern interpretations of the five laws of library science.

Unit 5

Library Legislation and Model Public Library Acts/Bills

NEED FOR LIBRARY LEGISLATION

Freedom, prosperity, and the development of a society and of individuals are fundamental human values. These values can be attained through well-informed citizens, who will be shaped through the utilisation of public libraries. It is recognised all over the world that education including the provision of free public libraries is the responsibility of the government at the national, state, and local levels. A public library is the "People's University". In the process of evolution, our country had established a good number of public libraries maintained by local bodies and voluntary organisations, and some libraries through subscriptions. But these libraries could not grow along modern lines because of a number of reasons like non-availability of sufficient funds, limitations in service deliverance and unstable nature, etc.

In modern times, the public libraries must provide services with a certain standard, and with an objective of reconstruction and development of a society. They cannot be achieved only through individual munificence. Library leaders, public men, and scholars have realised that the only way to establish and develop a public library system is through public law. Pioneers and men of vision like Edward Edwards, Dr. S.R. Ranganathan and many others spared no efforts to bring about a library legislation in their respective countries. Library Act/Legislation is a type of law or legislation that is passed by a country or a state government and implemented to establish a library system within its territory. The reason and need for a library legislation can be summed up as in this section:

1. It will constitute a proper administrative and supervisory body with executive powers;
2. It will provide a well-organised library system for the state, district and up to the remote village level with free access to all citizens;
3. It will provide a steady and permanent source of finance;
4. It will maintain standards in library service;
5. It will be obliged to meet the objectives and remain accountable.

Thus, it is only through a State and Union Territories Public Library Act that a public library system could be created, sustained and promoted, ensuring a smooth financial flow, properly governed and managed to provide modern library services to all.

COMPONENTS OF LIBRARY LEGISLATION

The Public Libraries Act/Library Legislation has the following components:

1. The Preamble: The preamble of the Act should clearly spell out the objectives of the library legislation and therefore, it should be precise and explicit.

2. State-level Authority: The Act should have the provision for the constitution of a Board as the State Library Authority. The minister-in-charge of libraries should be the State Library Authority, charged with the duty of implementing the Act. It will be her/his duty to supervise and promote the improvement of the library service, provided by the library authorities and to secure proper discharge of their functions.

3. Chief Executive of the State: In this component of the Act, the Chief Executive at the State level shall be called the Director of Public Libraries, who should be an information service professional. The director shall supervise and control the Public Library System of the State, with the guidance of the State Library Authority.

4. Network of Libraries: The Act should provide for the establishment and functioning of public libraries as a pyramidal structure from the village, or even a hamlet level, to the state level via the districts covering towns and tehsils, etc.

5. Financial Clauses: The Act should spell out the financial sources needed to ensure a regular flow of funds and their deployment. There should be a provision in the Act to collect library cess from all possible sources. Dr. S.R. Ranganathan, a pioneer in library legislation in India, advocated for the provision of a library cess in the Model Acts. It is to be recognised that the levying of library cess is essential for the planned and systematic growth of an authority through assured and established financial resources.

6. Manpower: A provision should be made to create a cadre of State Library Service, and all the members of the said service should be government servants, and their recruitment and conditions of service should be as per the provisions of the Article 309 of the Constitution of India.

7. Accountability: The activities and accounts of the Public Library System shall be open to public inspection, supervision and as per official audit rules.

8. Registration of Books: There must be a provision for the registration of books and newspapers/periodicals published in the State under the legal deposit rules.

9. Rules: Rules should be made by the State Library Authority for all the sections and for the smooth functioning, administration and control of the offices and the staff.

MODEL UNION LIBRARY ACT

The Government of India appointed a committee in the year 1948 to suggest the possibilities of establishing a National Central Library at New Delhi. Dr S.R. Ranganathan as a member of the committee drafted "The Library Development Plan—Thirty Year Programme for India with Draft Library Bills for Union and Constituent States", which contains Union

Library Bills. The salient features of the Model Union Libraries Act are given in this section:

(i) Constitution of a National Library Authority.

(ii) Establishment of a system of national central libraries, i.e. National Copyright Library.

(iii) Constitution of a National Library Committee for the purpose of advising the National Library Authority on all matters arising under this Act referring to it.

(iv) Constitution of a National Library Fund.

(v) Amendment to the Delivery of Books and Newspapers Act, 1954.

MODEL ACT OF S.R. RANGANATHAN

Dr S.R. Ranganathan initiated the Model Library Act as a conference paper during the All Asia Educational Conference held in Banaras in 1930 and later he revised it as the Model Public Libraries Act. Attempts were made to introduce this Model Act in West Bengal in 1931 and Madras in 1933. But it could not be enacted due to some compulsory clauses. The salient features of this Model Act are mentioned in this section:

(i) Model Libraries Act will provide a system of public libraries for the city, rural and other areas.

(ii) Minister of Education shall be the State Library Authority (SLA). It shall be the duty of the State Library Authority to provide for adequate library services in the state.

(iii) Constitution of a State Library Committee for the purpose of advising the State Library Authority on all matters arising under the Act.

(iv) Constitution of a Local Library Authority (LLA) for each city and one for each district.

(v) The State Library Authority and Government and a Local Library Authority may raise the library rate in such a manner and at such cess as may be determined from time to time.

Unit 6

Library Legislation in Indian States—Their Salient Features

LIBRARY LEGISLATION IN INDIAN STATES

In 1933 and 1937, the Madras Library Association first prepared and presented the Madras Library Acts, but for some reason, they couldn't be passed. In independent India, the same Act was passed in the state of Madras in 1948, becoming the first State in India to pass the Library Act. So far 19 States/UTs of India have passed the Library Legislation Act in their state. The list is as follows:

1. Madras Public Libraries Act, 1948 (5 paisa per rupee on property tax)
2. Andhra Pradesh Public Libraries Act, 1960 (8 paisa per rupee on property and house tax)
3. Karnataka Public Libraries Act, 1965 (3% on land revenue)
4. Maharashtra Public Libraries Act, 1967 (no library cess)
5. West Bengal Public Libraries Act, 1979 (no library cess)
6. Manipur Public Libraries Act, 1988 (no library cess)
7. Haryana Public Libraries Act, 1989 (surcharge on house and property tax, rate revision)
8. Kerala Public Libraries Act, 1989 (surcharge on house and property tax, rate revision)

9. Mizoram Public Libraries Act, 1993 (no library cess)
10. Goa Public Libraries Act, 1994 (no library cess)
11. Gujarat Public Libraries Act, 2001 (no library cess)
12. Orissa Public Libraries Act, 2001 (no library cess)
13. Uttaranchal Public Libraries Act, 2005 (no library cess)
14. Chhattisgarh Public Libraries Act, 2006 (no library cess)
15. Rajasthan Public Libraries Act, 2006 (no library cess)
16. Uttar Pradesh Public Libraries Act, 2006 (no library cess)
17. Lakshadweep Public Libraries Act, 2007 (no library cess)
18. Bihar State Public Libraries Act, 2008 (no library cess)
19. Arunachal Pradesh Public Libraries Act, 2009 (no library cess)

COMMON FEATURES OF THE LIBRARY ACT (OF ALL STATES)

All the state library acts/legislations share the following features (can be written to each Act):

1. It was established in the year as mentioned in the previous section.
2. Provision of library cess as indicated in the earlier section against each Act.
3. It facilitates the establishment of Public Libraries in the State.
4. It has the provision to constitute the State Library Authority for the purpose of advising the government on such matters related to libraries as they may refer to it.
5. It has the provision to appoint a Director of Public Libraries to manage the affairs.

6. Constitution of Local Library Authorities is recommended at different levels like Zilla, Block, etc.
7. Recommendation to nominate State Central Library in the state.
8. Declaration that libraries are eligible for government aid.
9. Provision for centralised units like:
   (a) Copyright collection of the State;
   (b) State Library for the Blind;
   (c) State Bibliographic Bureau, etc.
10. Creation of a State Library Service bestowing upon its employees all the benefits and privileges as are available to other State Government servants.
11. Provision for grant-in-aid for private libraries.
12. Provision for audit and accountability.

MISSING FEATURES IN PUBLIC LIBRARY LEGISLATION

Ever since the first Public Library Act was passed in India in 1948, different states and union territories have come forward to modify and amend it, so as to benefit the general masses. However, there still are certain missing features in the Act that are elaborated in this section:

1. A provision of the State Library Authority, with the Minister of Libraries as its head with executive powers conceived by Dr. Ranganathan or in the Western countries is missing in most of the Acts. This provision was made to a certain extent in Karnataka, Haryana, and Orissa Acts (2001). But they have not been implemented.
2. There is no clear provision to maintain, protect or save the heritage libraries, which have been in existence for more than one hundred years, more or less in all the States. In Maharashtra there are about 150 such great libraries.
3. Service to the people of slum areas, downtrodden people and people living in remote areas was never

thought of. But an attempt was made in Karnataka in 2007. All these years the public library service in India have remained a middle-class affair.

4. In our country, there are about 50% of illiterate people. There is no clear provision in the existing Acts to help them. It is to be noted that library cess or taxes are being collected from them, but spending of the same is done for the benefit of the literates. This is something unsocial.
5. In the states, where the library cess is being collected in all the cities, towns, and villages, but spending of the same is done mostly in the cities and towns. Only a small amount is being spent in the villages.
6. In the states, where the library cess is being collected, the development of libraries is linked with the income, which we are getting out of library cess. But this amount is not at all sufficient to develop the library service on a full scale. That is why there is a stunted growth of public libraries in states such as Tamil Nadu, Andhra Pradesh, etc.
7. Most of the public libraries still suffer from a lack of minimum facilities such as
   (a) a functional building, good ventilation, lighting, furniture, fittings, cleanliness, drinking water, toilets, etc.
   (b) a minimum core collection of books and periodicals.
   (c) a minimum salary structure for the staff.

Unit 7
Other Information-Related Legislations

RIGHT TO INFORMATION

The right to information is a fundamental human right which is made up of different rights and responsibilities, namely:

- Every person's RIGHT to request information from the government and even private bodies in some cases;
- The DUTY of the government to provide the requested information, unless defined exemptions apply; and
- The DUTY of the government to proactively disclose information that is of general public interest without the need for requests from citizens.

RIGHT TO INFORMATION ACT, 2005

The Right to Information Act, 2005 (No. 22 of 2005) received the assent of the President of India on 15 June 2005 and was subsequently published for general information. Right to Information Act, 2005 mandates timely responses to citizen requests for government information. It is an initiative taken by the Department of Personnel and Training, Ministry of Personnel, Public Grievances and Pensions to provide a RTI Portal Gateway to the citizens for quick search of information on the details of first Appellate Authorities, PIOs, etc. amongst others, besides access to RTI-related information/disclosures published on the web by various public authorities under the Government of India as well as the state governments.

OBJECTIVES OF THE RIGHT TO INFORMATION ACT

The basic objective of the Right to Information Act is to empower the citizens, promote transparency and accountability in the working of the government, contain corruption and make our democracy work for the people in its real sense. It goes without saying that an informed citizen is better equipped to keep a necessary vigil on the instruments of governance and make the government more accountable to the governed. The Act is a big step towards making the citizens informed about the activities of the government. The Act comprises six chapters. A brief description of all the chapters is provided in this section.

Preliminary (Chapter I): It provides meanings of appropriate terms like Government, Central Information Commission, Central Public Information Officer, Chief Information Commissioner, Information Commissioner, competent authority, information, prescribed, public authority, record, right to information, State Information Commission, State Chief Information Commissioner, State Information Commissioner, State Public Information Officer and third party.

Right to Information and Obligations of Public Authorities (Chapter II): The Chapter details the obligation of public authorities, designation of Public Information Officers, how to obtain information from public authorities, disposal of requests, exemption from disclosure of information, grounds for rejection to access in certain cases, severability and third-party information.

The Central Information Commission (Chapter III): It is fully devoted to the Central Information Commission and spells out the constitution of the Commission, terms of office and conditions of service of the Chief Information Commissioner.

The State Information Commission (Chapter IV): It deals solely with the State Information Commission and describes the constitution of the Commission, terms of office and conditions of service of the State Chief Information Commissioner and the State Information Commissioner and the grounds and procedures of their removal from office.

Powers and Functions of Information Commissions, Appeal and Penalties (Chapter V): It describes the powers and functions of the Central Information Commission and State Information Commission. The Act has provided for an appeal as well as penalties.

Miscellaneous (Chapter VI): The Chapter encompasses a number of items such as protection of action taken in good faith; overriding effects of the Act; bar of jurisdiction of courts; non-applicability of the Act in the case of certain organisations such as security and intelligent organisations; monitoring and reporting of the implementation of the provisions of the Act by the Central Information Commission or the State Information Commission; role of the appropriate government in the preparation of educational programmes and performing-related activities along with some other vital details.

INTELLECTUAL PROPERTY RIGHTS

Intellectual Property (IP) pertains to any original creation of the human intellect such as artistic, literary, technical, or scientific creation. Intellectual Property Rights (IPR) refers to the legal rights given to the inventor or creator to protect his invention or creation for a certain period of time. These legal rights confer an exclusive right to the inventor/creator or his assignee to fully utilise his invention/creation for a given period of time. It is very well settled that IP plays a vital role in the modern economy. It has also been conclusively established that the intellectual labour associated with the innovation should be given due importance so that public good emanates from it. There has been a quantum jump in research and development (R&D) costs with an associated jump in investments required for putting a new technology in the marketplace. The stakes of the developers of technology have become very high and hence, the need to protect the knowledge from unlawful use has become expedient, at least for a period, that would ensure recovery of the R&D and other associated costs and adequate profits for continuous investments in the same. IPR is a strong tool, to protect investments, time, money, and efforts invested by the inventor/creator of an IP, since it grants the inventor/creator an exclusive right for a certain period of time for use of his/her invention/creation. IP is divided into two categories:

industrial property, which includes inventions (patents), trademarks, industrial designs and geographic indications of source and copyright, which includes literary works such as novels, poems and plays, films, musical works, and artistic works such as drawings, paintings, photographs and sculptures, and architectural designs. Under IPR, we shall consider two acts which are of relevance to us: The Copyright Act of 1957 and the Patents Act of 1970.

THE COPYRIGHT ACT, 1957

Copyright is a type of intellectual property that protects original works of authorship as soon as an author fixes the work in a tangible form of expression. It is a type of intellectual property that gives its owner the exclusive right to copy, distribute, adapt, display, and perform a creative work, usually for a limited time. The creative work may be in a literary, artistic, educational, or musical form. Copyright is intended to protect the original expression of an idea in the form of a creative work, but not the idea itself.

The Copyright Act of 1957 as amended governs the subject of copyright law in India. The Act has been applicable from 21 January 1958. The history of copyright law in India can be traced back to its colonial era under the British Empire. The Copyright Act of 1957 was the first post-independence copyright legislation in India and the law has been amended six times since 1957. The most recent amendment was in the year 2012, through the Copyright (Amendment) Act of 2012. Copyright Act is a bundle of rights given by the law to the creators of literary, dramatic, musical, and artistic works and the producers of cinematograph films and sound recordings. The rights provided under the Copyright Law include the rights of reproduction of the work, communication of the work to the public, adaptation of the work and translation of the work. The scope and duration of protection provided under the copyright law varies with the nature of the protected work.

Salient Features of "The Copyright Act, 1957"

1. Scope of rights conferred to author: Under Section 13 of the Copyright Act of 1957, copyright protection is provided to literary works, musical works, dramatic works, artistic works, sound recording and cinematograph films. For example, books, manuscripts, poetry, and theses are protected under the Act as literary works.

2. Provisions to determine first ownership: According to Section 17 of the Copyrights Act of 1957, the first owner of the copyright is the author of the work itself. The exception to this rule is the case in which the employer becomes the owner of the copyright in circumstances where the employee creates a work in the scope of her/his employment.

3. Civil and criminal remedies: The civil remedies for copyright infringement are covered under Section 55 of the Copyright Act of 1957. These civil remedies include damages, injunctions, interpretation of accounts, destruction and delivery of infringed copies and damages for conversion. The criminal remedies, for infringement of copyright, are provided under Section 63 of the Copyright Act of 1957.

4. Creation of copyright office and copyright board: Provisions for setting up a copyright office, which is under the control of the Registrar of the copyright for the registration of books and other 'works' of art, and a copyright board to help in dealing with copyright-related disputes are also given in the Copyright Act of 1957. Section 9 of the Copyright Act of 1957 provides for the inception of an office which is to be called the Copyright Office for the purpose of the Act. Section 11 of the Copyright Act of 1957 provides for the inception of the Copyright Board.

THE PATENTS ACT, 1970

A patent is an exclusive right granted for an invention, which is a product or a process that provides, in general, a new way of doing something, or offers a new technical solution to a problem. To get a patent, technical information about the invention must be disclosed to the public in a patent application. A patent is a type of intellectual property that gives its owner the legal right to exclude others from making, using or selling an invention for a limited period of time in exchange for publishing and enabling the disclosure of the invention. In most countries, patent rights fall under private law and the patent holder must sue someone infringing the patent in order to enforce their rights.

The Patents Act of 1970 is the legislation that till date governs patents in India. It first came into force in 1972. The first Patent Act of British India was titled as "Indian Patents and Designs Act, 1911". That continued for about 60 years and then was amended as "The Patents Act, 1970". The words 'Indian' and 'Designs' were dropped. Since 1970, it has been amended several times. It was last amended in 2005.

Salient Features of "The Patents Act, 1970"

Following are some of the important features of "The Patent Act, 1970":

- Not only a product but also a process can be patented under act.
- On account of this Act, invention shall be useful, novel and something which is not obvious.
- The patented product shall be capable of getting used in the industry, if not then it may amount to revocation of the patent.
- Invention shall be new and shall not form part of Sections 3 and 4, which provide exceptions of ideas which cannot be patented.
- Term of patent—20 years (can be renewed and in some cases it may also be upto seven years).
- Patent examination can be conducted on request.
- Both pre-grant and post-grant opposition are enabled.
- Fast track mechanism shall prevail for disposal of appeals if any disparity exists.
- Values to protect integrity of the Indian Constitution's various clauses such as Article 51-A of Fundamental Duties is also taken into consideration by nurturing and keeping nature and rich heritage of culture in mind. Hence, provisions for protection of biodiversity and traditional knowledge is specified in act.

- Publication of applications after eighteen months with the facility for early publication enables getting patented rights as if it was registered from the day if reasonableness of time is observed.

EXERCISES: UNIT 5 – UNIT 7

1. Define the term "library legislation".
2. Highlight the need for the adoption of library legislation.
3. Highlight the major components of library legislation.
4. Highlight the major features of library legislation.
5. Explain the model library act of S.R. Ranganathan.
6. Trace the implementation of library legislations in India.
7. Write down some of the common features of library acts/ legislations across Indian states.
8. Highlight some missing features in public library legislations.
9. What do you understand by the term "Right to Information"?
10. Define the term "Act".
11. Discuss the "Right to Information Act, 2005" in detail.
12. What do you understand by Intellectual Property Rights (IPR)?
13. Define "The Copyright Act, 1957".
14. What are the salient features of "The Copyright Act, 1957"?
15. Define "The Patents Act, 1970".
16. Highlight some of the salient features of "The Patents Act, 1970".
17. Differentiate between "The Copyright Act, 1957" and "The Patents Act, 1970".
18. Enumerate the importance of the Copyright Act of 1957.
19. Enumerate the importance of the Patent Act of 1970.

Unit 8
Resource Sharing

DEFINITION AND NEED FOR RESOURCE SHARING

Resource sharing is a concept quite often talked about in the literature of LIS. Literally, the term implies, using each other's resources. Edmonds (1933) defines it as "the reciprocally beneficial sharing of resources, developed or pre-existing, by two or more bodies." In the context of libraries, it refers to libraries sharing their resources, including the sources of information, staff expertise, infrastructure, and finance. Thus, resource sharing can be considered as the sharing of library resources by certain participating libraries among themselves on the basis of the principle of cooperation. This is applicable in the sharing of documents, manpower, services, space, and equipment. Resource sharing enables libraries to function effectively and efficiently for the benefit of general users. The need for and effectiveness of resource sharing can be summed up in the following points:

1. To satisfy the information needs of maximum users, libraries would need to acquire all the relevant documents, thereby accounting for an increased demand of funds and space. To overcome such an issue, resource sharing is an ideal practice that would enable them to overcome the problem of increased prices (funds) and space for storing material.
2. Through sharing, libraries would have access to a large number of documents thus satisfying the increasing demand for documents.

3. It would also allow them to share the expertise of staff, thus saving costs as well as the time of the staff. They would now be comparatively freed from the routine technical procedures, as that would be done on a common basis between them.

OBJECTIVES OF RESOURCE SHARING

The objectives of resource sharing are to:

1. **Maximise the resource base of libraries:** The primary objective of resource sharing is to maximise the resource base, i.e. collection, staff, infrastructure, as well as services of the participating libraries. A library when functioning as part of a resource sharing programme would have at its disposal resources of other libraries besides its own to serve its users. In other words, the resources of any library would be the resources of every other library.
2. **Provide a democratic and wide access to information:** We are living in the information age where information is a commodity needed by one and all. We are highly dependent on information. It is required for learning, teaching, research, entertainment, and decision making at different levels. In view of this scenario, one should not be deprived of it. Libraries have different document collections to satisfy the information needs of their users. They are strong in some areas and poor in others. Thus, they lack resources to excel in all areas. If libraries share with each other, they can overcome this limitation of poor document collection and make available comprehensive information to their users.
3. **Development of core collection:** Resource sharing results in a rational acquisition of documents. A library should only acquire those documents that are core to the area of its organisation. It can satisfy minor or auxiliary needs of its users from other libraries with which it shares its resources. Similarly, it can satisfy the minor needs of other libraries.

4. **Save resources:** Libraries share their resources to save and use them optimally. Cooperative acquisition enables them to save on money spent on documents. Cooperative cataloguing and classification enable them to save on staff salaries, efforts, and time spent on technical processing.
5. **Enable uniform practices in routines:** A central agency can be entrusted with the task of cataloguing and classification, which can be followed by others which results in standardisation. Uniform practices are helpful to users as well as staff. It is a result of sharing and a requirement too.
6. **Rational acquisition:** Rationalisation of acquisition is one of the major functions of library networks. Libraries can come together to identify the duplication of resources thereby avoiding wastage. Funds could be diverted for resources which are found lacking in a particular geographical area. It would result in better allocation of funds and widespread availability of resources.

LIBRARY NETWORK

"Library Network" refers to the network among libraries for sharing sources and resources. It has been defined as "group of individuals or organisations that are interconnected to form a system to accomplish some specified goal. The linkage must include a communication mechanism and many networks exist for the express purpose of facilitating certain types of communication among members." Another definition of a network describes it in terms of its characteristics, viz.

- A network that functions to marshal resources from its environment to accomplish results beyond the ability of any one of its members.
- A network that develops an organisational design and structure allowing it to establish an identifiable domain and exercise appropriate influence over its members. It is based on communications technology.

NEED/ROLE OF LIBRARY NETWORKS

The term "Network" is increasingly used in place of "resource sharing" or "cooperative systems". Networking and modernisation are becoming very important in all types of libraries as they enable the users to have access to the resources of many other libraries in addition to their own. The developments in information technology have made it possible for libraries to network. But today library networks are a must because:

1. **Increasing amount of information in electronic form:** Information is stored in print, film, magnetic and optical storage media. However, an increase in the storage of information in digital media has forced libraries to develop a network, just to cope up with the issue of limited or insufficient funds.
2. **Bibliographic access to information is also in electronic form:** Access to information is provided through databases produced online and offline which require libraries to be networked and it also helps in easy retrieval of the information source.
3. **Internet:** The existence of the Internet is a major factor that has changed the way information is produced, published, stored, transmitted, and used. This requires libraries to be networked for accessing their information.
4. **Timely access to information:** It is difficult for an individual to lay hands on some specific information in the large mass of information available. Computer helps to process and easily access the required information. Networking is essential to access when the information is available at a distance. The networking of libraries has increased the feasibility of resource sharing by overcoming the barriers of distance and time involved in accessing information.

RESOURCE SHARING: ISSUES INVOLVED IN IMPLEMENTATION

The number and variety of libraries involved make it difficult to share the resources or create a network because policies have to be framed keeping in view the nature of documents for acquisition. The nature and variety of users make the framing and implementing the policy difficult. However, certain points hindering this process have been elaborated in this section:

1. **Inability to share all the documents:** It is neither required nor feasible to share all types of documents. A decision has to be taken in this regard taking into consideration the use and cost of the same. Libraries would like to share only costly and less used documents. Those documents that are in heavy demands in their libraries cannot be spared for other libraries. The requirements of their own users are primary.
2. **Terms and conditions for loan and return:** Documents are issued to users for a time period that enables them to use them effectively. A period of loan is decided by keeping this in view. It also depends on the type, cost, use and the number of copies of the document available. Similarly, these have to be formulated for sharing among a group of libraries.
3. **Deterrents and punitive measures to ensure safe and timely return of documents:** The biggest problem for a library in circulation service is to ensure the safe and timely return of documents to keep them in circulation. It is difficult if the user does not return the documents in time. It is all the more difficult when there are a number of libraries and hence users.
4. **Union catalogue production and maintenance:** The use of the combined collection of the participating libraries depends upon their knowing of the collection. The resources of the libraries should be made known to all through union catalogues. The responsibility for designing and maintaining the same should be entrusted to one of the participating libraries.
5. **Cooperative cataloguing:** Cooperative cataloguing is also expected in resource sharing. It needs to be decided as to who will be doing this work. It depends

on the resources of the library. A library that has the staff expertise to do this work should be entrusted this responsibility.

6. **OPAC:** The details of the documents along with their status should be made known to the users through OPAC. It is more important than for users of individual library because of the number of users involved as well as the distance between the participating libraries.

Library Consortia

Libraries and publishers come together for mutual benefits to enable the collaborative acquisition of e-documents to a group of libraries. Consortium of libraries is known for sharing of digital resources at the local, national, and international levels. Several libraries in India and foreign countries have formed consortia to share their human and e-resources in order to satisfy the user's needs and demands for rendering quality services. Library consortia are a part of library resource sharing and networking. A few well-known names of library consortia are:

- INDEST (for IITs, NITs, ISS and other Engineering and Technical Universities and Colleges), MHRD, India.
- FORSA (for Astrophysics/Astronomy), Raman Research Institute, 1981.
- UGC-INFONET (for E-Journals and database sharing), UGC, 2002.
- KERIS (Korea Education and Research Information System), 1999.

Unit 9
Library and Information Networks and Consortia

Library Networks

"Library Network" refers to the network among libraries for sharing sources and resources. It has been defined as a "group of individuals or organisations that are interconnected to form a system to accomplish some specified goal".

OBJECTIVES OF LIBRARY NETWORKS

Major objectives of a library and information network are to:

- Encourage interlibrary cooperation and resource sharing at all levels amongst members of the network;
- Provide help to member institutions in computerisation of their libraries, retro-conversion of bibliographic records and development of standardised databases for shared use;
- Develop union catalogues of various resources so as to provide reliable access to document collection available in member libraries;
- Provide effective access to combined holdings of library resources through computerised databases of various member institutions;
- Provide document delivery services to member libraries;
- Rationalisation of acquisition of information resources in member libraries and optimise their usage through resource sharing;

- Evolve/adapt protocols and standards, guidelines, methods and procedures for bibliographic records, their storage, inter-library loan hardware and software;
- Facilitate communication amongst users of member institutions;
- Provide training to members of library staff of participating libraries for effective use of libraries in the network;
- Guide member libraries in the effective implementation and utilisation of current and upcoming information technologies;
- Provide access to information resources at reduced rates through consortium arrangements; and
- Develop and promote collaborative digitisation projects.

CHARACTERISTICS OF A LIBRARY NETWORK

The library and information networks are characterised by the following aspects:

Equal Opportunity of Access to All Members: A library network provides equitable access to all its core resources to all its member libraries. However, resources that are licensed from a third party may be offered on subscription basis.

Interdependence: The members of a library network depend on each other for sharing their resources. The interdependency may go beyond sharing of document resources to sharing of expertise, manpower, equipment, etc.

Use of Standards and Protocols: The use of common standards and protocols are a pre-requisite for the successful implementation of a library and information network. The standards and protocols exist for network technology, database structure, information representation and for bibliographic records.

Shared Decision: The decisions of members of the executive committee of a library and information network are equitably applicable to all member institutions. All members of a library network are obliged to stand by the decision taken collectively.

Broad-based Library Services: Library and information networks generally offer a broad range of library services including a union catalogue of books and journals, access to union catalogues and licensed databases, licensing of e-resources from publishers, table of content services, database of experts in various disciplines, etc.

Centralisation: Network activities are generally centralised. Large bibliographic databases are centrally stored and maintained, although they have interfaces for online data feeding and updation.

Economics: The cost involved in maintaining the activities and the functioning of a library and information network including licensing and hosting of third-party databases get distributed amongst subscribers and members of the network. The products and services through the network, therefore, tend to be more economic than by the subscription directly by the libraries individually.

International Reach and Opportunity for Further Collaboration: The networks may be connected to other networks through which such networks can have an opportunity to learn from each other and work in collaboration.

Research and Development: The library and information networks, with their elaborate infrastructure and large number of databases, provide an opportunity for research and development work. The usage statistics of databases and electronic resources, feedback from participating libraries, etc. provides input for further research and analysis.

COMPONENTS OF A LIBRARY NETWORK

Major components of a library and information network are given in this section:

1. Human Network: While databases, databanks, computer, and communication infrastructure are important for the successful implementation of a library and information network, the most important component of a library network is manpower and their willingness to participate in the library network and share the resources of their respective libraries. While a library network focuses primarily on the availability and delivery of information, it is the human resource that makes it possible.

2. Online Databases: The emphasis within a library network is on the contents and users of the contents rather than on the technology of networking. Library networks lease communication and network infrastructure of other data networks and Internet service providers and concentrate on developing contents and making them accessible to member institutions. Databases and databanks are the backbone of a library network. The concept of online databases itself has emerged from the idea of sharing information. A database is non-redundant, multi-usable, independent and a physically available set of complete data, on a subject, stored in an organised and structured manner to allow users to search the information in an interactive mode. A library network may develop some of its own databases and licenses or acquire other databases from their producers. WorldCat, for example, is a worldwide union catalogue of books created and maintained collectively by more than 25,900 member institutions of OCLC with 302 million bibliographic records. DELNET's union catalogue of books, for example contains more than 30 lakhs records from 844 member institutions.

3. Computer Hardware and Software Infrastructure: A library and information network requires computer infrastructure to host the databases and databanks developed and maintained by it. The servers are used to host databases, digital objects, browse and search interfaces and to facilitate their access to the member institutions. Servers for a library network need to be computationally powerful; have adequate main memory (RAM) to handle the expected work; have a large amount of secured disc storage for the database(s) and digital objects. A library network may require a number of specialised servers for different tasks so as to distribute the workload onto different servers. It would require one or more computer server(s) to host indices and databases and one or more object server(s) to store digital objects and other multimedia objects. However, for a smaller library network, several distinct activities can be performed on a single server. A library network would also require communication equipment like communication switches, routers, hubs, repeaters, modems, and other items required for setting up a Local Area Network (LAN). These hardware and software items are required for setting up any network and need not be specific to a library network. A library network also requires a number of software packages to handle its highly specialised and diversified resources, activities, and services.

4. Data Networks: The servers of a library network are required to be hooked on to the Internet so as to make them accessible to its members. Most library networks use infrastructure of other data networks and Internet service providers. For example, National Knowledge Network, JANET and AARNET are important data networks in India, UK, and USA respectively.

5. Members: The number of members in a library network is a yardstick of its success. A library network is more meaningful and effective if it has a large number of members. The cost involved in maintaining the activities and the functioning of a library network including licensing and hosting of third-party databases are distributed amongst subscribers and members of the library network. The benefits of a large number of members in a library network are suitably distributed among them. The collective strength of the members of a library network provides it with the power to bargain with the publishers for better rates of subscription and terms of licenses.

TYPES OF LIBRARY NETWORKS

The library and information networks perform multiple activities including providing access to full text and bibliographic databases, creation, maintenance, and updation of catalogues on member libraries, document delivery services and promotion of resource sharing activities amongst member libraries. The library and information networks can be grouped into the following three categories:

(i) Types of library networks based on size.

(ii) Types of library networks based on geographical region.

(iii) Types of library networks based on their activities.

(i) Types of Library Networks Based on Size

Based on the size, a library network can exist in three forms, viz.:

(a) **Large networks** concerned primarily with computerised large scale technical processing, for example, OCLC, RLIN, etc.

(b) **Small networks** or consortia concerned with the acquisition of electronic resources for member libraries and training of staff, i.e. INFLIBNET.

(c) **Limited purpose networks** cooperating with respect to limited special subject areas, for example, FORSA, CERA.

(ii) Types of Library Networks Based on Geographical Region

The library and information networks can be divided into the following categories based on the geographical regions that they serve:

(a) **City or Metropolitan Library Networks:** The library networks confining their activities and membership to a given city or metropolitan area can be categorised as metropolitan area networks, such as CALIBNET, DELNET, ADINET, PUNENET, BONET, etc. in India.

(b) **Regional Library Networks:** There are regional academic groups founded by the member institutions for specific purposes. South Australian Public Library Network, Alberta Public Library Electronic Network (APLEN) in South Australia and Canada are examples of regional library networks.

(c) **National Library Networks**: Library networks whose activities are spread over the entire country can be categorised as national library networks. Information and Library Network (INFLIBNET) in India and

China Academic Library and Information System (CALIS) in China are examples of national library networks.

(d) **International Library Networks:** The library networks like OCLC can be considered as international networks with 25,900 libraries as its members in 170 countries.

(iii) Types of Library Networks Based on their Activities

The library networks can also be grouped under the following categories based on activities undertaken by them.

(a) **Umbrella or Supermarket Networks:** Some of the networks, such as OCLC, are "Umbrella" or "Supermarkets" type covering all fields and offer a multitude of services. Libraries can take membership of such networks for accessing selected databases or for using its union catalogue.

(b) **Bibliographic Utility Networks:** The most common purpose of a library network is library automation and resource sharing, which generally take multiple forms. Most other activities, such as creation of union catalogues, document delivery services and copy cataloguing are its by-products. They consist of a large union bibliographic database of member libraries, accessible online to members for copy cataloguing or for creation of new bibliographic records for new books. Such networks also provide cataloguing information on magnetic tapes or CD-ROM for retro-conversion of manual library catalogue into machine readable catalogues. The largest bibliographic utilities, such as OCLC provide a database for cataloguing records created by member libraries. These records are used for copy cataloguing, interlibrary loan, and other functions.

(c) **Online Search Service Networks:** Online search networks host a number of databases in machine readable form which are accessible online through telecommunication links. A user can directly interrogate the databases mounted on the host's computer through a computer terminal using a communication package and communication links in a two-way interactive mode. These databases are hired/leased to the online search services (also called vendors, spinners or retailers), from their owners (information provider—often the publishers of the printed version of databases). Some of the important online bibliographic search services networks include: DIALOG, ORBIT, STN, BRS and Datastar. Most of the online search services networks are now accessible over the Internet with a web interface.

(d) **Service Centre Networks:** Service centre networks concentrate on providing services to the member library in a networked environment. Such services may include cataloguing, literature search, database access, news service, etc. These networks act as a distributor or aggregator for online databases for offering computer-based online information retrieval services. Illinois Library and Information Network (ILLINET) is an example of service centre network.

(e) **Networks for Subscription to Electronic Resources:** Although most library networks undertake multiple activities, group licensing/purchasing of electronic resources is one of the major activities of modern library networks and consortia. Ohio Link, a state-wide network in USA and INDEST Consortium in India are examples of such networks.

ACTIVITIES AND SERVICES OF LIBRARY NETWORK

A library network can offer a number of services depending upon its objectives. It is advantageous for a network to take up multiple activities and services since the cost incurred on these services gets distributed amongst its members. Moreover, since a library network represents a large number of institutions, it has better bargaining power and economy of scales. A library network, therefore, can provide a large number of services in a highly cost-effective manner. Important services that a library network can provide are given in this section.

1. Cooperative Cataloguing: The catalogue of a library is an index to its collection like how a union catalogue of libraries in a network serves as an index for the combined collection of libraries in the network. The union catalogue was, therefore, taken up as one of the first activities by most of the library networks. Fully automated library networks offer interfaces for online cataloguing that allow member libraries not only to access the database but also create bibliographic records online for new books or download records for books that already exist. The centralised cataloguing saves time, avoids duplication, encourages inter-library loan and facilitates downloading of cataloguing information directly into the local library catalogue.

2. Database Services: The library networks can subscribe to electronic resources (including bibliographic databases, full text electronic resources and reference sources) on behalf of the member institutions on a cost sharing basis, host them locally on their own computer infrastructure and provide access to resources hosted locally to their member libraries on a payment basis. Besides being economic, local availability of international databases make access faster and reliable, reduces transpacific network traffic and bandwidth congestion, and costs incurred on it.

3. Document Delivery Services: The libraries depend on inter-library loan and document delivery services to meet the demands of their users for research articles that are not available in their collection. Libraries cooperate with other libraries to provide these services to their users. Library networks offer document delivery service as one of the services to its member institutions. They offer document delivery service for journal articles that are accessible electronically or available physically in the libraries of the member institutions.

4. Inter-Library Loan: Document collection in a library can broadly be classified into two groups, i.e. collection that caters to the core interest of the institution and the other that serves the peripheral interest of its users. With a financial crunch, the library could curb its acquisitions in the peripheral areas and depend on inter-library loan for meeting the demands of their users in areas of peripheral interest to the institute. The primary mechanism for sharing materials being practiced for centuries is known as inter-library loan which involves mutual lending and borrowing of materials among the libraries. Resource sharing through formal and informal arrangements helps a library to deliver a wide range of services.

5. Shared Electronic Reference/Real-time Reference Service: Electronic reference service/live reference service can be offered by a library network. Digital reference service, also called "Ask-An-Expert" or "Ask-A-Librarian" services are Internet-based question and answer services that connect users with individuals who possess specialised subject knowledge and skills in conducting precision searches. As opposed to static web pages, digital reference services use the Internet to place people in contact with other people who can answer specific questions and instruct the users on developing certain skills.

6. Collective Acquisition of Resources: The goal of a library network is to share equitably the collective resources of the member libraries. While the existing resources can be shared through inter-library loan, library networks can achieve greater benefits by implementing a centralised resource acquisition programme and through the rationalisation of its acquisitions. The process and operations where collaboration can be achieved include:

(i) pre-order searching;
(ii) integration of new bibliographic records in OPAC;
(iii) account keeping;
(iv) maintenance of address files for supplier/publisher name, etc.;
(v) negotiations for purchase of multiple copies of books; and
(vi) updation of databases when the documents are withdrawn.

7. Consortium Purchase: Consortia-based subscription to e-resources is a way of maximising access to e-resources at a minimum cost. It is a feasible strategy to increase the access to electronic resources across institutions at a lower cost. The consortia-based subscription can be successfully deployed to meet pressures such as diminishing budget, increased users' demands and the rising cost of journals.

8. Joint Archives and Cooperative Storage Facilities: Cooperative storage of documents is a recent trend, whereby a group of libraries funds the construction of a high-density facility with advanced climate control systems. Materials stored in such a facility are considered important for research but are not used often enough to justify space in the prime use area. The sharing of documents is in-built in the concept of cooperative storage, since there is little point in storing multiple copies of commonly owned documents.

9. Training of Users and Library Staff: The training programme is a crucial requirement for the functioning of a library and information network to facilitate the optimum use of subscribed electronic resources. It acts as a bridge to facilitate better communication amongst the members of a library network and find answers to common problems. Educational programmes are essential for both the user as well as for the library staff. Such programmes make users competent to conduct their own searches more effectively.

10. Technology Support to Member Institutions: It is a major challenge for libraries to select appropriate technology from several technological alternatives that are now available in the marketplace. All libraries invariably require consultation and expert advice in the implementation of new technologies. Technologies can be even shared within a network between the member libraries.

Unit 10

Library and Information Networks and Consortia: National and International

NATIONAL LIBRARY NETWORKS

INFLIBNET (Information and Library Network)

INFLIBNET Centre (Information and Library Network Centre) is an Inter-University Centre of the University Grants Commission (India) under the Ministry of Education (India). The organisation promotes and facilitates libraries and information resources for higher education in India. It started its operations in 1991, with headquarters in Ahmedabad, Gujarat. INFLIBNET has played an important role in the automation and modernisation of the university library system in India. It provided universities and research institutions with the bandwidth for accessing e-journals. It has become a major player in enhancing scholarly communication in India.

Objectives of INFLIBNET

The INFLIBNET Programme is directed towards the modernisation of libraries and information centres and the establishment of a mechanism for information transfer and access, to support scholarship, learning and academic pursuits. It was established with the following objectives:

- To promote and establish communication facilities for improving transfer and access capability of information. This in turn provides support to scholarship, learning, research and academic pursuits through the cooperation and involvement of agencies concerned;

- To establish a computer communication network for linking libraries and information centres in universities, deemed to be universities, colleges, UGC information centres, institutions of national importance and R&D institutions, etc. in order to avoid duplication of efforts;
- To promote and implement the computerisation of operations and services in the libraries and information centres of the country, following a uniform standard;
- To evolve standards and uniform guidelines in techniques, methods, procedures, computer hardware and software, services and promote their adoption in actual practice by all libraries, in order to facilitate pooling, sharing and exchange of information towards an optimal use of resources and facilities;
- To provide reliable access to document collection of libraries by creating an online union catalogue of serials, theses/dissertations, books, monographs, and non-book materials in various libraries in India;
- To provide access to bibliographic information sources with citations, abstracts, etc. through indigenously created databases of the Sectoral Information Centres of NISSAT, etc.;
- To create database(s) of projects, institutions, specialists, etc. for providing online information services;
- To encourage co-operation among libraries, documentation centres and information centres in the country, so that the resources can be pooled together for the benefit of helping the weaker resource centres by the stronger ones;
- To train and develop human resources in the field of computerised library operations and networking to establish, manage and sustain INFLIBNET;

- To facilitate academic communication amongst scientists, engineers, social scientists, academics, faculties, researchers and students through electronic mail, file transfer, computer/audio/video conferencing, etc.;
- To collaborate with institutions, libraries, information centres and other organisations in India and abroad in the field relevant to the objectives of the centre;
- To promote R&D and develop necessary facilities and create technical positions for realising the objectives of the centre;
- To generate revenue by providing consultancies and information services; and
- To do all other such things as may be necessary, incidental or conducive to the attainment of all or any of the above objectives.

Services Offered by INFLIBNET

(a) **Document Delivery:** INLIBNET provides inter-library loan and document delivery services from the comprehensive collection of subscribed journals under JCCC@UGC-INFONET. It has designated 22 libraries to fulfil ILL requests from the users, affiliated to 149 universities covered under the UGC. The ILL libraries together have subscription to 2,000 plus journals that are not available through consortia. Universities can request for articles from the journal holdings of those libraries wherever they find useful articles in JCCC search.

(b) **OJAS Open Journal Access System (OJAS):** It is an open-source journal management and publishing software developed and freely distributed by the Public Knowledge Project at the University of British Columbia. INFLIBNET has installed and configured the software at its server and provides the facility of uploading the e-versions of journals of universities and even individuals for open access.

(c) **Library Automation:** INFLIBNET has developed a library automation package called SOUL (Software for University Libraries). It has all the necessary modules which a library needs. Besides SOUL, INFLIBNET has developed several small utilities for day-to-day library operations. It also develops solution on demand by university libraries, like retro conversion, preparation of catalogue cards, duplicate checking of library records and so on.

(d) **Human Resource Development:** INFLIBNET runs several short-term courses for professionals in order to train them with new automated tools and techniques. It has conducted many programmes for working university library professionals. The course contains training modules in computer application for library and information centres.

Databases of INFLIBNET

INFLIBNET offers access to two kinds of databases—Bibliographic and Non-Bibliographic.

Bibliographic databases: INFLIBNET has developed the following bibliographic databases pertaining to the collection of participating libraries to enable the sharing of resources:

1. **Shodhganga:** It is a digital repository of theses and dissertations submitted in Indian Universities.
2. **Shodhgangotri:** This is a database of research-in-progress in universities across different disciplines.
3. **Infoport:** It is a subject gateway for Indian electronic resources. It is designed and developed to serve as a comprehensive gateway to all Indian scholarly content.

Non-bibliographic database: It has also developed non-bibliographic databases on research projects and experts in different fields by the name "Vidwan" to help improve communication and collaboration in research.

It also gives access to e-resources under NLIST (National Libraries Information Services Infrastructure for Scholarly Content) programme which is a project of the Ministry of Human Resource Development under the National Mission on Education through ICT being jointly executed by the UGC-INFONET Digital Library Consortium, INFLIBNET Centre and the INDEST-AICTE Consortium. The project has four distinct components, i.e.:

(i) to subscribe and provide access to selected UGC-INFONET e-resources to technical institutions (IITs, IISc, IISERs and NITs) and monitor its usage;

(ii) to subscribe and provide access to selected INDEST e-resources to selected universities and monitor its usage;

(iii) to subscribe and provide access to selected e-resources to 6,000 government/government-aided colleges and monitor its usage; and

(iv) to act as a monitoring agency for colleges and evaluate, promote, impart training and monitor all activities involved in the process of providing effective and efficient access to e-resources to colleges.

DELNET (Developing Library Network)

DELNET has been sponsored by the National Information System for Science and Technology (NISSAT), Department of Scientific and Industrial Research, Government of India and is currently being promoted by the National Informatics Centre, Department of Information Technology, Ministry of Communications and Information Technology, Government of India and India International Centre, New Delhi. Though it became a registered body in 1992, it has been functional only since 1988. DELNET was originally established as the Delhi Library Network and subsequently the name was changed to Developing Library Network. The Headquarter of DELNET is in New Delhi. Currently, DELNET has about 4,667 libraries as its members of which 241 are from Delhi, 4,402 from states and union territories outside Delhi and 24 outside India.

Objectives of DELNET

DELNET is fully functional with the following objectives:

- To promote sharing of resources among the libraries by developing a network of libraries, by collecting, storing and disseminating information and by offering computerised services to the users;

- To undertake scientific research in the area of information science and technology, create new systems in the field, apply the results of research and publish them;
- To offer technical guidance to the member libraries on collecting, storing, sharing, and disseminating information;
- To coordinate efforts for the suitable collection development and reduce unnecessary duplication wherever possible;
- To establish/facilitate the establishment of referral and/or research centres, and maintain a central online union catalogue of books, serials and non-book materials of all the participating libraries;
- To facilitate and promote delivery of documents manually or mechanically;
- To develop specialised bibliographic database of books, serials, and non-book materials;
- To develop databases of projects, specialists, and institutions;
- To coordinate with other regional, national, and international networks and libraries for the exchange of information and documents.

Services Offered by DELNET

(a) **Inter Library Loan:** Online member libraries can request online for a document using inter-library loan facility of DELNET through the DELNET server and the document is couriered to the requesting library. The member library needs to pay an annual subscription for this service.

(b) **Reference Service:** DELNET has a referral centre that provides reference service to participating libraries.

(c) **Access to Online Databases:** DELNET provides online access to several databases to its member libraries and information centres. This includes the Union Catalogue of Books, Union List of Current Periodicals, Database of Periodical Articles, CD-ROM Database, etc.

(d) **Training Programmes:** DELNET organises monthly training programmes with NIC on topics like web page design, Internet search strategies and other resources, etc. It also conducts courses on machine readable cataloguing and bibliographic standards like MARC21.

(e) **Publishing of Newsletter:** DELNET publishes a newsletter called the 'DELNET Newsletter' to communicate the activity of DELNET to professionals.

(f) **Research:** DELNET has actively played an important role in imparting knowledge of international standards by applying them in libraries particularly MARC21. Recently, it has been advocating the open source software and teaching their use by conducting training programmes in KOHA and D-Space.

CALIBNET (Calcutta Library Network)

The CALIBNET was envisaged as a metropolitan network in 1993, linking 38 libraries in Calcutta with financial support from NISSAT. The prime objective was to institutionalise systematic interlibrary co-operation and document delivery among the networked libraries for effective resource sharing. The applications to be supported are electronic mail, file transfer, remote logging to databases and document access. The participating libraries computerised their in-house functions such as cataloguing, serials control, acquisition and fund accounting, circulation, and user services. These have been interconnected through X.25 protocol. The network services centre provides global information services for all the users of the participating libraries. The services include current awareness, union catalogues and database access to national and international networks. CALIBNET provides libraries and their members an efficient solution for their information needs. The project was supported by NISSAT in 1986 and managed by the CALIBNET Society established under the West Bengal Government's Societies Registration Act of 1961. The centre is stationed at Jadavpur University Campus, Kolkata.

Objectives of CALIBNET

CALIBNET is established to pursue the problems of the Eastern region of the country, mainly West Bengal. The primary objective of the organisation is creating and facilitating access to available library and information resources in West Bengal. The main objective is supported by other objectives given in this section:

- Facilitating remote online access to the data held in Calcutta libraries and other specialised databases; and
- Providing electronic access to globally available information and imbibing its information centric approach.

Services Offered by CALIBNET

(a) **Software Development:** By intense in-house research and development two software have been developed for supporting library activities.

(i) Sanjukta: This in-house software has been developed for storage and retrieval which is used in the centralised database of CALIBNET for providing online access from remote locations.

(i) Parapar: Parapar has been developed to support the interchange of bibliographic data between different bibliographic standards like, USMARC, UNIMARC and CCF.

Current Content Service: It gives current awareness through a config service which covers almost 20,000 journals of different disciplines.

Document Delivery Service (Caliborder): Caliborder is a document delivery service which delivers the full text of any article and even patents on demand.

Selective Dissemination of Information: ConAlert service is designed to give current and tailored bibliographic information. A user profile is created based on the keywords. Notification about the arrival or availability of the document is sent to the user. On demand document is also delivered at the user's desk.

Institutional Resources Development Services: CALIBNET supports institutes to build a library. It also assists and provides consultancy services in library automation and creation of databases and electronic resources.

ADINET (Ahmedabad Library Network)

ADINET was established for developing cooperative mode of working amongst the libraries and information centres in and around Ahmedabad. It was established in 1994 with the help of NISSAT. ADINET promotes the sharing of resources and disseminates information among member libraries by networking them. It is stationed in INFIBNET Centre, Ahmedabad.

Objectives of ADINET

ADINET was established with the following objectives:

- To bring about a cooperative mode of working amongst libraries and information centres in and around Ahmedabad;
- To integrate the economic, scientific, and technical information systems into an effective network in and around Ahmedabad;
- To facilitate and promote the sharing of resources amongst the libraries and information centres in and around Ahmedabad by developing and maintaining a central online Union Catalogue;
- To coordinate with other regional, national and international networks, libraries, information and documentation centres for exchange of information and documents;
- To offer technical guidance to member libraries on selecting, storing, sharing, and disseminating information;
- To coordinate efforts for the suitable collection development and reduce unnecessary duplication whenever possible;
- To develop databases of projects, specialists and institutions in and around Ahmedabad;

- To create awareness amongst all users' groups and to educate them in the utilisation of information;
- To develop resources and to propagate information in ways appropriate to the needs of users in and around Ahmedabad; and
- To help library and information centre users and also individuals who practice different professions in getting specialised information of their interests.

Services Offered by ADINET

(a) **Document Delivery:** ADINET acts as a referral centre for finding any periodical, book, report, theses and non-book material like audio-video materials, etc.

(b) **Inter-Library Loan:** It facilitates inter-library loaning among the libraries within the Ahmedabad region. Besides, it procures and provides photocopies of articles from journals received by the libraries in the region.

(c) **Current Content for Library and Information Science (CUCOLIS):** ADINET prepares consolidation of content pages of library and information science journals and provides the list to member libraries. It is based on 5,000 journals received from 19 major publishers.

(d) **Access to Databases:** ADINET acts as a referral centre and maintains a database of all the databases available in different libraries in and around Ahmedabad. It also has a database of 5,500 current periodicals received by more than 140 libraries in and around Ahmedabad.

(e) **Continuing Education and Skill Enhancement of Library Professionals:** ADINET performs several professional activities around the year. It runs courses for fresh graduates of library science in Internet surfing and CDS/ISIS. It also maintains a database of available jobs and helps professionals in finding suitable jobs.

MYLIBNET (Mysore Library Network)

Mysore Library Network (MYLIBNET) was initiated in 1995 with the support of NISSAT. It is stationed at the Central

Food Technology Research Institute (CFTRI), Mysore. About 116 colleges/institutions are affiliated to the University of Mysore; of these 34 college libraries are located within Mysore. These were networked in the first phase.

Objectives of MYLIBNET

The objectives of the network are as follows:

- To share resources available with all the libraries;
- To provide a faster communication to all the libraries through electronic mail facility;
- To develop software tools for better library management;
- To create awareness in the field of latest information technology by conducting seminars/workshops/ training programmes;
- To setup an information base in collaboration with industries; and
- To flash the arrival of new books/journals, announcement of events like seminar/workshop/ training programmes.

Services Offered by MYLIBNET

(a) **E-Journals:** MYLIBNET provides links to several free online e-journals in the field of medicine, physics, mathematics and chemistry.

(b) **Union Catalogue of Journals:** In order to achieve the objective of 'Resource Sharing' for an optimum utilisation of the available resources and to avoid duplication as far as possible, a project was initiated in 1990 by the Academy of Information Science to conduct a survey and bring out a hard copy of the "Union Catalogue of S&T Serials in Mysore City Libraries". The project was completed, and a hard copy of the catalogue was published in 1991.

(c) **Experts Database:** The database contains the list of library professionals and their details. One can search for details of an expert either by selecting the name of the expert or by selecting the name of the institute. The database is not very exhaustive and is still being developed.

MALIBNET (Madras Library Network)

MALIBNET was established in 1993 with the support of the Indian National Scientific Documentation Centre (INSDOC). Now it is a registered society of Tamil Nadu Government. It provides information to the users in and around Chennai. Nearly 83 libraries in Madras are members contributing actively to the creation of various databases on MALIBNET. It has around 37 educational and research institutions as members.

Objectives of MALIBNET

The main objectives of MALIBNET are:

- To foster growth in the field of information science and technology;
- To undertake scientific research in the field of library and documentation;
- To evolve a network of libraries and information centres in India;
- To establish appropriate links to national and international libraries and networks; and
- To facilitate resource sharing and information dissemination through different networks.

Services Offered by MALIBNET

(a) **Content Search Service:** This service allows a search of the journal database of MALIBNET having 7,747 journals. It can be searched online through journal title, volume, year and issue number options.

(b) **Document Procurement Service:** MALIBNET provides the full text of articles from the journals available in its database. One needs to provide the journal's year, volume, and issue along with page numbers. The service is available upon the payment of ₹ 3 per page for members and ₹ 5 per page for non-members.

(c) **Internet Services:** MALIBNET provides facility of Internet search for which it charges the users for the time spent on searching. It prepares directories of current journals available in

Madras City in different areas like Engineering Sciences, Basic Sciences, Medical Sciences and Social Sciences.

BONET (Bombay Library Network)

Bombay Library Network (BONET) was established in 1994 with financial support from the NISSAT. It has 25 members in the city of Mumbai. It is located at the National Centre for Software Technology (NCST, now CDAC) and offers a number of computers and software for shared use to the members. The services offered include access to bibliographic databases, email, CD-ROM, etc. The BONET conducts seminars and training programmes for its member institutions.

NATIONAL LIBRARY CONSORTIA

INDEST (Indian Digital Library in Engineering Sciences and Technology)

INDEST stands for Indian National Digital Library in Engineering Sciences and Technology. It is a "consortia-based subscription to electronic resources for technical education systems in India", set up by the Ministry of Human Resource Development based on the recommendations made by the expert group appointed by the Ministry under the Chairmanship of Prof. N. Balakrishnan. The headquarters of the consortium is located at the Indian Institute of Technology, Delhi.

Objectives of INDEST

- To provide a common gateway of journal literature subscribed by seven IITs and the Indian Institutes of Science, to subscribe, access, and manage their journals.
- To provide common access and search interface for the journals subscribed by all its members.
- To provide access to the common database for the usage benefit of students and researchers in regional engineering colleges (National Institutes of Technology) and support them in sharing the collection of IITs and IIScs.

Features of INDEST

The common features of INDEST are:

(a) It provides common access to TOCs (Table of Contents) and full text articles;

(b) It allows to search common TOCs and database for both print as well as online journals with scholarly content subscribed by all the members of the consortium;

(c) It provides links to full-text articles, wherever available;

(d) It facilitates the search for articles and links to full texts in a bibliographic database;

(e) It has provisions to mirror the content in the server of each participating consortium member;

(f) It has also provisions to view the list of journals subscribed by each consortium member; and

(g) It is possible to send e-mail requests for photocopies from one consortium member to the other.

FORSA (Forum for Resource Sharing in Astronomy/Astrophysics)

In the early 1980s, librarians working in institutes where astronomy and astrophysics were two of the major research areas felt the need to establish a forum among the libraries to enable sharing of resources due to the reasons that very few institutes in the country were involved in the research of astronomy and astrophysics. A considerable amount of interaction already existed between astronomers of institutes doing research in astronomy and astrophysics, but no library can be self-sufficient in the resources. Based on the proposed plans made by the members of the Forum, the first meeting of the Forum for Resource Sharing in Astronomy/Astrophysics (FORSA) was held on July 29, 1981, at Raman Research Institute, Bangalore. This led to the emergence of a consortia called FORSA meant for sharing resources among institutions dealing with astrophysics/astronomy.

Objectives of FORSA

- To promote the collection development in an IT environment;
- To facilitate e-access to journals and books;
- To actively participate in resource sharing and ILL;
- To promote document delivery by fax, e-mail, speed post, courier, etc.;
- To support database merging by library holdings (books/journals) and facilitate access to merged databases;
- To ensure the digitisation of archival materials of the institutes and making them available on the website for everyone's access;
- To facilitate access to website of each institute's library;
- To participate actively in consortia plans for sharing e-journals, e-books and other databases with various publishers and academic societies' publications and joining existing consortia where forum members are benefitted;
- To come forward for open access and to develop institutional repositories; and
- To welcome new members of institutes where astronomy is one of the subjects and the library has a collection pertaining to the subject.

Services Offered by FORSA

All the participating libraries are well equipped with recourses and share them for mutual benefit. They provide the following services:

(a) Access to OPAC.

(b) Access to online journals.

(c) Inter-library loan.

(d) Document Delivery (by e-mail, speed post, courier and fax).

UGC-INFONET

University Grants Commission (UGC) is a national body for the coordination, determination, and maintenance of the standards of university education in India. It initiated a programme called the UGC-Infonet E-Journals Consortium to provide online access to electronic journals and databases in all disciplines to the universities in India. The programme aimed at increasing the accessibility of electronic resources to the universities. INFLIBNET is the coordinating and monitoring agency in the UGC-Infonet Project. INFLIBNET is also responsible for providing training to university library professionals in the use of this network for providing a variety of services to the users. The project aimed to provide e-resources and state-of-the-art technology for providing access to these resources. The part responsible for providing connectivity for the e-resources has been closed with effect from 31 March 2012.

NKRC (National Knowledge Resource Centre)

The National Knowledge Resource Consortium (NKRC), established in the year 2009, is a network of libraries and information centres of 43 CSIR and 26 DST institutes. NKRC's origin goes back to the year 2001, when the CSIR set up the Electronic Journal Consortium to provide access to 1,200 odd journals of Elsevier Science to all its users. Over a period of time, the consortium not only grew in terms of the number of resources but also in terms of the number of users as more like-minded institutions evinced interest to join the consortium. Today, NKRC provides access to more than 5,000 e-journals, patents, standards, citations, and bibliographic databases. It also provides access to a large number of open access resources in science and technology. Earlier it was called as CSIR E-Journals Consortium.

Objectives of NKRC

- To provide CSIR S&T staff electronic access to world S&T literature to strengthen the facilities for pooling, sharing, and electronically accessing the CSIR information resources;

- To provide access to world S&T literature to CSIR labs; and
- To nucleate the culture of electronic access with a view to catalyse the evolution of digital libraries.

Activities of NKRC

The following are the broad activities envisaged to be involved in carrying out the project:

(a) Identification of vendors.
(b) Invitation of proposals.
(c) Negotiation.
(d) Signing of agreement.
(e) Enabling access.
(f) Training.
(g) Payment to vendors.
(h) Monitoring.
(i) Usage statistics.
(j) Analysis.
(k) Reports.

IIM Consortium

The Indian Institutes of Management are premier national business management education institutions set up by the Government of India. They are independent societies governed by an independent Board of Governors. The major objective of the institutions is to train young graduates to become professional managers. The IIMs are available at six places—Ahmedabad, Bangalore, Calcutta, Indore, Kozhikode, and Lucknow. The concept of an IIM Library Consortium was floated a few years back. Since the year 2000, the librarians of all the IIMs had been interacting extensively on the possible resource sharing of the CD-ROM/digital databases being regularly subscribed to by them.

Objectives of IIM Consortium

The objectives of the IIM consortia are to:

- Ensure among the IIMs, optimum utilisation and enhancement of the resources;
- Minimise the expenditure by consortia-based subscriptions to the commonly subscribed databases and journals;
- Approach publishers of CD-ROM databases to begin with as a consortia for better pricing and services; and
- Cover other digital databases and journals by the programme.

HELINET (Health Sciences Library and Information Network)

The Rajiv Gandhi University of Health Sciences (RGUHS) launched HELINET (Health Sciences Library and Information Network) Consortium, on 15 March 2003. The importance and the role of quality medical journals in medical education are known. Moreover, according to a survey conducted in early 2002, the colleges of RGUHS were spending an enormous amount of money to get only about 150 journals each and even among these, many were duplicates. This spurred the need for reducing the cost while making the core medical journals more affordable and easily accessible. HELINET is a consortium of libraries dealing with health science.

Objectives of HELINET

The main objectives of the consortium are to:

- Network the libraries in the colleges affiliated to the university to promote resource sharing;
- Move these libraries gradually to the digital mainstream; and
- Bring all the libraries under HELINET for minimising the cost of acquisition and maintenance of learning resources and maximising their utilisation, among the faculty, students and researchers of the colleges and institutions affiliated to the university.

SPACENET

Spacenet is a communication network of the Indian Space Research Organisation (ISRO) using a Very Small Aperture Terminal (VSAT) network. The hub is located at the ISTARAC, Bengaluru and remote stations at 44 centres/divisions of ISRO at different places in India. It is a Closed User Group (CUG) network facilitating the transmitting and sharing of data, information, and other resources between the members. ISRO libraries exchange various resources including print and electronic. The libraries provide access to their resources by having their OPACs on the intranet. E-journals and e-books are also shared amongst the participating libraries. The divisions generate a lot of information internally in the form of reports, pre-prints, re-prints, conference proceedings, lectures, etc. which are shared amongst them. Effective document delivery services enable sharing and transfer of information amongst them.

CeRA (Consortia for e-Resources in Agriculture)

The Consortium for e-Resources in Agriculture (CeRA) was formed in November 2007 at the Indian Agriculture Research Institute (IARI), Pusa, New Delhi. It was funded by the National Agricultural Innovation Project (NAIP). It was set up to provide access to information in agriculture particularly the e-resources to researchers, teachers, scientists, students, extension workers, policy planners and administrators in the National Agricultural System (NARS).

Objectives of CeRA

To upscale the existing R&D information resource base of ICAR institutions/universities comparable to world's leading institutions/organisations;

To subscribe e-journals and create e-access culture among scientists/teachers in ICAR institutes/agricultural universities;

To assess the impact of CeRA on the level of research publications measured through NAAS ID and Science Citation Index.

ICMR e-Consortia

ICMR has two types of consortia, JCC@ICMR which covers all subscribed journals of ICMR along with free journals. The other, ICMR e-Consortia provides full text access to the journals subscribed by ICMR.

JCCC@ICMR: J-Gate C Custom Content for ICMR provides a single point access to all subscribed and free open access journals in medicine. It provides a platform to access the journals, search articles of interest, locate the library possessing it and put a request for acquisition. It acts as a common gateway and search interface to the journals. JCCC provides access to the table of contents, abstracts, full-texts, and facilities.

ICMR e-Consortia: It provides access to the subscribed journals to the users in different ICMR institutes through IP authentication. The consortia organises training programmes for the users to enable effective use.

INTERNATIONAL LIBRARY NETWORKS

OCLC (Online Computer Library Centre)

OCLC Inc. doing business as OCLC, is an American non-profit cooperative organization "that provides shared technology services, original research, and community programmes for its membership and the library community at large". It was founded in 1967 as the Ohio College Library Centre, then became the Online Computer Library Centre as it expanded. In 2017, the name was formally changed to OCLC Inc. OCLC and thousands of its member libraries cooperatively produce and maintain WorldCat, the largest online public access catalogue (OPAC) in the world. Researchers, students, faculty, scholars, professional librarians, and other information seekers use OCLC systems through libraries to obtain bibliographic, abstract, citation, and full-text information. The OCLC cataloguing and resource sharing system is the largest and most heavily used computer library system in the world. The OCLC and its member libraries cooperatively produce and maintain WorldCat, the Online Union Catalogue of Books available in the libraries of member institutions. Members of the OCLC can also get access to a wide range of services and databases, including WorldCat. The OCLC is the world's largest library network.

Services Offered by OCLC

The OCLC offers several products and services. A few of them are described in this section:

WorldCat: WorldCat is a worldwide union catalogue created and maintained collectively by more than 72,000 libraries representing hundreds of languages and cultures. Built from the bibliographic and ownership information of contributing libraries, it is the largest and most comprehensive database of its kind. WorldCat is the foundation of many OCLC services that facilitates libraries to process, manage, and share information resources. WorldCat holds 302 million bibliographic records for two billion items in 470 languages and dialects. Every ten seconds a new record is added to the catalogue and it is searched every second.

NetLibrary: The OCLC's NetLibrary platform provides access to electronic books from a wide range of publishers forming monographs and reference resources on hundreds of subject areas that can be accessed through an intuitive, easy-to-use interface that offers a single point of access.

OCLC's Electronic Collections Online: OCLC's Electronic Collections Online is a powerful electronic journals service that offers web-based access to a growing collection of more than 5,000 titles in a wide range of subject areas from over seventy publishers. It provides access to 4.2 million records from 1995 onwards.

OCLC Database Service (FirstSearch): The FirstSearch (FS) is an online service that provides web access to research databases consisting primarily of journals. The service provides seamless electronic access to more than eighty databases containing 258 million full text and full image articles via WorldCat in most subject fields. Some of the more important databases included in FirstSearch are:

- ArticleFirst
- Clase and Periódica

- Electronic Books
- ERIC
- Proceedings (PCF1)
- SCIPIO
- WorldCat (The OCLC Online Union Catalogue)
- WorldCat Dissertations and Theses (WorldCat Dissertations), etc.

EZproxy Authentication and Access Software: It is the world's leading access and authentication solution. EZproxy helps provide users with remote access to web-based licensed content offered by libraries and is easy to set up and maintain.

Question Point: Cooperative Virtual Reference Service: "Question Point" is a unique virtual reference service, supported by a global network of cooperating libraries as well as an infrastructure of software tools and communications.

RLG (Research Libraries Group)

The Research Libraries Group (RLG), a not-for-profit organisation consisting of over 150 research libraries, archives, museums, and other cultural memory institutions was founded in 1974 by the New York Public Library, Columbia University, Harvard University and Yale University. The reason for the formation of yet another consortium in the US when the OCLC already existed, was the dissatisfaction of research libraries with OCLC's record keeping. The RLG was founded to provide solutions to the challenges presented by information access and management of digital resources. It served researchers by providing them access to research materials held in libraries, archives, and museums. It designed and delivered innovative information discovery services, organised collaborative programmes and took an active role in creating and promoting relevant standards and practices. After three decades of serving libraries, RLG merged with the OCLC in 2006. After its merger, its catalogue merged with OCLC WorldCat and its databases merged with the OCLC FirstSearch service. RLG merged with the OCLC to be known as "RLG Programmes" as part of the OCLC Programmes and Research Division. The latter was renamed as OCLC research in 2009 and the former as RLG Partnership. RLG Partnership was renamed as OCLC Research Library Partnership in 2011.

JISC

JISC leads the further and higher education community in the use of ICTs for learning, teaching, research and administration. It is an advisory by nature and is funded by all higher education councils. It has the following sub-committees to facilitate work:

- JISC Organisational Support Committee.
- JISC Content Services Committee.
- JISC Integrated Information Environment Committee.
- JISC Learning and Teaching Committee.
- JISC Network Committee.
- JISC Support of Research Committee.

It works to develop solutions that help and enable education and research communities in the UK to keep their activities world class through the innovative use of Information and Communications Technologies.

JANET (Joint Academic Network)

JANET is dedicated to the needs of the education and research community in the UK. It connects education and research organisations in the UK to each other, as well as to the rest of the world through the Internet. In addition, JANET includes a separate network that is available to the community for experimental activities.

CALIS (China Academic Library and Information System)

The China Academic Library and Information System (CALIS), launched in 1998, is a nationwide resource sharing system among Chinese academic libraries. Its mission is to serve directly those universities, which are funded by the central government, by providing document and information services to the users through the China Education and Research

Network. The CALIS also serves users in other universities and colleges so long as they have network connections to the China Education & Research Network (CERNET). The CALIS is just like a nationwide academic library consortium in China, half supported by the government, half by the libraries themselves. At present, it provides service to 1,251 academic libraries and 792 journal content users in China.

INTERNATIONAL LIBRARY CONSORTIA

CARLI (Consortium of Academic and Research Libraries in Illinois)

CARLI was formed in July 2005 to serve the consortia needs of academic and research libraries in Illinois. CARLI took birth as a result of the consolidation of these three consortia. There had been consortia existing in Illinois since the 1980s prior to the formation of CARLI. These were Illinois Cooperative Collection Management Program (ICCMP) formed in 1986; Illinois Digital Academic Library (IDAL), formed in 1999 and Illinois Library Computer Systems Organization (ILCSO), formed in 1980. CARLI took birth as a result of the consolidation of these three consortia. Its mission is to create and maintain a rich, supportive, and diverse knowledge environment to facilitate teaching, learning and research by sharing collections, expertise, and programmes.

Services Offered by CARLI

E-Resource Program: Participating libraries are provided access to a large number of e-resources in a consortium mode enhancing the collections of individual libraries.

Access to I-Share database: I-Share database is the union catalogue of all participating libraries. It contains 11.5 million unique bibliographical records and thirty-six million item records. These pertain to eighty-two CARLI I-Share member institutions.

Document Delivery: I-Share libraries allow users to borrow documents from other libraries. Libraries are assigned a User ID which can be quoted to borrow documents from other libraries.

Training: CARLI organises training programmes for the staff of participating libraries. It also conducts training programmes for the users.

CONCERT (Consortium on Core Electronic Resources in Taiwan)

The CONCERT was set up in 1990 to take advantage of the growing popularity of web-based full-text documents. It consists of members mainly from universities, colleges as well as research institutes in Taiwan. As the coordinator of the CONCERT, Science and Technology Policy Research and Information Centre (STPI), tries its best to fully exploit the economies from group purchase and resource sharing. In the year 2002, CONCERT leased twenty-two international database systems, partly funded by the Ministry of Education and National Applied Research Laboratories.

Objectives of CONCERT

- To enhance sci-tech policy research and establish a knowledge bank: major themes include critical national issues; and
- To establish a national integrated information service mechanism.

Features of CONCERT

To Sustain Academic Research Progress—It develops and integrates national information resources and introduces international information resources to foster domestic research.

To Support Policy Decision Makers—It provides critical insights for governmental policy decision makers by undertaking policy research of S&T development and value-added analysis.

To Facilitate Circulation of Industrial Innovation—It serves as a major gateway of knowledge innovation in support of cutting-edge technology research by taking part in nation based nanotechnology programmes, etc.

To Enhance S&T Cooperation Across Nations—It helps in accelerating bilateral and multilateral collaboration by participating in the information activities worldwide.

SANLIC (South African National Library and Information Consortium)

SANLIC is a consortium of higher education and research libraries in South Africa. It works with a mission to provide high quality research materials to participating institutions at cost-effective rates. Its mission is to "facilitate, on a non-profit basis, affordable access to scholarly electronic information in support of the learning, teaching and research activities of its members. This is achieved mainly through collective negotiations with publishers and aggregators. It also promotes the use of high quality, open access electronic information resources". It offers access to e-journals, e-books and open access resources. It also publishes regularly its newsletter titled "SCANLiCTALK" informing its clientele about its activities and resources.

CURL (Consortium of University Research Libraries)

The CURL is a Consortium of University Research Libraries in the UK. Several activities of CURL are funded by the JISC. The CURL helps member institutions to build a distributed and hybrid research library in their institutions with an aim to help researchers all over the world:

(i) to search, locate and request resources of all kinds in different formats, easily and quickly from their desktops;

(ii) have quick and easy access to an increasing number of electronic resources, both born-digital and digitised;

(iii) have physical access to manuscripts, archives or printed items that have not been digitised and cannot be moved, wherever these are held; and

(iv) have other printed items from outside their own institutions delivered to them efficiently.

The CURL's mission is to increase the ability of research libraries to share resources for the benefit of the local, national, and international research community. The total membership of the CURL has grown to twenty-eight libraries in the UK including twenty-two university libraries, as well as the British

Library, the National Library of Scotland, and the National Library of Wales.

EIFL (Electronic Information for Libraries)

EIFL is a not-for-profit organization based in Europe to provide access to knowledge through a global network to developing countries and countries in transition in Africa, Asia, Europe, and Latin America. Starting with providing access to e-journals to libraries in Central and Eastern Europe in 1999 it has spread wings enabling access to knowledge for learning, teaching, research, and sustainable development to sixty countries.

Programmes of EIFL

EIFL-Licensing: EIFL negotiates with publishers to provide access to scholarly materials for research and education on discount rates.

EIFL-OA-Open access: EIFL is a strong advocate of open access. It helps institutions to build and sustain open access repositories.

EIFL-FOSS (**Free and open-source software for libraries):** EIFL helps libraries to install and use free and open-source software. It also provides training to professionals to use open-source software.

ICOLC (International Coalition of Library Consortia)

ICOLC refers to the International Coalition of Library Consortia. It is a consortium of consortia and first met informally in 1997. It comprises over two hundred library consortia across the world and the Coalition represents thousands of member libraries worldwide. The Coalition serves primarily higher education institutions by facilitating discussion among consortia on issues of common interest. Additional information about the ICOLC can be found at http://www.icolc.net.

Activities of ICOLC

- It conducts meetings twice a year generally in the month of March/April in North America and in September/October in Europe to keep the participating consortia informed about new electronic information resources, pricing practices of electronic providers and vendors, and other issues of importance to directors and governing boards of consortia.

- The Coalition meets with members of the information provider community, providing a forum for them to discuss their offerings and to engage in dialogue with the consortial leaders about issues of mutual concern.
- It also maintains listservs and web pages for the benefit of its members.

EXERCISES: UNIT 8 – UNIT 10

1. What do you understand by "resource sharing"?
2. Highlight the need for resource sharing within the context of libraries.
3. What are the different objectives of resource sharing?
4. What is a library network?
5. Highlight the need for the establishment of a library network.
6. Highlight some of the major issues and challenges associated with the establishment of a library network.
7. Describe library consortia with some examples.
8. Define a "Library Network".
9. What are the objectives of a library network?
10. Highlight some of the characteristics of a library network.
11. Discuss the major components of a library network.
12. Highlight the hardware/software requirements of a library network.
13. What are the different types of library networks?
14. Define "cooperative cataloguing".
15. Explain the role of a library network.
16. Write down the full form of INFLIBNET.
17. Explain the objectives of INFLIBNET.
18. Write down some major services offered by INFLIBNET.

19. What do you understand by DELNET?
20. What are the objectives of CALIBNET?
21. Write down the objectives and services offered by ADINET.
22. Explain MYLIBNET and BONET.
23. What do you understand by INDEST? Write down its objectives and features.
24. Explain FORSA in detail.
25. What is UGC-INFONET?
26. Write down the objectives and activities of NKRC.
27. Explain in detail the services offered by OCLC.
28. Define "Research Libraries Group".
29. Write down the names of some library consortia at the international level.

Unit 11

Librarianship as a Profession

DEFINITION OF PROFESSION

A profession is a field of work that has been successfully professionalised. It can be defined as a disciplined group of individuals or professionals, who adhere to ethical standards and who hold themselves out, and are accepted by the public as possessing special knowledge and skills in a widely recognised body of learning derived from research, education and training at a high level and who are prepared to apply this knowledge and exercise these skills in the interest of others. In other words, a profession is any calling or occupation other than commercial, manual, etc., involving special attainments, or disciplines, such as editing, music, teaching, etc. and also the collective body of those following such vocations.

DEFINITION OF OCCUPATION

According to *Merriam-Webster Online Dictionary*, the term "occupation" means "an activity in which one engages" or "the principal business of one's life".

DEFINITION OF VOCATION

Merriam-Webster Online Dictionary defines "vocation" as "the work in which a person is regularly employed". It involves a routine activity of some kind—physical or scholarly and needs certain or no skills.

A profession differs from a vocation in the following aspects: A profession is mainly service based and not job based. Professionals acquire skills by virtue of intellectual training and not on the job training. A profession must have associations at the national and state level which a vocation does not have.

CHARACTERISTICS OF A PROFESSION

Several authorities attempted a closer review and identified specific elements, which go into characterising a profession. Following are some of the specific elements/characteristics that constitute a profession:

- Availability of a systematic theory which delineates and supports the skills that characterise the profession;
- A level of authority which comes from extensive education in the systematic theory;
- Research and continuous in-service updating of specialised knowledge;
- The interest of the client and the public must be placed above the immediate interests of the practitioner;
- Presence of a code of ethics which regulates relations of professional persons with clients and colleagues;
- A professional culture sustained by formal associations, consisting of values, norms and symbols and having at its centre the career concept; and
- A service orientation.

LIS AS A PROFESSION

A librarian conserves the cultural and intellectual heritage of mankind and acts as an agent of communication from the point of information generation to the point of its use. Her/his services are indispensable in the information transfer chain. This opinion was shared by many social and information scientists like Melvil Dewey, Butler, Greenwood, Schaffer et al. and they tried to prove that librarianship is a profession as it has many attributes of a profession. Ever since the librarianship has been considered as a profession because it has the following attributes/characteristics:

- A body of knowledge imparted in LIS schools;
- Intensive training and continued practice to gain mastery over the skills for knowledge organisation and retrieval;

- Oriented at service to the society;
- Associations to bind the professionals;
- Standard terminology and practices; and
- A code of ethics.

Purpose of LIS Profession/Librarianship/Library Science

The primary purpose of the LIS profession is to provide access to information pertinent to user requests with great speed and thus, achieve user satisfaction. Hence, it is service based. Keeping this basic purpose in view many LIS scientists define the LIS profession (librarianship) in different ways. In essence, it is the science and art of managing libraries. Mayors defines librarianship as "That branch of human knowledge which is concerned with the production, care and use of recorded human knowledge". Dakhole characterises librarianship in the following words:

(1) "Librarianship is a branch of human knowledge.
(2) It is a profession.
(3) It is tool for information or knowledge.
(4) It involves social service.
(5) It is a department of scholars not mere a craft".

STAGES INVOLVED IN THE EVOLUTION OF THE LIS PROFESSION

Custodian: The library custodians are keepers of culture, preservers of creation and defenders of the future. Their duty earlier was to keep the books intact rather than allow them to be circulated freely among readers. Thus, the first generation of librarians were mere custodians/keepers of recorded knowledge and culture.

Librarian: With the invention of printing in the 15th century there was less need for the protective function of libraries. The librarian moved away from being just a "custodian of books" to being the information/knowledge collection manager. The philosophy changed, that library resources were meant to be put into use and the need was felt to circulate the books for better utilisation of knowledge. So, the diffusion of knowledge by lending books became the predominant function of the library in the 20th century. It was also realised that the utility of library resources depends upon the skills and knowledge of the people who direct, operate, and manage the library. Hence, a human agent, called the librarian was felt as a necessity to provide personal assistance to users in the form of providing relevant information and assisting them in its utilisation. Thus, the traditional librarianship started shifting from material handling to information handling. In this process of transmission of knowledge, the librarian stood as a mediator between the originator (author) and the end user. With the bombarding of the generation of information termed as "information explosion" and the need for the same growth in a big way, the importance of librarianship has been realised among people in the society.

Documentation Officer: With changing times, users expect specific information to be culled out from sources to be provided to them. This gave birth to the concept of documentation activities in libraries. Increasing specialisations resulted in the making of the post of a documentation officer in libraries. Documentation centres have been set up to meet the requirements of specialised users in research organisations. The job of the documentalist is to collect, organise, and disseminate information from books, monographs, serial publications and non-print sources and provide information pin-pointedly and precisely according to the users' requirements. Bibliographical, information consolidation and digest type of services are provided in documentation centres to serve the specific needs of users.

Information Officer/Scientist: It is the responsibility of the library to build up a collection of information in anticipation of its future use. The increasing amount of information and its increasing importance have led to the evolution of libraries into library and information centres. Identification of distinct user groups and developing suitable information services like providing access to the virtual collection through a website at anytime and anywhere is the responsibility of the information scientists. As the use of information increases in the society, the importance of library and information centres also increases. This demands for special skills in information professionals to create, collect, communicate, and consolidate the information on behalf of the clients. The speedy and radical explosion of information has greatly transformed the role of libraries and information centres. Thus, the change in the mission of librarianship has significant implications for the library profile in the 21st century.

Digital Librarian: Digital libraries are electronic libraries wherein all the collections in full text are in digital form and access to the collection is through networks. The very mission of digital libraries is to create new approaches to acquisition of resources, new storage and preservation, classification and cataloguing, intensive use of electronic systems and networks. Thus, the present role of the digital librarian extends her/his services far beyond physical boundaries. They provide innovative resources and services and play an important role as digital librarians in connecting old graphic records, to machine readable forms and create new records of text, graphics and sounds and multi-media. They integrate all the memory institutions like libraries, archives, and museums. Thus, they have stemmed out of the traditional brand of gatekeepers of information, to information gateways and information skill developers.

DIFFERENT CATEGORIES OF LIS PROFESSIONALS/JOB PROFILES/PROFESSIONAL POSTS

LIS professionals are generally involved in the process of acquisition, processing, organising, and maintaining documents in a library and providing various types of information services based on these documents and their experiences. In certain cases, say, in a small library, all these activities are performed by a single individual. In certain other cases, an individual may be involved only in a single activity, say cataloguing. Generally, these personnel are trained by certain institutions like universities and associations and are paid for the jobs they perform. Library professionals include among others library administrators, classifiers, indexers, cataloguers, reference librarians, classificationists, teachers of library and information science, and thesaurus constructors. Some are briefly described below:

Library Administrator: A library administrator is responsible for the administration of a library. The head of a library is usually designated as the chief librarian and his/her subordinates as deputy librarian, assistant librarian, etc. Sometimes, he/she is simply called a librarian, a library manager or a director. He/she possesses expertise in planning, organisation and management of various activities and services of a library and is considered to be a good source of information in these areas.

Classifier: A classifier generally classifies books by following certain schemes of classification, say the Dewey Decimal Classification. While classifying, first of all the classifier has to ascertain the subject that the book is dealing with. For this purpose, he/she has to go through the title, contents and sometimes even through the text and index of the book.

Cataloguer: One who catalogues documents by following a catalogue code or a set of cataloguing rules is a cataloguer. While cataloguing, a cataloguer gathers information about the title, author, collaborator, edition, imprint, collation, ISBN, price, etc. of the book. He/she also gathers information usually from the class number about the subject of the book.

Classificationist: One who designs and builds up a scheme of classification on the basis of sound principles is a classificationist. For example, Melvil Dewey, S.R. Ranganathan, H.E. Bliss were all classificationists. A classificationist is an expert not only in the principles of classification but also in epistemology.

Indexer: An indexer compiles indexes based on some principles, guidelines, and tools. To aid indexers standard lists of subject headings, thesauri, etc. are being developed and updated from time to time.

Reference Librarian: Reference librarian is the library professional who is in charge of the reference section and the one who readily provides referential information to users.

Library and Information Science Teacher: An LIS teacher takes classes in various courses of library and information science. Many of them guide research students as well. They also write textbooks, course materials, etc.

Thesaurus Designer: A person who designs a thesaurus is called a thesaurus designer. This is a new group of professionals that emerged several decades ago especially with the advent of computers in the field of library and information science. For deciding the descriptors for the thought content of a particular document and for its subsequent retrieval from a computerised database, a thesaurus provides immense help.

Bibliographer: Compilation of bibliographies is one of the important library activities. Many libraries of the world, especially special libraries provide bibliographical services to its users. Compilation of a bibliography is an interesting job and is the responsibility of a bibliographer.

Librametrician: An expert on librametrics is termed as a "librametrician". The word 'librametrics' was coined by S.R. Ranganathan in 1949. Later on A. Neelameghan elaborated its scope. Librametrics is a discipline that measures library activities, library collection, personnel, building, furniture, etc.

Bibliometrician: An expert on bibliometrics is called a bibliometrician. Bibliometricians study among others the growth of literature in a subject, scattering of literature of a subject in various types of documents, ranking of journals from various angles, ranking of authors of a subject depending on their output, active life of literature, obsolescence and so on.

Content Developer: With the advent of the Internet, the idea of content development became engendered. It started involving designing, creation, and deployment of the content as well in the cyber space. Usually, it includes text, sound, images, animation, and provision for interaction.

Unit 12
Ethical Issues in Librarianship

ETHICS

The word "ethic" is derived from the Latin word 'ethicus' meaning the custom or character or attitude of a community or people. Ethics is the science of morals. It is one of the branches of the subject of philosophy. Each facet of this branch is concerned with character, attitude, and conduct.

PROFESSIONAL ETHICS

Every profession establishes a code of conduct to govern ethical behaviour within that profession. Professional ethics is considered as an expression of the ethos (i.e. character, spirit, culture, practice) of an occupation. In other words, it should reflect or be based upon, all the basic values associated with the occupation. It should reveal what the occupation is, what the practitioners think of themselves and of their place in society.

Objectives of Professional Ethics in Library and Information Science

According to P.S.G. Kumar, the motto of professional ethics in library and information science is to:

Provide a dedicated service; build up the knowledge base of the professionals; maintain neutrality to caste, creed, religions and idealisms; uphold the six freedoms—study, thought, speech, press, dissemination of knowledge and instruction and voice the convictions relating to library legislation, censorship, etc.

CODE OF ETHICS FOR LIS PROFESSIONALS

Johan Bekker a leading authority on ethics in librarianship stated that "a code of ethics should be an expression of ethos of an occupation. It should reflect or be based upon all the basic values associated with occupation. It should reveal what the occupation is, what the practitioners feel and of their place in society. It should indicate what is distinctive about a group. The code should reflect the nature of library and the library like agencies as one of the functioning systems." He has suggested a few broad principles for designing a code.

(1) Librarians should exercise their best professional judgment on behalf of the users. They should therefore provide the highest level of service not only complying with requests, but also anticipating needs; consider the needs of the users the central focus of their work; assist actively in preventing incompetence and misconduct in their profession and in encouraging adherence to this code and other standards and protect each user's right to privacy.

(2) Librarians should strive to improve libraries and library services. They should therefore be active members of local and national professional associations; pursue continuing education in order to improve their: skills, knowledge, and qualifications; protect and enhance the reputation of libraries by exemplary professional conduct and service; involve themselves in research and other systematic efforts to understand and improve library service and avoid situations that could compromise professional judgement or provide personal benefits at the expense of the library and its users.

(3) Librarians should help to create and maintain conditions under which learning and scholarship can flourish freedom of inquiry and of thought and its expression. They should therefore ensure the free flow of information between libraries; allow access to the library holdings and services to everyone in

need of information; avoid bias in the acquisition and presentation in information; resist efforts to censor library materials or restrict intellectual freedom.

(4) Librarians should be sensitive to the concerns of the larger society of which they are a part. They should therefore protect and preserve sources of information for future use; assure that confidential and proprietary information are safeguarded and avoid transgression into the practice of other professions.

The word 'ethics' was first used in 1908 during a discussion on the topic in Boston. The results pronounced as 'Librarian's Canons of Ethics' 1909 was the first set of 'Code of Ethics' in librarianship in the USA. These were revised by Botton in 1912 and published as an article in *The Annals of American Academy of Political and Social Sciences* entitled "The Ethics of Librarianship". The first code of ethics from ALA was prepared in 1938 by Ms. Flora B. Ledington.

THE AMERICAN LIBRARY ASSOCIATION CODE OF ETHICS

Since 1939, the American Library Association has recognised the importance of codifying and making known to the public and the profession the principles which guide librarians in action and revised the same from time to time to reflect changes in the nature of the profession and its social and institutional environment. The ethical statements help when values are in conflict.

The statements of code provide a framework. They cannot and do not dictate conduct to cover particular situations. It states:

(i) We provide the highest level of service to all library users through appropriate and usefully organised resources; equitable service policies; equitable access; and accurate, unbiased and courteous responses to all requests.

(ii) We uphold the principles of intellectual freedom and resist all efforts to censor library resources.

(iii) We protect each library user's right to privacy and confidentiality with respect to the information being sought or received and resources consulted, borrowed, acquired or transmitted.

(iv) We respect intellectual property rights and advocate balance between the interests of information users and rights holders.

(v) We treat co-workers and other colleagues with respect, fairness and good faith and advocate conditions of employment that safeguard the rights and welfare of all employees of our institutions.

(vi) We do not advance private interests at the expense of library users, colleagues or our employing institutions.

(vi) We distinguish between our personal convictions and professional duties and do not allow our personal beliefs to interfere with fair representation of the aims of our institutions or the provision of access to their information resources.

(vii) We strive for excellence in the profession by maintaining and enhancing our own knowledge and skills, by encouraging the professional development of co-workers and by fostering the aspirations of potential members of the profession.

CODE OF ETHICS OF LIS PROFESSIONALS IN INDIA

1. Libraries have demonstrated their ability to enrich community life. The librarian should retain the belief in his/her job. One must believe that libraries are good for people and that he/she is good for libraries. One must not expect gratitude.
2. In our cultural work, all branches of learning play a role. Librarians must be trained to know the essence of culture and do their work of promoting culture.
3. The librarian enjoys perfect freedom and autonomy of individual judgment. She/he should uphold the sanctity of six freedoms of our creed—the freedom

of study, freedom of thought, freedom of speech, freedom of press, freedom of the circulation of knowledge and the freedom of instruction.

4. The librarian must have the conviction that libraries are indispensable to society. They should never be apologetic about their profession.
5. A good librarian must herself/himself be an avid reader and eager to help others find their way in the collection. Techniques can be learned quickly by those who are keen to learn. The important factor is enthusiasm for the job. Librarians must be book men quite distinct from administrators in general.
6. The function of the library is to serve as a store of information from which each reader can draw the required information. A store requires a key so the librarian and his professional technology only can provide it.

Unit 13
Role of Professional Associations

LIBRARY ASSOCIATIONS

Library associations are the learned societies that play a vital role in the development of the library movement in a country. They continuously strive for better provisions of library and information services. During this process, library associations also work for the advancement of the profession and the professionals. Professional associations are established by and for the professionals. Their membership is open to librarians, library staff members, library science teachers, libraries, library associations and even users of libraries. An association is what its members make it through their active collaboration and participation in its programmes and activities.

ROLES/AIMS/OBJECTIVES OF LIBRARY ASSOCIATIONS

- To herald the library movement in a country to spread knowledge and information and ultimately contribute to human resource development;
- To work for the enactment of public library legislation, drafting of the bills along progressive lines and based on sound principles; to make people library conscious so that they demand the right of access to public library services and mobilise social pressure for the healthy development of library services;
- To strive for the evolution of an integrated national library and information system based on a national policy and bring to the attention of the authorities

the deficiencies, defects, etc., in the existing library infrastructure;

- To provide a common forum for library professionals for the exchange of information, ideas, experience and expertise and work for the betterment of salaries, grades, service conditions, status, etc. of library professionals;
- To hold the image of the library profession high in society and promote cooperation among libraries and library professionals;
- To share resources and avoid duplication of efforts; and
- To contribute towards manpower development for library and information work by organising education and training programmes and promoting research, incentives, awards and rewards, etc.

PROGRAMS AND ACTIVITIES OF A LIBRARY ASSOCIATION

Library associations undertake many important programmes and activities which vary from association to association. These include:

Conferences: By organising conferences, seminars, lectures, etc. they offer opportunities for library professionals to meet, discuss and exchange information, ideas, experiences, and expertise.

Library Publicity and Advocacy: Organising a library week, exhibitions, book fairs, competitions, etc. for promoting library consciousness and reading and learning habits among citizens. Library associations also play a vital role in greater visibility of libraries and librarians.

Service Conditions: Taking up with the management at all levels, through appropriate means, the issues relating to improvement of salary grades, service conditions and status of library professionals and also help in the recruitment of library personnel.

Education: LIS associations conduct training courses that are necessary to supplement university education in library and information science as well as continuing education programmes for working professionals.

Publications: Library associations publish professional literature like professional journals and newsletters as well as ad hoc publications such as proceedings, directories, catalogues, bibliographies, course manuals, textbooks, reference books and others.

Standards, Services, and Research: Library associations are involved in: Formulating standards, guidelines, codes and manuals with regard to practices, procedures, techniques, tools and equipment, as a step towards fostering cooperation among libraries; undertaking bibliographical projects on their own and through outside contract; offering advisory and consultancy services and undertaking research surveys of library facilities and services, user demands, learning and reading habits, book production, etc.

Ethics: Library associations formulate codes of ethics for library professionals in order to set high values in conduct and service.

Cooperation: They establish cooperation with international and national associations of other countries having similar objectives. They maintain liaison with book and publishing trade for attending to mutual problems in library acquisitions.

INDIAN LIBRARY ASSOCIATION (ILA)

The Indian Library Association was formed on 13 September 1933 on the occasion of the First All India Library Conference held at Calcutta (now Kolkata). The Indian Library Association is the largest professional body in the field of library and information science in the country. It is a premier national association representing the library profession in the country. ILA, right from its inception in right earnest has identified itself with the library movement in the country. In due course of time, it has also worked for the upliftment of the professional education and cadre-based status by providing the necessary training and education avenues. It has made consistent efforts to provide an opportunity for the development of library and information professionals at all levels, all over the country.

Objectives of ILA

The association aims at establishing high standards of librarianship and library services in the country. It has the following objectives:

- Promotion of library movement in the country and enactment of library legislation;
- Improvement of library services;
- Development of library science education and training and accreditation of library schools towards maintaining proper standards of education;
- Betterment of salaries, service conditions and status of library personnel;
- Promotion of cooperation among the libraries and professionals;
- Promotion of research and bibliographical studies;
- Affiliation with the state and other library associations;
- Cooperation with international and other national associations with similar objectives;
- Publication of serials and other publications for dissemination of information;
- Providing a common forum by organising conferences, seminars, and meetings;
- Promotion and formulation of standards, norms, guidelines, etc., for the management of library and information systems and their services;
- Establishments of libraries, documentation and information centres and assistance in their development; and
- Carrying out all such other activities that are incidental or conducive to the attainment of the above objectives.

Activities/Role of ILA

Meetings/Conferences: An all-India Library Conference is held every year at some place in the country. The host institution is usually a university, an institution or a local library association. A national seminar, on one or more themes of importance is a part of the programme. In addition to this, national seminars on themes of topical interest are also held from time to time. The programmes are generally organised during the national library week in November each year.

Publications: The association brings out a quarterly journal entitled *Journal of Indian Library Association* as an official organ and a vehicle for publishing learned articles contributed by professionals in the library and information science field. Another monthly publication called *ILA Newsletter* keeps ILA members abreast with activities of the ILA.

Continuing Education: The association conducts need-based continuing education programmes from time to time for the benefit of working professionals.

Professional Issues: The association takes up with the state governments, at every conceivable opportunity, the issue of enacting the library legislation in order to develop the public library system. It has been repeatedly sending a memorandum persuading the state governments to initiate action on the library legislation. It has been active in pursuing the government, the University Grant Commission (UGC) and other bodies on matters related to the profession.

Participation in Official Bodies: The ILA represents the profession to discuss various policy level issues with the government.

Relations with Other Associations: ILA plays a leading role in the Joint Council of Library Associations (JOCLAI) in India towards evolving a coordinated approach and a common strategy on professional issues of concern to all library associations in the country.

INDIAN ASSOCIATION OF SPECIAL LIBRARIES AND INFORMATION CENTRES (IASLIC)

The Indian Association of Special Libraries and Information Centres (IASLIC) was founded in 1955. It is a registered society with its headquarters located in Kolkata. It was formed with the aim of having an association in India similar to the Association for Information Management (ASLIB) in the UK and the Special Libraries Association (SLA) in the USA. At a largely attended meeting of librarians held in Calcutta on 25 June 1955 under the Chairmanship of Dr. S.L. Hora, the idea of starting an all-India association devoted to the progress of special libraries and information centres was mooted. Following this initiative, another meeting held on 3 September 1955 formalised the decision to establish the Indian Association of Special Libraries and Information Centres (IASLIC). Over the years, it has earned recognition for its regular and systematic work.

Objectives of IASLIC

- To undertake, support and coordinate research and studies;
- To organise general and special meetings, seminars, workshops, and conferences at the national and regional level;
- To publish journals, monographs, manuals, newsletters, papers, proceedings and reports;
- To conduct short-term training courses;
- To coordinate with other fraternal bodies in promoting the interests of the library and information profession; and
- To undertake other similar activities which are incidental and conducive to the attainment of its objectives.

Activities/Role of IASLIC

Programs: IASLIC holds biennial seminars and a conference every alternate year in different parts of the country at the venue of the host organisations that are usually university libraries/

departments of library and information science, institutions, associations, etc. It has Special Interest Groups (SIG) devoted to areas like Industrial Information, Social Science Information, Computer Application, Humanities Information, Informatics and Library and Information Science Education. The SIGs choose themes for discussion during the conferences/seminars. Library and information professionals meet at the time of the annual conference/seminar to discuss problems of common interest.

Publications: The IASLIC Bulletin (started in 1956 with a quarterly periodicity) is the official organ of the association and is devoted to the advancement and dissemination of the fundamental and applied knowledge of library and information science in an accessible form. The "IASLIC Newsletter" is the official newsletter of the association and is aimed to inform members about the professional activities in general and IASLIC in particular. It is published on a monthly basis. The "Indian Library Science Abstracts" (annual), another publication of the association covers literature published in the country in the field of library and information science.

Information Services: The IASLIC undertakes the work of compiling bibliographies and translation of documents from Russian, German, French, Chinese, Japanese, etc., to English and the imaging of documents for archiving purposes. All these services are provided on a non-profit basis.

Awards for Excellence: The IASLIC has instituted different awards for librarians. These are awarded to the best librarian of the year, best teacher in LIS, best young teacher in LIS, a retired librarian, and the best article award.

Professional Issues: The association strives to improve the standards of service in special libraries and information centers. In this connection, it has made attempts to evolve a code of ethics for librarianship. It brings to the attention of authorities, issues which call for improvement and corrective measures.

Education and Training: The association in its continuing education programmes conducts short-term courses, workshops, round tables, seminars, etc. Organising short-term training courses in various topics is now a regular feature of the continuing education programme to improve professional competency.

Relation with Other Bodies: IASLIC maintains a healthy relationship with the Indian Library Association and other library associations. It has taken a leading part in the formation of the Joint Council for Library Associations in India (JOCLAI). It took an active interest in implementing the common programmes of this Joint Council for Library Associations in India. IASLIC in different ways had cooperated with the erstwhile National Information System for Science and Technology (NISSAT).

AMERICAN LIBRARY ASSOCIATION (ALA)

The American Library Association (ALA) has the uniqueness of being the oldest and largest library association in the world. It was founded in 1876 with its headquarters in Chicago. A group of 103 library activists, at a meeting held in Philadelphia in the fall of 1876 to coincide with the nation's centennial celebrations, resolved on a motion moved by Melvil Dewey, the father of librarianship, to form the American Library Association. ALA, thus born, has been a success story through the dedicated efforts of eminent librarians who steered the association in its formative periods. The ALA grew in strength steadily and became even in the early part of this century the national voice for library interests. Today, with a solid foundation, wide base expanding programmes and activities and social impact, ALA plays a dynamic role to foster American library interests with great success.

Objectives of ALA

- Increase awareness and support for libraries by increasing their visibility in a positive context and by communicating why libraries are both unique and valuable;
- Update the image of libraries, librarians and all library staff for the 21st century, sustaining and strengthening their relevance;

- Bring renewed energy to the promotion of libraries and librarians;
- Bring library messages to a more diverse audience;
- Create turnkey tools, resources and materials that could be utilised by all types of libraries;
- Provide an opportunity to share public relations/ marketing/advocacy practices within the library community;
- Tie together ALA promotions into one unified brand, reinforcing key messages;
- Quickly respond to emerging issues such as library funding cuts;
- Develop more cross-collaborations across the association to ensure that new campaign projects and initiatives are inclusive and effective;
- Work more closely with ALA chapters and affiliates to help them achieve their public awareness objectives;
- Promote the contributions of all library staff, including both librarians and support staff.

Activities of ALA

Programmes: ALA holds its annual conference every year in the month of June which is attended by more than 25,000 librarians, educators, writers, publishers, friends of libraries, trustees, and special guests. The conference includes more than 2,000 meetings, discussion groups, programmes on various topics affecting libraries and librarians.

Publications: The American Library Association develops many resources for the library and information services communities. Almost 3,00,000 of ALA products are purchased every year and the proceeds help to support the ALA's general programmes. The ALA store features titles from ALA Editions, the general publishing operation of the Association and ALA Graphics, the unit specialising in promotional products supporting libraries, literacy, and reading, as well as other products from around the association. ALA's serial publications

include: American Libraries, Book List, Book Links, ALA Tech Source, Library Technology Reports and Guide to Reference. Apart from these, different divisions, offices, roundtables, and sections bring out various newsletters, magazines, and journals.

Awards for Excellence: Each year, the American Library Association and its member units honour people and institutions through an awards programme that recognises the distinguished services of libraries and their librarianship.

International Activities: International Relations Office of the ALA coordinates international activities. It acts in support of official ALA delegations to international events such as book fairs and congresses; promotes international library exchanges and partnerships; recruits international librarians to become members of ALA and attend ALA conferences; responds to international inquiries concerning library issues and activities in the United States; serves as a point of contact for ALA's routine communication with international organisations to which ALA belongs, including IFLA and provides support for the ALA International Relations Committee (IRC) and the International Relations Round Table.

CHARTERED INSTITUTE OF LIBRARY AND INFORMATION PROFESSIONALS (CILIP)

CILIP (The Chartered Institute of Library and Information Professionals) is the leading professional body of library and information professionals in the UK. It came into existence in 2002 with the merger of the erstwhile Library Association (UK) and Institute of Information Science. CILIP provides practical support for members throughout their entire careers, helping them with their academic education, professional qualifications, job hunting, and continuing professional development.

Objectives of CILIP

The CILIP aims at activism and enterprise to build its community, a strong voice to advance the profession and modern professionalism to develop the workforce. Its objectives are to:

- Set, maintain, monitor and promote standards of excellence in the creation, management, exploitation and sharing of information and knowledge resources;

- Support the principle of equality of access to information, ideas and works of the imagination which it affirms is fundamental to a thriving economy, democracy, culture and civilisation; and
- Enable its members to achieve and maintain the highest professional standards in all aspects of delivering an information service, both for the professional and the public good.

Activities of CILIP

Programmes: CILIP organises one-day conferences with expert speakers, demonstrations from suppliers of associated technology and unrivalled networking opportunities. It also organises and manages events like two and three-day conferences, often with associated exhibitions, organised on behalf of CILIP's special interest groups.

Education and Training: Professional development underpins every successful career. CILIP members benefit from certification, charter ship, fellowship, revalidation, and course accreditation to get their careers started and to make all their achievements and learning count. CILIP's training and development provides the widest range of training for the LIS community in the UK.

Publications: CILIP brings out the "CILIP Update" magazine. It is published both in print and digital formats on a monthly basis. Using state-of-the-art page turning technology, the digital edition has live web links and is available prior to Update's print publication date.

Awards: CILIP promotes excellence by recognising the best practices awards. Different groups manage these awards, for example, Publicity and Public Relations Group offers the International Library and Information Group Award.

Information and Advice Enquiry Services: The Information and Advice Team provides support to members on a range of practical and professional issues related to library work. It provides different services, for example, Current Awareness Services (CAS), Employment, Law Helpline, and Information Centre Online database. CILIP gives general advice to its members on employment-related subjects such as pay, job evaluation or redundancy. Individual members also have access to a range of e-journals and online databases, which can be searched for. These include:

- Emerald journals.
- IRWI (Information Research Watch International).
- LISA (Library and Information Science Abstracts), etc.

Policy and Advocacy: CILIP has developed a new resource for its members to demonstrate the value of their professional skills. The campaigning toolkit is a resource designed by CILIP to help members create an effective grassroots action plan to demonstrate their value as a library and information professional.

International Relations: CILIP is an association member of the IFLA and encourages its members to involve in IFLA activities such as contesting elections for the Standing Committees and other bodies. CILIP had organised an IFLA conference in 2002 just after its emergence. CILIP takes up an opportunity to publicise its activities by participating in exhibitions during the IFLA conferences.

ASSOCIATION OF SPECIAL LIBRARIES AND INFORMATION BUREAUX (ASLIB)

The ASLIB (Association of Special Libraries and Information Bureaux) was founded in 1924 with the aim of coordinating the activities of specialist information services in the UK. It is presently known as the Association for Information Management. Its members are private and public sector companies and organisations across the world, concerned with managing information resources efficiently. ASLIB had special interest groups to cater to the needs of particular subjects/areas. These have evolved into communities of practice.

Objectives of ASLIB

- To stimulate awareness of the benefits of good management of information resources and its value;

- To represent and lobby for the interests of the information sector on matters which are of national and international importance varying from copyright and data protection to the role of scientific journals; and
- To provide a range of information-related products and services to meet the needs of the information society.

Activities of ASLIB

Consultancy Activity: Consultancy activities drawn principally from the network of leading information professionals range from giving answers to specific questions for individuals or small companies, to major studies for the British Government.

Managing Information: "Managing Information", the association's colour magazine, is the magazine for everyone who uses information. It combines the successful print magazine with a web-based news service, doubling the impact of the publication.

Training: ASLIB provides training in key aspects of information work in the form of public courses, on-site training, conferences, and distance learning.

Publications: ASLIB publications are an important element in their mission of supplying practical, leading-edge support in managing information and knowledge. ASLIB titles are produced by Emerald and Europa Publications.

Consultancy: ASLIB has a consultancy group that undertakes projects for organisations for information support. The projects have included IT selection and implementation, user needs surveys, business information, and online sources.

INTERNATIONAL FEDERATION OF LIBRARY ASSOCIATIONS AND INSTITUTIONS (IFLA)

IFLA (The International Federation of Library Associations and Institutions) is the leading international body representing the interests of library and information services and their users. It is the global voice of the library and information profession.

Founded in Edinburgh, Scotland, in 1927 at an international conference, IFLA celebrated its seventy fifth birthday at its conference in Glasgow, Scotland in 2002. IFLA now has more than 1,600 members in approximately 150 countries around the world. IFLA was registered in the Netherlands in 1971. The Royal Library, the National Library of the Netherlands, in The Hague, generously provides its facilities for their headquarters.

Objectives of IFLA

IFLA is an independent, international, non-governmental, not-for-profit organisation. Its aims are to promote the international support, cooperation, exchange of information, education, research and development within the scope of the library and information services sector in general. In addition, the foundation seeks to protect, preserve and document written and printed cultural heritage and all that is in connection with these purposes.

Activities of IFLA

Programs: IFLA general conference and council is held in the month of August or early September in a different city each year. More than 3,000 delegates meet to exchange their experiences, debate professional issues, see the latest products of the information industry, conduct the business of IFLA and experience something of the culture of the host country.

Publications: The results of the programmes developed by IFLA's professional groups are recorded and disseminated in the publications. The IFLA Journal is published four times a year. Each issue covers news of current IFLA activities and articles, selected to reflect the variety of the international information profession, ranging from freedom of information, preservation, services to the visually impaired and intellectual property. The Biennial Council Report records IFLA's achievements in five key areas: access to information, the electronic environment, preservation and conservation, services and standards and professional development.

Awards for Excellence: IFLA offers the following awards and fellowships/prizes:

- Dr Shawky Salem Conference Grant.
- The Margreet Wijnstroom Fund for Regional Library Development.
- Jay Jordon IFLA/OCLC Early Career Development Fellowship.
- IFLA International Marketing Award.
- Guust Van Wesemael Literary Prize.

Resources: Many librarians and information professionals throughout the world, who contribute their time, expertise, and financial resources, make its achievements possible. About 80% of IFLA's income is derived from its membership fees. Other sources of income include sales of publications, contributions in cash and kind from the corporate partners, grants from foundations, and government agencies.

IFLANET: The web site IFLANET has rapidly become a prime source of information not only about IFLA, but also on a broad spectrum of library and information-related issues.

Relations with other bodies: IFLA has established good working relations with a variety of other bodies with similar interests, providing an opportunity for a regular exchange of information and views on issues of mutual concern. It has formal associate relations with the UNESCO, observer status with the United Nations, associate status with the International Council of Scientific Unions (ICSU) and observer status with the World Intellectual Property Organisation (WIPO) and the International Organisation for Standardisation (ISO).

Unit 14

Organisations and Institutions Involved in the Development of Library and Information Services

UNITED NATIONS EDUCATIONAL, SCIENTIFIC AND CULTURAL ORGANISATION (UNESCO)

The United Nations Educational, Scientific and Cultural Organisation is a specialised agency of the United Nations (UN) aimed at promoting world peace and security through international cooperation in education, arts, sciences and culture. It has 193 member states and twelve associate members, as well as partners in the non-governmental, inter-governmental and private sector. Headquartered at the World Heritage Centre in Paris, France, UNESCO has fifty-three regional field offices and 199 national commissions that facilitate its global mandate. Its constitution establishes the agency's goals, governing structure and operating framework. UNESCO's founding mission, which was shaped by the Second World War, is to advance peace, sustainable development and human rights by facilitating collaboration and dialogue among nations. It pursues this objective through five major areas: education, natural sciences, social/human sciences, culture and communication/information.

The Constitution of the United Nations Educational, Scientific and Cultural Organisation (UNESCO), signed on 16 November 1945, came into force on 4 November 1946 after its ratification by twenty countries including India. Today, UNESCO functions as a laboratory of ideas and a standard setter to forge universal agreements on emerging ethical issues. It also serves as a clearinghouse—for the dissemination and sharing of information and knowledge—while helping member states to build their human and institutional capacities across diverse fields. Article I, clause 1, sub-clause (c) of its Constitution stipulated that the "Organisation shall maintain, increase and diffuse knowledge by assuring the conservation and protection of the world's inheritance of books, works of arts and monuments of history and science, and recommending the nations concerned the necessary international conventions; by encouraging cooperation among the nations in all branches of intellectual activity, including the international exchange of persons active in the field of education, science and culture and the exchange of publications, objects of artistic and scientific interest and other materials of information; by initiating methods of international cooperation calculated to give the people of all countries access to the printed and published materials produced by any of them".

UNESCO Public Library Manifesto

The Public Library Manifesto of the UNESCO was adopted in 1994. It proclaims its belief in the public library as a living force for education, culture, and information and as an essential agent for the fostering of peace and spiritual welfare through the minds of men and women. UNESCO, therefore, encourages national and local governments to support and actively engage in the development of public libraries. The following key missions which relate to information, literacy, education, and culture should be at the core of public library services:

- Creating and strengthening reading habits in children at an early age;
- Supporting both individual and self-conducted education as well as formal education at all levels;
- Providing opportunities for personal creative development;
- Stimulating the imagination and creativity of children and young people;

- Promoting awareness of cultural heritage, appreciation of the arts, scientific achievements and innovations;
- Providing access to cultural expressions of all performing arts;
- Fostering inter-cultural dialogue and favouring cultural diversity;
- Supporting oral traditions;
- Ensuring access for citizens to all sorts of community information;
- Providing adequate information services to local enterprises, associations and interest groups;
- Facilitating the development of information and computer literacy skills; and
- Supporting and participating in literacy activities and programmes for all age groups and initiating such activities if necessary.

School Library Manifesto of UNESCO runs on similar terms.

Activities of the UNESCO

Access to Information: The UNESCO aims at helping individuals and organisations in improving access to information and knowledge. It strives to create conditions conducive to the free flow of information.

Archives: Archives are important components that help at improving information access, both for the public at large and for specialised groups. Since its creation, the UNESCO has contributed to the reinforcement of these types of services. The UNESCO, through its Records and Archives Management Programme—RAMP (established in 1979) aims at: "making the general public and decision makers aware of the importance of records and archives for planning and development safeguarding of the national heritage".

Memory of the World: The UNESCO established the "Memory of the World" programme in 1992. It provides access to the documentary heritage of the world.

Community Multimedia Centres: UNESCO's International Initiative for Community Multimedia Centres (CMCs) promotes community empowerment and addresses the digital divide by combining community broadcasting with the Internet and related technologies.

E-Governance: E-governance is the use of ICT by different actors of the society with the aim to improve their access to information and to build their capacities. E-Governance Capacity Building project of the UNESCO aims at promoting the use of ICT tools in municipalities to enhance good governance.

Information Processing Tools: The UNESCO develops, maintains, and disseminates, free-of-charge, two interrelated software packages for database management (CDS/ISIS) and data mining/statistical analysis (IDAMS).

Public Domain Information: UNESCO strongly promotes access to public domain information, also known as the "information commons".

E-Heritage: The UNESCO Charter helps and guides members in the preservation of the cultural heritages, rare information sources as well as digital heritage.

General Information Programme: The General Information Programme was created by bringing together two series of activities UNISIST Intergovernmental Programme dealing with scientific and technical information and NATIS to integrate national information concerned with documentation, libraries, and archives.

Information Accessibility: The UNESCO has encouraged global efforts in the direction of removing different barriers, like lack of funds, metadata, Creative Common License, etc. to access information. The outcomes have been projects granted in the areas such as Free and Open Source Software (FOSS), Open Educational Resources (OER), etc.

UNIVERSITY GRANTS COMMISSION (UGC)

The University Grants Commission (UGC) is a statutory body set up by the Department of Higher Education, Ministry of Education, Government of India in accordance with the UGC

Act of 1956 and is charged with the coordination, determination and maintenance of standards of higher education in India. It provides recognition to universities in India and disbursements of funds to such recognised universities and colleges. The headquarters is in New Delhi. It also frames regulations such as those on the minimum standards of instruction and qualifications of teachers on the advice of subject specialists and academicians with whom it frequently interacts in connection with the formulation, evaluation and monitoring of programmes.

The Commission, being an apex body in maintaining higher education in the country, has also played a major role in promoting library and information services in these universities and colleges. Besides, it has also established and constituted a number of libraries/information centres/study centres and committees to provide quality education/services in the field of library and information science.

Activities of UGC in the Field of Library and Information Science

Financial Assistance to University and College Libraries: Financial assistance is given to universities and colleges including central universities, state universities, deemed universities, government and affiliated colleges, for building and updating libraries.

Curriculum Development Committee (CDC) on Library and Information Science: The UGC constituted the CDC on Library and Information Science in 1990 to restructure the courses of studies in LIS.

Establishment of National Information Centres: Different centres like Indian Institute of Science have been established to provide improved access to information and bibliographic support to teachers and research scholars in their respective fields.

Establishment of INFLIBNET: The UGC established an Information and Library Network (INFLIBNET) Programme with headquarters in Ahmedabad as part of a project of the Inter-University Centre for Astronomy and Astrophysics (IUCA), Pune in April 1991. The INFLIBNET Programme aims at the establishment of a national network of libraries and information centres in institutions of higher learning including universities, colleges, R&D institutions and national organisations like CSIR, ICMR, ICSSR, ICAR, DOE, etc.

Modernisation of University Libraries: Giving funds to the university libraries for their overall upgradation.

National Review Committee on University and College Libraries: The purpose of constituting such a committee is to review the utilisation of grants to central universities and some state university libraries.

RAJA RAMMOHUN ROY LIBRARY FOUNDATION (RRRLF)

Raja Rammohun Roy Library Foundation (RRRLF) was established in May 1972 by the Department of Culture, Government of India to spread library services all over the country in cooperation with state governments, union territory administrations and organisations working in the field. It is a central autonomous organisation established and financed by the Ministry of Culture, Government of India. It is the nodal agency of the Government of India to support public library services and systems and promote public library movement in the country. The supreme policy making body of RRRLF is called the Foundation. It consists of members nominated by the Government of India from amongst eminent educationists, librarians, administrators, and senior officials. The Foundation has twenty-two members. The Minister of the Department of Culture, Government of India or his nominee is the Chairman of RRRLF.

Objectives of RRRLF

RRRLF functions as a promotional agency, an advisory and consultancy organisation and a funding body for public library development in India. Some of its significant objectives are to:

- Promote the library movement in the country;
- Enunciate a national library policy and to help build up a national library system;
- Provide financial and technical assistance to libraries;

- Provide financial assistance to organisations, regional or national, engaged in the promotion of library development;
- Publish appropriate literature and to act as a clearing house of ideas and information on library development in India and abroad;
- Promote research in problems of library development; and
- Advise the government on all matters pertaining to the library development in the country.

Activities and Events of RRRLF

RRRLF is constantly trying to achieve its objectives which are reflected in its programmes and activities. The following are their activities/events:

1. The Assistance to Libraries: Assistance to libraries is provided:

- Towards the building up of an adequate stock of books and reading materials;
- Towards the development of Rural Book Deposit Centres and Mobile Library Services;
- Towards the organisation of seminars, workshops, training courses (orientation/refresher), books exhibitions and library awareness programmes;
- Towards increasing accommodation to public libraries;
- To acquire computers with accessories for library application and TV, CD player, DVD player for educational purposes for public libraries;
- To public libraries towards celebration of Golden/ Diamond/Platinum, Jubilee years, etc.;
- Towards the collection and compilation of library statistics through official and non-official agencies.

(2) **Grant to Book Associations:** RRRLF provides financial assistance from time to time for organising seminars and conferences for book associations.

(3) **Library Act:** RRRLF continues to endeavour that various states implement the Library Act in their area. In these efforts, the chairman of RRRLF maintains contact with the education minister and concerned departments of the states through constant correspondence.

(4) **National Library Policy:** The RRRLF formed a working team in 1981 to draft the National Library Policy under the chairmanship of Dr. B.P. Varua. As a result, in 1983, a draft National Policy on Library and Information System was prepared, on the basis of which the Department of Culture, Government of India issued a draft policy statement and a review was chaired by Dr. D.D.P. Chattopadhyay.

(5) **Promotional Activities:** RRRLF has undertaken several promotional activities for qualitative improvement of library services. It has played a major role in the preparation of National Policy on Library and Information System (NAPLIS). It has also issued guidelines on public library systems and services.

(6) **Research Project:** The Research Cell of RRRLF renders advisory and consultancy services whenever required, besides carrying on research projects on public library or allied subjects.

(7) **RRRLF Publications:**

(i) Books for the million at their doorstep.

(ii) Directories of public libraries in India.

(iii) Indian Libraries: Trends and perspectives.

(iv) Newsletter.

UNITED NATIONS INTERNATIONAL SCIENTIFIC INFORMATION SYSTEM (UNISIST)

The UNISIST model of information dissemination was proposed in 1971 by the United Nations. The UNISIST (United Nations International Scientific Information System) is a model of the social system of communication, which consists of knowledge producers, intermediaries, and users. These groups of people (or actors) are different kinds of professionals. The social system also contains institutes such as research institutes, publishers, and libraries. The actors and institutions perform information services such as writing, publishing, storing, and retrieving documents and information. The actors are communicating in both formal and informal ways and they are producing different kinds of documents such as journal articles, books, book reviews, proceedings, bibliographies and catalogues, dictionaries, handbooks, encyclopedias and review articles.

The UNISIST model can be used to define the relation between various kinds of scientific and scholarly documents and to compare various domains and their discursive practices. It provides a classification of documents and information services into primary, secondary, and tertiary services and products.

INTERNATIONAL NUCLEAR INFORMATION SYSTEM (INIS)

The International Nuclear Information System (INIS) hosts one of the world's largest collections of published information on the peaceful uses of nuclear science and technology. INIS was established in 1970 in response to the International Atomic Energy Agency's (IAEA's) mandate "to foster the exchange of scientific and technical information on peaceful uses of atomic energy". The INIS represents a wealth of experience and an extensive pool of information in the nuclear field. The first INIS output products, the printed Atom index and associated magnetic tapes, were issued in April 1970. It has since grown into one of the successful and comprehensive information systems on the peaceful uses of nuclear science and technology. INIS is operated by the International Atomic Energy Agency (IAEA) in collaboration with, at present, 128 Member States and twenty-four International Organisations.

Activities of INIS

INIS Database: INIS has operated on cooperative principles since 1970 as a service to its members. It consists of a bibliographic database and a collection of non-conventional literature (NCL) and is the largest IAEA information source in nuclear science and technology.

Non-Conventional Nuclear Information: INIS has a unique collection of seven lakh full-text documents of non-conventional "grey" literature, available on microfiche and is being upgraded to digital format and made available through the INIS online database to users in its member states.

Document Delivery Service: INIS has arrangements with seventy-two national INIS Centres to provide document delivery services to users within their countries.

INIS Multilingual Thesaurus: INIS specialists from its member states and the IAEA have developed a controlled vocabulary for indexing and searching the INIS Database.

Capacity Building: To assist its member states, the IAEA transfers knowledge and know-how in data collection and information processing, in particular, to developing countries and new INIS Members.

AGRICULTURAL INFORMATION SYSTEM (AGRIS)

AGRIS (Agricultural International System) is a global public domain database with more than twelve million structured bibliographical records on agricultural science and technology. It was created by the Food and Agriculture Organisation (FAO) of the United Nations in 1974, to facilitate information exchange and to bring together world literature dealing with all aspects of agriculture. The database was maintained by the Coherence in Information for Agricultural Research for Development, and its content is provided by more than 150 participating institutions from sixty-five countries. The AGRIS Search system allows scientists, researchers and students to perform sophisticated searches using keywords from the AGROVOC thesaurus, specific journal titles or names of countries, institutions and authors.

NATIONAL INFORMATION SYSTEM FOR SCIENCE AND TECHNOLOGY (NISSAT)

NISSAT is National Information System for Science and Technology. The role of NISSAT is important for linking and coordinating information resources, information systems and services available in India. Firstly, due to efforts to establish an information system in the field of science and technology, NISSAT was established in 1975 and the programme started completely in 1977, which was under the Department of

Science and Technology. The role of science and technology in the economic and social development of the country has increased extensively. In this situation, the transfer of technology has become necessary so that in addition to the information produced in our country, the information produced abroad can be benefited from research and development work. NISSAT is playing an important role in this direction and is fulfilling the information needs of various industries and research work, etc.

Objectives of NISSAT

1. To obtain national scientific information.
2. Coordination of scientific information sources, information services and information systems of the nation.
3. Detection and removal of defects in information sources, information equipment and information services.
4. To provide support in research work.
5. To fulfill the information requirement of various sections.
6. Establish a scientific information system at the national level.
7. To use the latest information technology and technology for the advancement of information services.
8. To create a standard for information exchange at the international level.
9. Availability of at least one copy of the publication in the scientific literature.
10. To arrange training, seminars, etc. for information scientists.

NISSAT Activities and Functions

- Acquisition: To make available a copy of all scientific literature published in the national science library.

- Union Catalogue: To make a union list of documents available in various information centres.
- C.A.S. Services: For the development of information services, the present information tools and services have been developed.
- S.D.I. Service.
- Information Service for Industries.
- Training in Information Science.
- Promotion of Research Work.
- International Cooperation: Its main function is international cooperation. Through this, UNESCO, FID, INIS, etc. participate in many programmes.

NATIONAL INSTITUTE OF SCIENCE COMMUNICATION AND INFORMATION RESOURCES (NISCAIR)

The National Institute of Science Communication and Information Resources (NISCAIR) came into existence on 30 September 2002 following the merger of two establishments: Council of Scientific and Industrial Research (CSIR), i.e. National Institute of Science Communication (NISCOM) and Indian National Scientific Documentation Centre (INSDOC). INSDOC was established in 1952 for providing scientific and technical information and documentation services including abstracting and indexing services, design and development of databases, translation, library automation, access to international information sources, human resource development, consultancy services in setting up modern library and information centres. NISCOM, earlier known as Publications and Information Directorate (PID) had been involved in diverse publications in science and technology ranging from those for the common man to researchers and policy makers. NISCAIR has its core activities to acquire, organise, store, publish and disseminate scientific and technical information for the benefit of the society. It has the following mandate:

- To provide formal linkages of communication among the scientific community in the form of research journals in different areas of science and technology;

- To disseminate S&T information to general public, particularly school students, to inculcate interest in science among them;
- To collect, collate and disseminate information on plant, animal and mineral wealth of the country;
- To develop human resources in science communication, library, documentation and information science and scientific and technical information management systems and services.

Services and Activities of NISCAIR

National Science Library (NSL): NISCAIR serves as a single window to provide scientific and technical information. Its role as the national information resource is fulfilled through the National Science Library (NSL) that has a comprehensive collection of S&T publications in the country.

Access to Online Databases: NISCAIR has access to international databases. Information is sought through online searching from over 1,500 international databases.

Access to E-journals: NISCAIR is the nodal agency for the e-journals consortium of CSIR and DST known as the "National Knowledge Resource Centre (NKRC)".

Development of Traditional Knowledge Digital Library (TKDL): Repository of traditional knowledge.

National Science Digital Library: NSDL is a learning repository developed by NISCAIR. It provides access to course material for undergraduate students in different areas of science and technology.

Foreign Language Translation and Interpretation Service: Translation of S&T documents from twenty foreign languages into English are being provided.

National Centre for ISSN: NISCAIR is the national centre of ISSN International Centre for assigning ISSN to serials published in India.

Human Resource Development: NISCAIR develops human resources in library and information science and documentation.

NATIONAL SOCIAL SCIENCE DOCUMENTATION CENTRE (NASSDOC)

NASSDOC was established in 1969 as a division of the Indian Council of Social Science Research (ICSSR). Its objective is to provide library and information support services to researchers in social sciences working in academic institutions, autonomous research organisations, policy making, planning and research units of government departments, business, and industry, etc. Its functions include:

- Providing guidance to libraries of ICSSR regional centres and ICSSR-supported research institutes;
- Providing study grants to doctoral students for collection of research materials from various libraries located in different parts of India;
- Rendering financial assistance for taking up bibliographical and documentation projects;
- Providing document delivery service by procuring books and journals on inter-library loan or by photocopying the documents; and
- Organising short-term training courses for research scholars, social scientists, librarians, and IT professionals.

Services Offered by NASSDOC

Consultation Facility: Research scholars visiting NASSDOC for their research work can access various online databases, International Political Science Abstracts, Socio file, Psycinfo, etc.

Reference Service: Reference queries received in person, via e-mail, telephone, fax, are answered to by the staff.

Referral Service: In case of non-availability of materials in the library, research scholars are referred to other institutions/ libraries.

Literature Search: NASSDOC has a good collection of bibliographic data, both in printed as well as in digital format, including online and CD-ROM databases.

Document Delivery Service: NASSDOC provides copies of research materials from its own library and other libraries and institutions in India and abroad.

Bibliographic Service: Bibliographic service is provided on demand.

Union Catalogue of Social Science Periodicals and Serials in India: The union catalogue work was undertaken in 1970 by NASSDOC. The complete database was published in thirty-two volumes, holding records of 31,125 journals in 550 libraries, in seventeen states and two UTs.

Directory of Social Science Libraries and Information Centres in India: The Directory provides details of libraries and information centres attached to government agencies.

DEFENCE SCIENTIFIC INFORMATION AND DOCUMENTATION CENTRE (DESIDOC)

DESIDOC started functioning in 1958 as the Scientific Information Bureau (SIB). It was a division of the Defence Science Laboratory (DSL) which later on became the Defence Science Centre. In 1967, SIB was reorganised with augmented activities and named as the Defence Scientific Information and Documentation Centre (DESIDOC). It became a self-accounting unit and one of the laboratories of the Defence Research and Development Organisation (DRDO) on 29 July 1970. It provides scientific and technical information, based on its library and other information resources, to the DRDO Headquarters and its various laboratories located all over the country. Today, DESIDOC is functioning as a central information resource for DRDO laboratories which are deeply engaged in developing defence technologies covering various disciplines, like aeronautics, armaments, combat vehicles, engineering systems, missiles, advanced computing and simulation, naval systems, information systems, etc. The main objectives of DESIDOC are to:

- Function as a central resource for providing scientific and technical information to DRDO headquarters and laboratories;
- Develop an information system for defence science and technology;
- Provide training and user education programmes in the field of scientific information;
- Provide consultancy and referral services; and
- Publish scientific and technical journals, books, and monographs of DRDO.

Activities of DESIDOC

Defence Science Library (DSL): DSL is a unique specialised library caters to the information needs of researchers in defence science and technology.

Training Programmes: Short-term training programmes and workshops are being conducted by DESIDOC every year for DRDO personnel.

Database Development: DESIDOC develops and maintains bibliographic databases of books, conference proceedings, etc.

Multimedia Service: This facility has been created to facilitate multimedia authoring.

Printing Service: DESIDOC has a full-fledged high quality printing facility including designing, layout, etc.

e-Journals: This service is available only at DESIDOC premises, DRDO users visit DESIDOC to avail this facility.

Publications: Defence Science Journal, Technology Focus, DRDO Newsletter and DRDO Samachar.

EXERCISES: UNIT 11 – UNIT 14

1. Define the term "profession".
2. Write down some important characteristics of a profession.
3. Name few professional categories in LIS.
4. Define the term "professional ethics".
5. Write down the code of ethics for LIS professionals.

6. Highlight the American Library Association (ALA)'s code of ethics.
7. Define a "library association".
8. Highlight the role played by a library association in the upliftment of the profession.
9. Highlight some of the programmes and activities of a library association.
10. Discuss in detail ILA. Highlight its objectives and activities.
11. What do you understand by the IASLIC?
12. Explain the objectives of the IASLIC.
13. Discuss in detail the activities of the American Library Association (ALA).
14. What do you mean by the CILIP?
15. Discuss the role of the IFLA in LIS.
16. Write down the objectives of the IFLA.
17. Discuss the role played by the UNESCO in the development of LIS.
18. Explain the Public Library Manifesto of UNESCO in detail.
19. Highlight some of the prominent activities of the UGC.
20. Discuss the role of the RRRLF.
21. What do you mean by the NISSAT?
22. Discuss the INIS.
23. Write down the services offered by the NASSDOC.
24. Discuss the DESIDOC along with its role and objectives.

PART II

INFORMATION SOURCES AND SERVICES

PART II
INFORMATION SOURCES AND SERVICES

Unit 15
Categorisation of Sources

INFORMATION SOURCE: DEFINITION AND TYPES

An information source is a person, thing or place from which information comes, arises or is obtained. In other words, an information source is a source of information for somebody, i.e. anything that might inform a person about something or provide knowledge to somebody. Information sources may be observations, people, speeches, documents, pictures, organisations, etc. It is different from an information resource, which is defined as a set of resources required to produce information. It includes hardware, software, technical support, users, facilities, data systems and data.

Types of Information Sources

Different epistemologies have different views regarding the importance of different kinds of information sources. Empiricism regards sense data as the ultimate information source, while other epistemologies have different views. Information sources can be divided into two broad categories.

(A) Documentary Sources

(B) Non-Documentary Sources

(A) Documentary Sources: These are generally published or are recorded documents of knowledge. Documentary sources may be as mentioned here:

- **Primary Sources of Information:** Primary sources of information are the first published records of original research and development or descriptions of new applications or new interpretations of an old theme or idea. These are original documents representing unfiltered original ideas. Research reports, patents, conference proceedings, manuscripts, periodicals, standards, theses, personal diaries, etc., are primary information sources of information.

- **Secondary Sources of Information:** Secondary sources of information are those which are either compiled from or refer to primary sources of information. The original information having been casually modified, selected or reorganised so as to serve a definite purpose for a group of users. Textbooks, reference works, indexing services, abstracting services, treatises, monographs, etc. are secondary sources of information.
- **Tertiary Sources of Information:** Tertiary sources of information are those materials in which the information from secondary sources has been digested, reformatted, and condensed, to put it into a convenient, easy to read form. This includes sources which are once removed in time from secondary sources, works which index, organise and compile citations and show you how to use secondary sources. Tertiary sources of information contain information distilled and collected from primary and secondary sources. The primary function of tertiary sources of information is to aid the searcher of a particular information in the use of primary and secondary sources. Bibliography of bibliographies, directories, yearbooks and guides to literature, etc. are tertiary sources of information.

(B) Non-documentary Sources: Non-documentary sources of information form a substantial part of communication especially in science and technology. These are generally unpublished or unrecorded documents of knowledge. User studies have underlined the importance of such sources. These sources provide information that other sources do not. There are two kinds of non-documentary sources:

(1) **Formal Sources:** It includes research organisations, societies, industries, government departments and universities.

(2) **Informal Sources:** It includes conversations with colleagues, visitors, and attendants at professional meetings.

Other Categorisations of Non-Documentary Sources of Information

There are three types of non-documentary sources of information, i.e. humans, organisations, and the World Wide Web.

Humans: It includes information professionals, consultants, experts, resource persons, extension workers, etc.

Organisations: It includes international agencies, government ministries and departments, research and development organisations, academic institutions, societies, publishing houses, libraries, and information centres, etc.

World Wide Web: It includes contents available on the World Wide Web like chats, pages, websites, etc.

OTHER CATEGORIES OF INFORMATION SOURCES

Other categorisations of information sources include print and non-print, published and unpublished, macro and micro, conventional and non-conventional.

Print Sources: All sources that are in print form are print sources. Some of the examples of print sources are books, periodicals, patents, standards, conference documents, etc.

Non-print Sources: Documentary sources that are not printed are all non-print sources. These include manuscripts, theses, diaries, letters, office files, laboratory notebooks, microforms, etc.

Published Sources: These sources are documentary sources, both printed and non-printed. They are brought out by publishers in a large number of copies, usually priced and sold. Some of the examples are books, periodicals, patents, standards, conference documents, etc.

Unpublished Sources: These documentary sources are neither published nor produced in a large number of copies and usually are not for sale. Unpublished sources, at times, can turn into published sources as well. Some of the examples of unpublished sources are manuscripts, theses, project reports, diaries, letters, etc.

Macro and Micro Sources: Ranganathan, the father of library science in India, conceived the idea of macro documents and micro documents. Documents embodying macro thoughts such as books are macro documents and those embodying micro thoughts such as journal articles are micro documents. It is to be noted that documents in microforms are not always micro documents since a microfilm can harbour a book, a macro document or a journal article.

Conventional and Non-conventional Sources: Ranganathan termed traditional documents such as books printed on paper as conventional sources and modern documents like microfilm, reprography, etc. as non-conventional sources.

DIFFERENT CATEGORISATION OF SOURCES BY EMINENT LIS PROFESSIONALS

Categorisation of Sources by Grogan

Grogan attempted to categorise documents relating to scientific literature only. He classified all the scientific information sources into three categories:

1. Primary Sources (as defined earlier, only primary periodicals fall under this group).
2. Secondary Sources (as defined earlier, non-primary periodicals are included in this group).
3. Tertiary Sources (as defined earlier).

Categorisation of Sources by Bonn and Smith

The categorisation by George S. Bonn and Linda C. Smith is for scientific and technical literature. It only covers published sources and include:

Primary Sources: Periodicals, Festschriften, conference proceedings, research reports, research monographs, preprints, patents, standards, dissertations, manufacturers' literature, etc. (Festschriften not ideally suited here in this group.)

Secondary Sources: Handbooks, encyclopaedias, dictionaries, treatises, monographs, indexes, bibliographies, reviews, databanks, translations, indexing serials, abstracting serials, etc. (most secondary sources are listed in this group).

Tertiary Sources: Guides to literature, directories (of persons, organisations, products, etc.), textbooks, etc. (most tertiary sources are missing here, books fall under this group).

Categorisation of Sources by Giljarevskij

R.S. Giljarevskij, a Russian information scientist, categorised all information sources as either primary or secondary. He stated that there is no tertiary category. Moreover, his categorisation covers all forms of literature, not only scientific and technical.

Primary Sources: Monographs, collection of papers, conference proceedings, textbooks and manuals, official publications, invention specifications (for example, patents), technical catalogues, information leaflets, scientific and technical reports, theses, serials, journals and magazines, newspapers, standards, information cards, preprints, manuscripts, galleys, and data files (uncommon sources are covered here).

Secondary Sources: References, literature reviews, abstract journals, express information bulletins, standard indexes, invention bulletins, secondary publications on patents, library catalogues and bibliographic files (few are missing in the group like translations).

Categorisation of Sources by Subramanyam

Subramanyam included micro documents (journal articles, preprints, etc.) in his categorisation. It is more exhaustive than the others.

Primary Sources: Laboratory notebooks, diaries, notes, medical records, personal correspondence, videotapes of experiments and surgical operations, graphs, charts and tables usually machine-generated during experiments, transcripts and audio or videotapes of lectures and discussions, letters to the editor or short communications in primary journals, preliminary communications in letters, journals, preprints and reprints of conference papers, conference proceedings, technical reports, theses and dissertations, journal articles, preprints, reprints, newsletters, house organs, memoranda, company files, patent specifications and computer programs.

Secondary Sources: Bibliographies, indexes, abstracts, current awareness services, dictionaries, directories, tables, handbooks, catalogues, yearbooks, almanacs, reviews, monographs, textbooks, and encyclopaedias.

Tertiary Sources: Bibliography of bibliographies, directory of directories and guides to literature.

Categorisation by Ranganathan

Ranganathan has categorised the documents from two different angles:

(i) by the volume of thought content and

(ii) by recording media.

Documents according to the first categorisation are termed as macro and micro documents; and those by the second categorisation are conventional and non-conventional documents.

Macro Document: When a work expressing macro thought is embodied into a document all by itself, it is called a macro document. A book may be considered as a macro document.

Micro Document: A work expressing micro thought, say a journal article, is referred to as a micro document. Several micro documents comprise a macro document when they are printed together in the macro document.

This is an extremely broad categorisation based on the volume of thought content. It does not go into the numerous types of documents prevalent in the world. Neither does it take into account the various forms the content of a document takes while passing from primary to secondary to tertiary phases.

Conventional Documents: A conventional document is one in which paper forms the basic material on which recording is done by phonetic symbols forming the script of an articulate natural or artificial language or non-conventional script such as Braille or non-phonetic symbols such as drawings or simply by writing. These documents are used for the communication of thought content. Some examples of conventional documents are journals, serials, books, articles, Braille books, stenographs, books with musical notations, etc.

Non-conventional Documents: A non-conventional document is one:

(i) which is reproduced from a conventional document either on paper (for example, a photocopy) or on any other non-paper material (for example, a microfilm); and

(ii) which records sound on non-paper media (for example, gramophone record) or sound and picture together on non-paper media (for example, A/V materials, video recordings, etc.).

Categorisation of documents here is predominantly based on the medium of recording—paper and non-paper. It does not take into account the content of the document.

LACK OF UNANIMITY IN CATEGORISATION

Going through the categorisation by various authors, it becomes evident that Ranganathan has categorised documents firstly by the volume of the thought content and secondly by the recording medium. It may be construed that the categorisation is in the context of cataloguing. Grogan, Bonn and Smith, Giljarevskij, and Subramanyam have categorised documents on the basis of the forms the content of a document take while passing from the primary to secondary to tertiary stages. It has been noticed that in the categorisation by aforesaid authors, there is no unanimity in the categorisation of certain sources like textbooks, monographs, manuals, yearbooks, bibliographies, and directories. It makes it amply clear that criteria for categorisation are not yet fixed firmly and naming of the sources in certain cases has not been precise.

USEFULNESS OF CATEGORISATION

(i) To judge the soundness of a collection, categorisation of documents renders positive help. Take for example the periodical collection of a research library. If the library contains more primary periodicals compared to secondary, then the collection will be considered balanced and more helpful for research.

(ii) Using categorisation it is possible to determine to what extent a particular field is research-oriented. Take the current periodicals of a particular field. Categorise them in primary and secondary sources and then find out the percentage of periodicals in each category. The percentage will indicate to what extent the field is research oriented. If in a field more than 50% periodicals are primary, then the field is surely research-dominated.

Unit 16

Primary Sources

Primary Sources: Primary sources of information are the first published records of original research and development or description of new applications or new interpretations of an old theme or idea. Some of the primary sources of information are discussed in this section.

PRIMARY PERIODICALS

A primary periodical is one that contains, either wholly or mostly, research papers. *Indian Journal of Chemical Technology* and *Pramana—Journal of Physics Features* are its examples. The features of primary periodicals are as follows:

- They are brought out by learned bodies, private or commercial organisations and sometimes by a government.
- The articles contain something original and new interpretations.
- Articles published are of high standards which are ensured by refereeing procedure.
- Usually, the address of the author is provided.
- The date of receipt of the article is generally indicated.
- The abstracts of the articles are generally given.
- The articles include a list of references.

Types

1. **Primary periodicals proper:** Published by learned institutions to publish their complete research work.

2. **Letters journals:** Include short communications which are often called 'letters to the editor'.
3. **Data periodicals:** Contain only or mostly numerical data and nothing else. For example, water resource data.
4. **Previews:** These periodicals contain summaries of forthcoming full-length articles, titles of short communications and preliminary notes. For example, preview of heat and mass transfer.
5. **Synopsis journals:** These publish only condensed forms of the research work. For example, *Journal of American Chemical Society*.
6. **Electronic journals:** Electronic journals are also known as e-journals. Journals brought out in electronic form are termed so.

REPORTS

A "report" is a specific form of writing that is organised around concisely identifying and examining issues, events or findings that have happened in a physical sense, such as events that have occurred within an organisation or findings from a research investigation. It can be categorised as technical reports, administrative reports, and trip reports.

Technical reports: These are possibly the most important of the three categories. These reports are the ones that originate through mission-oriented research projects of governments, industrial organisations or other agencies. Often, the agencies themselves do the experimentation. Sometimes they are assigned to some other bodies who have the necessary infrastructure to carry out the experiment. Reports brought out depicting the various stages of the project are termed progress report, interim report, final report, etc.

Administrative reports: These are the reports that are usually brought out by ministries, departments, institutions, associations, etc. The most common form of these reports is the annual reports. They are brought out every year and contain, among others, the details of the activities performed during the preceding year, plans for the next year, financial statements regarding income and expenditure, etc.

Trip reports: These are the reports that are usually submitted by government officials, company executives, businessmen, scholars, scientists and many others after visiting different parts of the world on various missions and purposes. During their visits, they hold talks with their counterparts, sign agreements, finalise business deals, attend conferences, study markets, go around various establishments, sites, trade fairs and places of their interest, examine machineries and other products, etc. On their return, they usually submit such a report to the authorities concerned.

ANTHOLOGIES OF PAPERS

"Anthologies of Papers" is a collection of previously published articles and research papers on a specific subject, usually written by many authors. When this collection of writings is published in the honour of a learned person, it is referred to as Festschrift. In addition, a number of articles contributed by her/his professional colleagues, students, friends, and others are also included in it. Sometimes, the articles are contributed on a specific topic. There is another kind of anthology of papers known as collected works. For example, *The Collected Papers of Albert Einstein* brought out by Princeton University, USA is a publication of this category.

CONFERENCE DOCUMENTS

The reported recordings of an entire conference are referred to as "conference documents". Conference documents are important sources of information as they often contain nascent ideas. Thousands of conferences are held every year throughout the world. According to the scope, these conferences are categorised as international, national and provincial. Conference documents include conference proceedings, list of delegates, discussions, speeches, minutes of the papers presented and resolutions.

MONOGRAPHS

A "monograph" is a specialised work of writing or exhibition on a single subject or an aspect of a subject, often written by a single author or an artist and usually on a scholarly subject. A monograph presents a detailed study on a single subject, class of subjects, or on a person and is usually accompanied with a bibliography. Some publishers bring out a monograph series as well. Examples, Roy S.C.'s monograph on the gur industry of India.

OFFICIAL PUBLICATIONS

Government publications are referred to as "official publications". A government generates both primary and secondary documents. *Defence Science Journal*, brought out by the DESIDOC, Delhi is a primary publication. On the other hand, *Indian National Bibliography* brought out by the Central Reference Library, Kolkata, is a secondary publication.

PATENTS

A "patent" is a type of intellectual property and primary information source that gives its owner the legal right to exclude others from making, using or selling an invention for a limited period of time in exchange for publishing an enabling disclosure of the invention. The word "patent" means an official right given to a person to make, use or sell a product, process, design, etc. invented by her/him for a fixed number of years. In other words, a patent is a government grant to a patentee conferring on her/him for a stated period of time the exclusive privilege of using the patented invention.

STANDARDS

A "standard" is something set up and established by the authority as a rule for the measure of quantity, weight, extent, value or quality. A standard is an information source that provides detailed description of a standard published by a standard-issuing institution of a country like our Bureau of Indian Standards. These documents are also termed as standard specifications. Standards are always categorised as primary sources of information. These documents appear in A4 (210 mm × 297 mm) or A5 (148 mm × 210 mm) size and in most cases are pamphlets.

TRADE LITERATURE

"Trade literature" is an information source that refers to printed matters such as catalogues, sales brochures, operating manuals and lists of parts. It is produced by manufacturers to encourage sales of their goods and to inform and assist their customers.

Broad Characteristics of Trade Literature

- Provides application-oriented descriptive information;
- Provides primary sources of information about products and processes, much of the literature is not published in any other form;
- Loses currency very quickly;
- The amount of information varies from a very brief announcement in a sheet to a very elaborate description of the product, process or service. The elaborate description at times takes the form of a pamphlet or a book; and
- The literature is distributed for free.

THESES AND DISSERTATIONS

The two words "thesis" and "dissertations" are used sometimes as synonyms, sometimes separately and sometimes in such a way as to indicate that one term totally embraces the other. A thesis or a dissertation is a document (usually unpublished) that contains details of a research conducted under the guidance of an expert. Apart from the hypotheses, objectives, scope, methodology and results of the study, a thesis contains a detailed literature survey which is useful for the compilation of a bibliography on the subject. Moreover, sometimes a thesis indicates the areas where further research can be conducted. In some cases, the researcher gives birth to a new methodology, which becomes useful in subsequent research.

Features of Theses and Dissertations

- Doctoral theses/dissertations are usually considered as original work.

- The findings reported in a thesis/dissertation in most cases appear as articles in learned journals, conference papers or even as monographs.
- For a research degree, a thesis/dissertation is examined by an expert in the field and the candidate has also to defend it.
- A thesis/dissertation is not required to be printed in India, the UK, the USA, etc. for the award of the degree. In many European countries, it needs to be printed before the degree is awarded.
- Theses/dissertations are usually available on inter-library loans and also as microforms.
- The structure of a thesis/dissertation is more or less the same across the world.

PROJECT REPORTS AS PARTIAL FULFILMENT OF ACADEMIC DEGREES

A "project report" is simply a document that provides details on the overall status of the project or specific aspects of the project's progress or performance. Regardless of the type of the report, it is made up of project data based on economic, technical, financial, managerial or production aspects. For the completion of a Master's degree, in many universities and institutions, there is a mandatory requirement because of which a student has to work on a project approved by the authorities concerned. The duration for the completion of the project varies from three months (for example, University of Delhi) to one year (for example, NISCAIR and DRTC). Accordingly, the size of the project report varies from about fifty pages to several hundred pages. The components of project reports are almost similar to theses.

REPRINTS

After the publication of an article in a journal, the author is supplied with a few printed copies of the article for her/his own use. These printed copies are called "reprints". If these reprints pertain to research articles, then they are primary sources of information.

INFORMATION LEAFLETS

Information leaflets are sources of information that are usually intended to inform a wide audience, including the laboratory staff, managers, and laboratory customers. Like guides, information leaflets are developed by different working groups, often in cooperation with other organisations. Information leaflets are also carriers of information. There is an abundance of information leaflets for parents, kids, young people, patients, etc. Suppose a dentist extracts the infected tooth of a patient. After the job is done, the dentist may hand over an information leaflet to the patient which will tell them how long the pain will continue, the healing process will take, what should be done if any emergency arises, etc.

PREPRINT MANUSCRIPTS

A "preprint" is a typewritten scientific paper, i.e. the manuscript, that is yet to be published in a scientific journal. This means that the paper is yet to be peer-reviewed. From the initial submission in typewritten form to the publication of a paper, the process often takes weeks, months or even more because manuscripts are to undergo peer review.

OTHER PRIMARY SOURCES

Laboratory Notebooks

A "laboratory notebook" is an information source in which a researcher maintains a complete record of procedures (the actions taken), the reagents used, the observations (the data) and the relevant thought processes that would enable another scientist to reproduce observations.

Diaries

Writers, scholars, rulers and many others maintain "diaries". These diaries provide the most authentic biographical material and plenty of other information. Normally, these diaries are handwritten and sometimes depending on their importance they are published also. The diaries of Fanny Burney, English novelist, titled *Early Diary* (1768-78) and *Diary and Letters* (1778-1840) beautifully depict the background of the period.

Memoranda

A "memorandum" or memo in short is usually a document that aids our memory by recording events or observations on a topic, which may be used in a business organisation. The plural form is either memoranda or memorandums. There are various types of memoranda such as memorandum of agreement, memorandum of association, memorandum of understanding (MoU), etc.

Internal Research Reports

Often companies, institutions, and organisations conduct research to survey the market, consumer behaviour, sale of a particular product, etc. It is also possible that a country is closely watching the defence activities of a neighbouring country. The results of such research are recorded in a document. This document is for internal use only and hence called "internal research reports".

Minutes of Meetings

In an office, apart from the governing body there is an executive committee, purchase committee, staff selection committee, etc. All these committees hold meetings from time to time. The agenda of the meeting, members present in the meeting, deliberations that took place and the decisions taken in the meeting are all meticulously recorded in a document. This document is called the "minutes of the meeting".

Official Files

In every office one can find a collection of files that have been accumulated over the years. In certain offices the collection is huge. If you classify the files, you will notice that they broadly belong to personnel, capital items like buildings, machineries, books, and periodicals, etc., maintenance and repair, stationeries, etc. These files contain notes, drafts or copies of letters, clippings of printed tenders, advertisements and others. The vital decisions taken by a government, chairman of a company, head of an institution or organisation, a general and many others are also recorded in these files.

Correspondence

Ever since the system of writing developed, humans have been writing letters. Of late, with the advent of e-mail, the usual practice of writing letters on materials like paper has greatly diminished. Letters written by litterateurs like Rabindranath Tagore have been published in several volumes. Apart from its literary value, many of the letters have got not only biographical but historical significance. Such sources documenting such information are referred to as "correspondences".

Information Cards

A card containing information is an "information card". A postcard harbouring a letter, an invitation card to attend a marriage or a meeting, a report card from the teacher of a child, a menu card of a restaurant, are all information cards.

Medical Records

Medical records comprise prescriptions, pathological reports, X-ray reports, ultrasonographic reports, MRI reports, surgical reports, electroencephalograms, mammograms, colour doppler test reports, etc. All these carry valuable information using which the doctors diagnose various ailments, defects, fractures, presence of foreign bodies inside the body, etc. The prescription is a valuable document for the patient as well. Such information sources are called medical records.

Audio and Video Tapes

Audio-video tapes are information sources that may contain lectures by eminent professors, scientists, authors, politicians and others. Often, debates in legislative bodies, cross-examinations of criminals, are also audio-taped as they authenticate the statement of a person. Hence, these act as primary sources of information.

Computer Programs

A "computer program" is an information source with 'a series of coded software instructions to control the operation of a computer' (program). Everyday numerous programs are written either for a new job to be executed by a computer or for the new version of an old program. These programs are the property of companies who have produced them. Usually, it is for their exclusive use. As such there is practically no bibliographical control of these programs.

Data Files

A "data file" is 'a set of related records (either written or electronic) kept together'. Examples of data files are databases, spreadsheets, and e-mails (data files). It is to be noted that all databases are not primary sources. There are databases of secondary and tertiary sources as well. A database devoted to a primary periodical is a primary source.

Unit 17

Secondary and Tertiary Sources

Some important secondary information sources are elaborated in the next section.

SECONDARY PERIODICALS

A "secondary periodical" may be defined as a periodic publication that disseminates information, contained in primary sources in various forms such as index, abstract, digest, account, etc. Some secondary periodicals are defined below.

Abstracting periodicals: An abstracting periodical is a periodic publication that contains an abstract of the publication in addition to the bibliographical details. The abstract may be informative or indicative.

Indexing periodicals: An indexing periodical is a periodic publication that includes the bibliographical details of an article or any other document. It does not provide any abstract. Entries are arranged either under class numbers or under subject headings.

Popular periodicals: A popular periodical, as the name suggests, is a periodic publication that usually serves common people, students, technicians, teachers and others. These periodicals contain popular articles written in a lucid style on a particular area of knowledge.

Technical periodicals: A technical periodical is a periodic publication devoted to a technical subject. In many cases, a technical periodical embraces the features of both a primary periodical and a secondary periodical.

Trade journals: As the name implies, these journals are meant for persons related to trade and contain matters of trade interest. The technical journals also provide a great deal of trade information creating at times difficulty in drawing a sharp line of distinction between both.

House journals: Often, an industrial house, a scientific organisation, an educational institution or other bodies bring out different categories of periodicals reflecting mainly the various activities of the house. These periodicals are usually called house journals and appear in various forms.

BIBLIOGRAPHIES

A "bibliography" is a list of documents arranged in a systematic order. Each entry provides the bibliographical details of the document. Some of the important types of bibliographies are defined in this section.

Universal bibliography: A universal bibliography is that 'which lists all documents of all kinds of materials, produced in all countries, in every language, at any time and on all themes'.

National bibliography: A national bibliography lists the publications produced in a nation. They may appear in the form of a book or a periodical. It does not, however, list all sorts of publications. For example, the Indian National Bibliography.

Trade bibliography: Trade bibliographies are brought out by commercial publishers, booksellers, distributors, printers, and others. Normally, these bibliographies list books which are meant for sale. For example, Books in Print.

Selective bibliography: A selective bibliography does not cover all the documents on the topic. They are selected on the basis of some criteria. These bibliographies may appear in the form of a book or a periodical. For example, ASLIB booklist.

Subject bibliography: A subject bibliography lists the documents on a given subject. The subject may be a place, a person or any other topic. For example, the *Asian Social Science Bibliography*.

Author bibliography: An author bibliography is also known as biobibliography or individual bibliography. It lists the works of a single author. For example, R.B. Freeman's *Works of Charles Darwin: An Annotated Bibliographical Handlist.*

LISTS OF RESEARCH IN PROGRESS

In research laboratories, universities and institutes of higher learning, researchers are engaged in research projects. If researchers in the world remain unaware of these projects, it is quite likely that there will be some duplication in the research work. To minimise the duplication, a new type of publication has evolved that lists the research projects providing information about the name of the researchers, the name of the institute where the research work is going on, the title of the project, when the work has started, when it is likely to be finished, etc. Such an information source is called "lists of research in progress". For example, the Current Research Projects in CSIR Laboratories.

REFERENCE SOURCES

"Reference sources" are meant for ready reference. The purpose of these sources is to readily provide information practically on any topic. There are many types of reference sources. Some of them are described in this section.

Encyclopaedias: Encyclopaedias are sources that provide information on any topic in such a way whereby one can get a holistic view of the topic. Articles contained in them are informative and of varying length, ranging from a few lines to one hundred pages or more. That is why encyclopaedias are used not only as reference sources but also for self-education. Broadly, there are two types of encyclopaedias—general encyclopaedias (covering all subjects) and subject encyclopaedias (covering a particular subject).

Dictionaries: A dictionary, as you know, provides 'a list of words of a language in alphabetical order and explains what they mean or gives a word for them in a foreign language'. Dictionaries are of many types: general dictionaries (covering all areas and fields), subject dictionaries (covering one field), monolingual dictionaries (term and meaning in the same language), bilingual dictionaries (use two languages for term and meaning), and multilingual dictionaries (with multiple languages).

Handbooks: It is an information source containing concise information and are small enough to be held in the hand, but is strictly a book written primarily for practitioners and for serving as constant references. It is also called a "manual". It is to be noted that there is no general handbook. A handbook is always devoted to a particular subject or subjects.

Manuals: A manual is 'a book that gives instructions about how to use a machine' (manual). The definition is quite clear and does not create any confusion with handbooks. However, the definition is narrow as manuals give instructions not only for the use of a machine but for other things as well.

Directories: A directory lists the names of persons, institutions or organisations of a particular area. The area may be a locality (for example, residents' directory), a town (for example, telephone directory), a country (for example, Directory of British Associations and Associations in Ireland).

Yearbooks: A yearbook, as the name suggests, appears annually and updates information every year. Yearbooks are of various types and can be categorised as, general and subject-oriented, or as national, regional and international. *The Statesman's Yearbook* is an example.

Maps: A map is a sheet of paper or similar material on which the earth's surface, or part of it is shown indicating countries, oceans, seas, mountains, rivers, deserts, roads, etc.

Atlases: An atlas is a book that usually contains maps and an index of places and other geographical entities indicating their locations in particular maps.

Globes: A globe is a sphere, the surface of which shows countries, oceans, seas, mountains, rivers, deserts, etc. just like a map. It is mounted on a stand and can be rotated around its axis. The surface of globes is generally plain.

Gazetteer: A gazetteer is a dictionary of names of places and other geographical entities with descriptive, statistical, economical, geographical, and historical information. Sometimes a gazetteer is called a "geographical dictionary". For example, *Webster's New Geographical Dictionary*.

Biographical sources: A biography is an account of someone's life. Biographical sources appear in the form of biographical dictionaries and individual biographies.

Who is who: Provides biographical information about various persons who are living. For example, *International Who's Who* gives information about names, addresses, occupations, etc.

TREATISES

A "treatise" is 'a long and serious piece of writing on a particular subject'. For example, *A Treatise on Heat* by M.N. Saha and B.N. Srivastava (4th ed. Allahabad, Indian Press, 1958) is a veritable source of information on heat for advanced learners.

TEXTBOOKS

A "textbook" is an information source that is 'used by students as a standard work for a particular branch of study'. Throughout our educational career we have studied textbooks to gain knowledge on various subjects. In student life, the textbook acts as a major source of information for students. Teachers in schools, colleges and universities also use textbooks to update their knowledge, prepare class notes, clarify doubts, etc.

TRANSLATIONS

A primary source when translated into another language becomes a secondary source. Many Russian primary journals are translated into English. For example, *Soviet Geology* is a cover-to-cover translation of the Russian journal *Sovetskaya Geologiya*. Books are also translated from one language to another. For example, *Ramayana* by Valmiki was translated into Hindi by Tulsidas as *Ramcharitamanas*.

OTHER SECONDARY SOURCES

Computer Files

A "computer file" is a collection of records or programs stored under a single filename. For the computerisation of a library catalogue, we create a record for each and every book in a computer. All these records are stored in a computer under a single name. The collection of these records constitutes a file and the name given to it is called a "filename". The digitised form of a book, a periodical, a thesis, etc. can be a computer file. Depending on the content, a computer file can be a primary, secondary or a tertiary source.

Bibliographic Databases

A "database" is a collection of cross-referenced files designed to retrieve information from a number of access points. A large number of indexing and abstracting services in the world have created their own databases which can be searched from any part of the world on a payment basis to retrieve desired information. For example, Medline is the database of the indexing service called "Index Medicus".

Databanks

There are a number of vendors that possess a large collection of online databases. The collection is sometimes referred to as "databanks". After obtaining a password from the vendor one can search all these databases from a single access point. For example, DIALOG, a service of The Dialog Corporation, has been serving users since 1972. Its collection of over 900 databases handles more than 7,00,000 searches and delivers over seventeen million document page views per month. Thus, a databank is a collection of multiple databases.

CD-ROMs

A "CD-ROM" becomes a source of information only when it contains data. The data accommodated on CD-ROMs may include colourful pictures, sound, animation, and facilities for interaction. Many a time, the matter on CD-ROM is in hypertext that facilitates surfing from one item to another with ease.

The next section will elaborate on some important tertiary sources of information.

LIBRARY CATALOGUES

A "library catalog" or "catalogue" is a register of all bibliographic items found in a library or group of libraries, such as a network of libraries at several locations. A catalogue for a group of libraries is also called a "union catalogue". A bibliographic item can be any information entity (for example, books, computer files, graphics, realia, cartographic materials, etc.) that is considered library material (for example, a single novel in an anthology), or a group of library materials (for example, a trilogy), or linked from the catalogue (for example, a webpage) as far as it is relevant to the catalogue and to the users (patrons) of the library.

BIBLIOGRAPHY OF BIBLIOGRAPHIES

A "bibliography of bibliographies" is a list of bibliographies. They may be classified or arranged alphabetically subject-wise or otherwise. Most of them are in the form of a book. However, there are some which are issued periodically. For example, the *Bibliographic Index: A Cumulative Bibliography of Bibliographies*.

GUIDES TO LITERATURE

A "guide to literature" helps a researcher, reader and the like to find the primary, secondary, and tertiary sources of literature on a specific subject. These guides are in the form of books and are available for many fields. It should be noted that these 'guides to literature' are totally different from 'guidebooks for tourists' which we have dealt with earlier. Guides to literature are available for fields like social sciences, history, biology and others. For example, L.J. Anthony's *Sources of Information on Atomic Energy*.

DIRECTORY OF DIRECTORIES

A "directory of directories" is an information source that lists the directories available on a particular topic or pertaining to a particular area. For example, the Guide to Scientific and Technical Directories is devoted to science and technology.

GUIDES TO REFERENCE SOURCES

"Guides to reference sources" is an information source that lists reference books of all types usually subject-wise. Guide to reference books is a reference source.

Unit 18
Criteria of Evaluation

CHECKLIST OF EVALUATION

A book evaluation is an assessment of the suitability of a book for a particular purpose. Most books are evaluated by an editor before they are deemed fit for publication. Books from major publishers and those selected for research and university libraries may be evaluated many times. For the evaluation of a reference book, the authorities prepare a checklist which includes past records of the publisher, authority, scope, treatment, arrangement, index, special features, book reviews, limitations, format, and conclusion. These criteria have been discussed in this section.

1. Past Record: There are many publishers like Oxford University Press, Wilson, Europa, and McGraw-Hill who are bringing out well-known reference books for decades or centuries. If the past record of a publisher is found to be good, then it becomes easy to decide about the procurement of the book. On the other hand, if the publisher is new, little known or unknown, then it becomes essential to read the reviews about the book before taking a final decision.

2. Authority: The authoritativeness of a reference book is usually judged on the basis of the qualifications, reputation, and experience of the author, compiler, and editor responsible for the book and the reputation, experience, and past records of the publisher/corporate body. For example, Encyclopaedia Britannica, Inc. is publishing *The Encyclopaedia Britannica* since 1768.

3. Scope: When we talk of scope, we generally take into account the subject, geographical area, time span, forms of documents, language, target user, etc. For example, the Indian National Bibliography (INB) covers publications on all subjects, published from India.

4. Treatment: Here the term treatment implies thoroughness, completeness, reliability, bias, style, illustrations, etc. Apart from thoroughness and completeness, reliability of information contained in a reference book is of great importance. In the reference books brought out by well-known publishers generally you will not find any factual error, grammatical error, stylistic error, etc. Data from these books are freely quoted by people without any hesitation.

5. Arrangement: A variety of arrangements are noticed in reference books. Alphabetical arrangement is quite common. The pattern of arrangement is also an essential criterion for the selection of a reference book.

6. Special Features: Many reference books have some unique features which others do not have. For example, some reference books are updated at regular intervals, others irregularly. There are some which are not updated at all. Apart from unique features and mode of updation, presence of bibliographies, supplements, appendices, etc. are also considered as special features. These also define the selection of a reference book.

7. Format: Format takes into account the binding (paper binding, cloth binding, rexine binding, half leather binding, full leather binding, etc.), quality of paper (newsprint, bond paper, book paper, and magazine paper), font, page makeup and illustrations (photograph, portrait, map, plan, facsimile, table, chart, etc.).

8. Book Reviews: Book reviews are published in newspapers, journals, magazines, etc. There are even book review periodicals which publish only book reviews. Book reviews are written by scholars and many people of eminence. Hence, book reviews must be given due importance while evaluating a book.

9. Limitations: All reference books have some limitations however comprehensive they may be. Take for example,

Webster's Third International. This dictionary is one of the most comprehensive English language dictionaries currently available. Yet this dictionary does not contain any phrase or idiom. Moreover, a dictionary cannot cover all the words that have come into use very recently. Identification of limitations is yet another criterion for the evaluation of a book.

10. Conclusion: The overall judgment on a reference source is to be reflected in the conclusion whereby the authorities concerned are able to take a decision about its procurement after evaluating the above-mentioned criteria. The conclusion is written point-wise.

EVALUATION OF DIFFERENT REFERENCE SOURCES

Bibliographies, Abstracting and Indexing Periodicals

A systematic bibliography lists the bibliographical details of documents in a particular order. When these bibliographies are brought out periodically, they are called "indexing periodicals", for example, the "Index Medicus". Some bibliographies include abstracts along with the bibliographical details of documents. They are called "abstracting periodicals". For example, the "Indian Science Abstracts". For evaluation of the bibliographies, abstracting and indexing periodicals all the ten criteria mentioned in the previous section are considered. These can be mentioned one by one with suitable and appropriate modifications (for demonstration, this one can be completed).

Past record: For the purpose of selection, past records may be examined to see whether there have been frequent changes in the periodicity or frequent interruptions in the publication, etc. The reputation of the publisher is also verified.

Authority: In this case, both the publisher and the sponsor are to be examined. If these periodicals are brought out by a lesser-known publisher or a sponsor, adequate care has to take before finally selecting the periodical for a library.

Scope: The scope of bibliographies varies. For example, the scope of Indian Science Abstracts is national and that of Chemical Abstracts is international. Many bibliographies cover various types of documents in diverse languages. It is evaluated before selection.

Treatment: In an abstracting periodical the abstract may be informative or indicative. Its coverage may be exhaustive or selective. The same is applicable to an indexing periodical.

Arrangement: The arrangement of entries varies from bibliography to bibliography. The arrangement is taken into consideration before selection.

Special features: Usually, bibliographies provide indexes. Indexes vary from bibliography to bibliography. Author index and subject index are quite common. Buyer is supposed to verify this criterion as well.

Format: See the format as discussed in the previous section.

Limitations: For international abstracting and indexing services, achieving exhaustivity in terms of coverage is a difficult task due to various factors. Similar kind of limitations like language, etc. are verified before selection.

Other criterion can be taken into consideration as well including treatment, format, and book review. These have been discussed earlier.

Dictionaries

For the evaluation of dictionaries, the past record of a dictionary, authority, scope, arrangement, word treatment, specific features, revision, format and conclusion are taken into consideration.

Past record: Most dictionaries of the world have got a past record. Many dictionaries have started in a modest way and gradually became more voluminous. In some cases, utilising the same base resulted in the springing up of different dictionaries.

Word treatment: Here, we take into account, spelling, pronunciation, definition, quotation, synonyms and antonyms, phrases, derivatives, etymology, gender, etc. These are defined one by one.

- **Spelling:** In the English language, American and British spellings are prevalent. Dictionaries published in the UK and Commonwealth countries use British spelling and those produced in the USA use American spelling. It is to be noted that British dictionaries include words with American spellings and vice versa.

- **Pronunciation:** The pronunciation of certain words in the same language varies from region to region and from country to country. It is checked for evaluation.
- **Definition:** The definition given in a dictionary should be accurate and easily understandable. Keeping in view the level of users, lexicographers try to define a word.
- **Synonyms and antonyms:** To express the meaning of a word, many dictionaries use one or more synonyms along with or without the definition. In some dictionaries, the synonyms and antonyms are given at the end of the main entry.
- **Phrases and idioms:** Many dictionaries include phrases and idioms which occur under the headwords.
- **Etymology:** It provides 'an account of the origin and the history of the developments in meaning of a word'. For example, the word 'zero' has originated from the Arabic word 'sifr'.
- **Gender:** In certain languages like Hindi, the gender of the word is usually mentioned in the dictionaries.

Other criteria have been discussed in the first section of this unit.

Conclusion: It is to be remembered that all that has been discussed about a dictionary will not be available in a single dictionary. A dictionary may give definitions of words and not the synonyms. Another may include only the words (single or compound) and not the phrases and idioms. When there are several options available, we can use the checklist and then decide which one is to be taken.

Encyclopaedias

Encyclopaedias are generally costly publications. The number of encyclopaedias are also many. The multi-volume general encyclopaedias in English are quite a few in the market such as *The New Encyclopaedia Britannica*, *Encyclopaedia*

Americana, etc. The cost of all these encyclopaedias run into thousands/lakhs of rupees which most libraries cannot afford to purchase. In such a situation, a checklist for the evaluation of encyclopaedias is of real help. The criteria include past record of a dictionary, authority, scope, arrangement, word treatment, index, specific features, revision, format, and conclusion.

Index: The index is an indispensable part of an encyclopaedia. Initially, *The New Encyclopaedia Britannica* was without an index as it was hoped that the Micropaedia will serve the purpose. In reality, it did not. Finally, in order to meet the demands of the users an index was provided.

Special features: Each encyclopaedia has some special features. For example, *The New Webster's International Encyclopaedia* has a separate section of maps and an index of place names figuring in the maps, etc. These are taken into consideration for evaluation.

All the other criteria including the conclusion are already defined in the first section of this unit.

Yearbooks and Almanacs

For the evaluation of yearbooks and almanacs, the scope, treatment, arrangement, special features, limitations, authority, and format are all taken into consideration.

Special features: "India: A Reference Annual" provides information only about India. It does not practically have any special features. On the other hand, *Manorama Yearbook 2006* (41st ed. Kottayam: Malayala Manorama, 2006) not only provides information about India but also of the world. In addition, it provides information about one hundred books, one hundred literary characters, one hundred eminent persons, a dictionary of 600 terms, 500 places of interest and other things. This helps in the selection of an information source.

Limitations: All yearbooks will have some limitations. *Manorama Yearbook* is biased towards India. On the other hand, *Statesman's Yearbook* is biased towards the UK.

All the other criteria including conclusion are already defined in the first section of this unit.

Directories

For evaluation of directories the past record, authority, scope, compilation, treatment, arrangement, information content of an entry, indexes, special features, limitations, and format are taken into consideration.

Compilation: A directory is usually compiled on the basis of the replies to the questionnaires mailed to the concerned persons or institutions. This method ensures a great degree of authenticity.

Treatment: It differs from directory to directory. For example, the information given on a periodical is much more in *Ulrich's International Periodicals Directory* compared to the *Directory of Indian Scientific Periodicals*.

Information content of an entry: It also differs according to the type of a directory. The information content of a telephone directory is—name of the person/institution/organisation, address and the telephone number.

Indexes: A telephone directory generally is without an index. Many directories in which the entire gamut of entries is not in the alphabetical order, usually provide one or more indexes to ensure the easy location of information.

Special features: Some directories have some special features. For example, *Ulrich's International Periodicals Directory* includes information on abstracting and indexing services, money symbols and a list of periodicals that have ceased publishing, etc.

Limitations: Generally, directories are compiled on the basis of information obtained from the concerned people, institutions, organisations, etc. Sometimes, some persons, institutions or organisations do not provide the required information. Most of them are not updated.

All the other criteria including conclusion are already defined in the first section of this unit.

Geographical Sources

Geographical sources usually comprise geographical dictionaries, geographical encyclopaedias, gazetteers, guidebooks, atlases, maps, and globes. At times, a gazetteer has been termed as a geographical dictionary. A geographical dictionary compiles definitions of geographical terms such as island, river, valley, and mountain while a gazetteer, the descriptions of specific places, rivers, valleys and mountains. For the evaluation of geographical sources past records, authority, scope, date, compilation, treatment, limitations, arrangement, items of information, special features and format are taken into consideration.

Date: Throughout the world different types of geographical changes occur around the year. The birth of a new country (for example, Bangladesh) or a new state (for example, Jharkhand), the change in the name of a place (for example, Calcutta to Kolkata), etc. are common geographical phenomena. A backdated geographical source will not be able to include the latest changes.

Items of information: A geographical dictionary like any other dictionary, provides the definition of geographical terms. An international gazetteer may provide against the place name, the variant name/s of the place, pronunciation, population, geographic and political location, altitude, trade, industry, agriculture, mineral and other natural resources, irrigation works, river lengths, communications, history, cultural institutions and monuments, battles and other facts pertinent to the place. These are taken into consideration for evaluation.

Special features: In all geographical sources, black and white and colourful maps are usually provided. The more the number of maps, the more useful will be the source. This should be borne in mind while selecting a source.

Format: Maps, atlases and globes are usually produced in colour. Maps in many cases are of big size and meant for hanging on the wall. Similarly, the other dimensions in format are also verified.

All the other criteria including conclusion are already defined in the first section of this unit.

Biographical Sources

Biographical sources are also of various types, of which, biographical dictionaries are most important. These dictionaries are published as who's who, who was who, biographical dictionary, etc. The scope of these dictionaries may be national or international, they may be devoted to particular subjects, particular gender (for example, women), particular a class of persons, for example, presidents, kings and queens, prime ministers, parliamentarians or they may be current or retrospective or both current as well as retrospective. In addition, there are individual biographies written by the person herself/himself or by a biographer. In the case of the selection of biographical sources, past records, authority, scope, method of compilation, treatment, arrangement, items of information, indexes, special features, limitations, updation, and format are taken into consideration.

Method of compilation: Currently, who's who is compiled on the basis of filled in questionnaires received from the biographers. This authenticates the information given in the source as the information is given by the biographer herself/himself.

Items of information: Usually, the following items of information are found in a sketch type entry figuring in a biographical dictionary: name, pronunciation of the name, highest qualification, present position, date of birth, parent's name, education, services, publications, recreation or hobbies, address, telephone number, e-mail address, etc.

Indexes: Biographical sources that are arranged alphabetically do not usually provide any index. If it is arranged otherwise, usually a biographer index is provided.

Special features: Some biographical dictionaries provide a photograph or a portrait or a sketch of the biographer along with her/his biographical details. Apart from this, some biographical sources provide a list of abbreviations, etc.

Limitations: All biographical sources have some limitations. The coverage of none of these sources can be considered to be comprehensive. One has to select biographies on the basis of some criteria, whereby, many others are left out. There is also bias in selection.

Updation: There are some biographical sources which appear annually. They are updated regularly. Other biographical sources are updated after long intervals. As a result, the information contained in them is often outdated.

All the other criteria including conclusion are already defined in the first section of this unit.

Textbooks

Textbooks are the backbone of school, college, university and other educational institutions' libraries. Numerous authors write textbooks and known, little-known and well-known publishers publish them. As such, they are of varying quality. The first thing that should be checked in a textbook is whether the textbook covers the prescribed syllabus adequately. This apart from authors, publishers, the edition and error-freeness are to be given greater importance. Students know textbooks by the name of the authors. Hence, for procuring a textbook for a library, the first element to be checked is the author. If the author is famous, the textbook may be procured without any problem. The corporate body is no less important. The problem arises in selecting the first edition of a textbook by a new author and a new publisher. It may contain a lot of grammatical and factual errors. A glance through the first few pages may reveal the quality of the book. If you fail to judge the purchase worthiness of a book, take the help of a good teacher. The judgment of a teacher will be valuable for making a decision. A glance through the reviews may also help.

Handbooks and Manuals

Checklist/criteria in the first section of this unit are taken into consideration for the evaluation of handbooks and manuals.

Trade Catalogues

Trade catalogues are distributed free of charge. They contain a lot of information not available elsewhere. Their evaluation is generally not necessary as you are not purchasing them. If you find some information missing in the catalogue, you may suggest to the producer to include them.

Statistical Information Sources

Statistical information sources are generally brought out by international bodies like the United Nations, UNESCO, FAO, government bodies and departments like the Central Statistical Office, Great Britain, Central Statistical Organisation of India, Office of the Census Commissioner, India, State Statistical Bureaus of Indian States, etc. The information they provide is authentic and the authority is unquestioned. Hence, the procurement of a statistical publication, if required by the library, does not pose any problem. Data contained in the statistical publications generally cannot be updated every now and then. Hence, they may be backdated by a year or at times a decade. Our population census is taken once every ten years. It was last taken in the year 2011. Next it will be taken in 2021. Hence till 2021, books will provide our population data based on the 2011 census only.

Sources of Information on Current Affairs

Newspapers are the primary sources of information on current affairs. Based on newspapers, various types of secondary sources are being published in the world which has considerable reference value. Some of the types of sources are as follows:

(i) Indexing services based on individual newspapers. For example, *The New York Times Index*.

(ii) Indexing services based on many newspapers. For example, *The Canadian Index*.

(iii) News digests. For example, *Keesing's Record of World Events*. All such sources can be evaluated using the checklist elements given in the first section of this unit.

Primary Periodicals

Checklist/criteria in the first section of this unit are taken into consideration for the evaluation of handbooks and manuals.

Reviewing Periodicals

Checklist/criteria in the first section of this unit are taken into consideration for the evaluation of handbooks and manuals.

EXERCISES: UNIT 15 – UNIT 18

1. Define "information sources".
2. What are the different types of information sources? Illustrate with examples.
3. Define a "documentary source".
4. Differentiate between a primary and a secondary source of information.
5. Discuss in detail the categorisation of information sources by S.R. Ranganathan.
6. Discuss the usefulness of the categorisation of information sources.
7. Define a "primary source of information".
8. What is a "primary periodical"?
9. Discuss the different types of "reports".
10. Define "monographs".
11. What is a "patent"?
12. Write down the characteristics of trade literature.
13. What are the features of theses and dissertations?
14. Define "memoranda".
15. What is a "secondary source of information"?
16. Name some important secondary periodicals.
17. List some important types of bibliographies.
18. What is a "reference source"?
19. Define "tertiary sources of information" with some examples.
20. Highlight some common criteria for the evaluation of an information source.
21. How would you evaluate reference sources?
22. How would you evaluate directories?

Unit 19
Humans as Source of Information

HUMAN SOURCE

A human source is a person who has been deliberately recruited and is managed to collect information to satisfy an intelligence requirement. All sensible human beings possess information and usually deliver the same when needed. Thus, they become a 'human source' of information.

HUMAN RESOURCE

The term 'human resources' is defined as

(i) 'the people that staff and operate an organization'; and

(ii) 'the personnel employed in an organization.'

Information Generators: This group includes researchers, inventors, innovators, authors, writers, planners, policy makers, executives and such others who have an assigned role to generate knowledge or create information. These people are involved in different kinds of activities.

Information Gatherers: These people do not generate knowledge or information but gather information for various purposes and organise the collected information for a given purpose. Reporters, correspondents, detectives, spies, police, compilers, enumerators, etc. are information gatherers by profession. All these people receive training for the job they do.

Information Compilers: Bibliographers, lexicographers, encyclopaedists and reviewers stand prominently among the set of compilers. Compilers are also gatherers of information. Once

the details are collected, a compiler prepares a standard entry for each of the items. The entries are then organised in a helpful sequence which may be alphabetically author-wise, subject-wise or year-wise. Thus, a compiler gathers and then compiles the information in a helpful sequence.

Information Processors: These are the professionals that refine and filter the available information and transform it into more comprehensive and convenient form. Editors and their varieties and also the information technologists especially software specialists who write programs for data processing, fall under this category. When books, articles, reports, etc. are received for publication, in many cases plenty of inconsistencies, inaccuracies, redundancies, incompleteness, etc. are observed. The editorial process becomes essential to give it a final phase.

Information Recorders: This category of professionals record/document different sources of information relating to their activity and environment. The author and the reporter in most cases are found to be the first recorders of information. Inscribers, engravers, scribes, calligraphers, printers, data entry operators, typists, stenographers, compositors, proofreaders, videographers, photographers, painters, sculptors, etc. are other professionals that belong to this category.

Information Disseminators: Professionals that spread or give out something, especially news, information, or ideas, to a lot of people are referred to as information disseminators. The professionals belonging to this category are library professionals, documentalists, information officers, extension workers, publishers, representatives of firms, receptionists, consultants, marketing officers, broadcasting professionals, press professionals, advertisers, teachers, doctors, lawyers and hawkers.

Translator: A translator is someone who conveys materials communicated in one language such as English into another language like French, Chinese or Spanish, without losing the literal meaning or nuances of the original work.

Information Condensers: Professionals having transliterator or interpreter skills whereby the source message is reduced in length without impacting the meaning or grammatical accuracy of the information are referred to as information condensers. An important consideration in condensing is the retention of key vocabulary.

Information Retrievers: In this category, we usually include those personnel who retrieve information on demand by searching reference books, databases, the Internet, etc. We call these people reference librarians, database searchers, Internet searchers, etc. All these people are experts in their respective fields and good sources of information in the sense that they know where the information is available and can search for it on demand.

Informaticians: Every moment new information is being continuously generated in the world and is cumulating day by day. It is necessary, for various purposes, to know the rate of growth, decay and many other properties of information. To study all these phenomena a new species of information professionals has emerged called informaticians. They possess information about the generation, growth, propagation, use and obsolescence of information, various laws governing these factors, the efficiency of information systems, services and products and various types of relationships existing among subjects.

Information Preservers: Man since time immemorial has been trying to preserve information through various means. Even today man is discovering and inventing new methods and mediums of preservation. These professionals are good sources of information about document preservation. Such professionals that preserve information by various means are referred to as information preservers.

INFORMATION PROFESSIONALS/PROFESSIONS

Lawyer: A lawyer (also called attorney, counsel or counsellor) is a licensed professional who advises and represents others in legal matters. Today a lawyer can be young or old, male or female. From the purchase of assets, to solving disputes, getting a society registered and for various other purposes, we require legal help. Lawyers are the persons who provide us with the necessary information in such situations.

Doctor: A doctor is a person who is a professional skilled in the science of medicine. Such a person is trained and licensed to treat sick and injured people. The doctor first of all gathers information from the patient about their symptoms. Thereafter, the doctor examines the patient. If the doctor can diagnose the disease, s/he informs the patient about the disease s/he is suffering from.

Teachers: A professional whose job is to teach, especially in a school or college is called so. A teacher possesses information on the subject they teach, books and journals on the subject, institutions where the subject is taught within the country and abroad, other teachers on the subject, availability of scholarships, job opportunities, research facilities available within the country and abroad, etc. They also possess information about the students of their classes and many students whom they have taught earlier.

Experts: An expert is a professional who possesses sound knowledge on a particular subject, technique, etc. On many occasions, we need their help. For example, for appointing an information scientist in an organisation, we set up an interview board comprising experts. They interview the candidates, judge their suitability for the post and finally choose the best candidate depending on her/his knowledge, skill, qualification, and experience.

Resource Persons: The connotation of the term "resource person" varies depending on the context. Normally, a resource person enriches a programme by virtue of her/his vast knowledge. S/he provides the main intellectual inputs to the course for which s/he is the resource person by delivering lectures and enriching others' lectures by her/his comments and suggestions.

Technological Gatekeepers: A "technological gatekeeper" is a well-informed person in a particular field. Usually, some scientists, technologists, and professionals in business, etc. have the tendency (possibly inborn) to acquire information from various sources, to keep herself/himself abreast of the development in the field and to disseminate the information to a person or group who may be interested in that information. There is no formal course to train a person as a technological gatekeeper. Almost automatically, they grow into a technological gatekeeper.

Invisible College: "Invisible college" is the term used for a small community of interacting scholars who often met face-to-face, exchanged ideas, and encouraged each other. One group that has been described as a precursor group to the Royal Society of London consisted of a number of natural philosophers like Robert Boyle.

Common People: Common masses also become sources of information as discussed under the following headings.

Children: A growing child starts picking up information while exploring her/his house, meeting relatives, playing with toys, etc. By the time a child is three, s/he can tell where a particular toy s/he has kept. In the school, a child gathers a great deal of information and can provide information about the location of the school, school compound, school uniforms for boys and girls, classmates, teachers, books, school library, etc. In many cases, the information given by an innocent child is considered highly trustworthy.

Head of a Family: During census operations and other surveys, usually the head of the family is consulted for collecting information. The information obtainable from her/him includes among others the name, age (date of birth, if available), sex, educational qualification, profession, marital status, health status, etc. of each family member.

Village Head: The village head possesses information about libraries or reading rooms (if any), non-government organisations working in the village, newspapers that the villagers read, religions that the villagers follow, religious and other festivals which they organise, shrines that the village has, the castes of the village people, political affiliations of the villagers, panchayats, financial status of the villagers, availability of banks and loan providing institutions, household industries and small-scale industries, development plans being executed, etc. Similarly, a postman, police officer, etc. are all information professionals or information sources.

Biography of a Celebrity: For the biography of a celebrity different humans become information sources like parents (if alive), brother(s), sister(s), son(s), daughter(s), relatives, friends, co-workers, personal secretaries and aides. For a freedom fighter's biography, jailers at times become a potential source of information.

Events: Everyday countless events are taking place in the world such as meetings, conferences, festivals, fairs, exhibitions, games, births, deaths and so on. In addition, there are events which have happened in the past and there are many others that will take place in the future. To gather information on many of these events humans are considered the best sources and in some cases the only source of information.

Accidents and Disasters: Various types of accidents and disasters take place every day on earth. Information regarding these is usually gathered from eyewitnesses or the survivors. Thus, humans act as information sources in such situations.

Unit 20

Institutions as Sources of Information

Among the many non-documentary sources of information, institutions are a major source of information. An institution is a large important organisation that has a purpose. A university for example is an educational institution and a bank is a financial institution. In addition to the people who manage and run the institution, other components such as its various resources including files, documents and the organisational website cumulatively make an institution a rich source of information.

GOVERNMENT MINISTRIES AND DEPARTMENTS

The various ministries of the government are authentic sources of primary data and information. The executive, legislature, judiciary, states, union territories and districts of the Indian Government have a structured mechanism for carrying out its many activities and disseminating much-needed information through its various institutions and organisations. The Ministry of Earth Sciences, the Ministry of Environment and Forests, the Ministry of External Affairs and the Ministry of Finance are a few examples.

INTERNATIONAL AGENCIES

There are numerous international agencies that are authentic sources of primary data and information. These include the UNO, UNESCO, IFLA, WHO, ADB, etc.

R&D ORGANISATIONS

There are several research and development (R&D) organisations in the country under the aegis of many government departments such as the Department of Science and Technology (DST), the Council of Scientific and Industrial Research (CSIR), the Indian Council of Medical Research (ICMR), and the Defence Research and Development Organisation (DRDO), etc. There are also many private R&D organisations. Many of the laboratories of these umbrella organisations are not only well known but have been recognised as important sources of information in specific areas. In the case of CSIR, many of the laboratories' libraries and information centres function as national information centres.

ACADEMIC INSTITUTIONS

Schools, universities, colleges, and other specialised academic institutions not only impart knowledge but also play an important role in moulding the lives of youngsters for their future careers and also for being a part of a good citizenry. Academic institutions, particularly the higher education institutions such as universities are sources of various kinds of information.

LEARNED SOCIETIES

A "learned society" is an organisation that exists to promote an academic discipline or group of disciplines. Most learned societies are non-profit organisations. Their activities typically include holding regular conferences for the presentation and discussion of new research results and publishing or sponsoring academic journals in their discipline. The formation of a society is an important step in the emergence of a new discipline or sub-discipline. Historically, the learned societies have played a very important role in furthering research and most vitally, serving as a body for information dissemination and knowledge sharing. One of the finest examples of a renowned learned society is the Royal Society of London.

OTHER INSTITUTIONS

Publishing Houses: Publishing houses are in the information business by way of publishing a variety of documentary sources, predominantly books and of course others such as maps, atlases, and other documents. Publishing by itself is a process of production and dissemination of literature or information. Traditionally, publishing referred to printed materials. However, with the advent of ICT applications, especially the Internet, publishing is being redefined. Types of publishing include newspapers, periodicals, books, directories, and academic publishing. Academic publishing distributes academic research and scholarship.

Press: Like the publishing house, the press or the print news media are also institutions in the information business, although the difference being that the press and print news media focuses on current news and events. Newspapers are a valuable documentary source of current information. In addition to the general newspapers, sports, business, trade, science, and other such narrow areas also have newspapers and news magazines that aim to disseminate information to the users.

Broadcasting Stations: Broadcasting stations include the radio and television stations that broadcast programmes for entertainment and news. In the present times, the television, in particular, has become an integral of part of one's life as a source of entertainment and general awareness. From modest beginnings, radio and television stations in India have proliferated so much that India is one of the countries that have the highest number of news channels. Today, many broadcasting stations, including several private ones and air programmes, have enormous information value. Other than for entertainment, the broadcasting stations are also being used to support education through the various radio and television programmes. For example, IGNOU's Gyan Vani and Gyan Darshan are educational broadcasting stations on the radio and television respectively.

Museums: 'A museum is a building or institution which houses a collection of artifacts. Museums collect and care for objects of scientific, artistic or historical importance and make them available for public viewing through exhibits that may be permanent or temporary. Most large museums are located in major cities throughout the world and more local ones exist in smaller cities, towns and even the countryside. Early museums began as the private collections of wealthy individuals, families or institutions of art and rare or curious natural objects and artifacts. There are museums all over the world. The museums of ancient times, such as the Museum of Alexandria, would be equivalent to a modern graduate institute. Unlike the press and broadcasting houses that help to serve current information, museums are organisations that are a major source of ancient and historical information. There are different kinds of museums in different areas such as science museums and rail museums. There are a number of museums in India. The National Museum, in New Delhi is the prime museum in the country.

Archives: Archives, like museums, are storehouses of documents that have great historical value. An archive is a collection of historical records. Archives consist of records which have been selected for permanent or long-term preservation on grounds of their enduring cultural, historical or evidentiary value. Archival records are normally unpublished and almost always unique, unlike books or magazines for which many identical copies exist. Archives are quite distinct from libraries with regard to their functions and organisation, although archival collections can often be found within library buildings as well. The National Archives of India is the repository of the non-current records of the Government of India and is holding them in trust for the use of administrators and scholars. It is an attached office of the Department of Culture under the Ministry of Tourism and Culture. It was set up in March 1891 in Calcutta (Kolkata) as the Imperial Record Department and subsequent to the transfer of the National Capital from Calcutta to New Delhi in 1911. The records were made available for bonafide research in 1939 and by 1947 all pre-1902 records were available for consultation. After independence, the Imperial Records Department was rechristened as the National Archives of India.

Non-Governmental Organisations: A non-governmental organisation is defined as an independent voluntary association of people acting together on a continuous basis, for some common purpose, other than achieving government office, making money or illegal activities. Further, it is legally constituted and operates independently from any government and thus does not have government status. Some NGOs are funded totally or partially by governments and such NGOs maintain their non-governmental status by excluding government representatives from taking membership in the organisation.

All NGOs irrespective of their areas of work create information materials which range from simple brochures to elaborate reports. With many NGOs receiving grants from funding agencies for executing projects, the NGOs have to prepare project reports which are a valuable source of primary information. All NGOs bring out one or the other information product, including directories, yearbooks, proceedings, etc.

Unit 21
Media as Sources of Information

MEDIA

Media is the plural form of medium, which (broadly speaking) describes any channel of communication. This can include anything from printed paper to digital data and encompasses art, news, educational content, and numerous other forms of information. Media refers to the mass media communication such as newspapers, magazines, radio, television, recordings of audio-visual aids like CD, DVD, etc. which are vital sources of information of mass communication. The impact of media has totally transformed human life in modern societies. They are not just the carriers of information and knowledge but also the means by which they have been communicated are the main cause of the sea changes in society, which is heading towards a knowledge society.

MASS MEDIA

Mass media is defined "as the institutions of public communication that have as their physical channel of transmission a mass medium, which include the television, radio, motion pictures, newspapers, books, music and recordings". It is these institutions and organisations that use print and electronic devices to produce content for the use of audiences. When mass medium become the channels in mass communication, they bring three characteristics to the process, namely:

(1) A complex technology becomes involved;

(2) The velocity of the process increases in order to reach a huge audience; and

(3) The amplitude increases because the potential to be read, heard or viewed, is powerful.

MASS COMMUNICATION

Mass communication is the process whereby mass-produced messages are transmitted to large, anonymous, and heterogeneous audiences. The word 'mass' refers to people in a large number. The large number, usually, indicates or implies mostly to the lower strata of society who are unlettered or ignorant in many ways. But in today's context, 'mass' includes every section of society, irrespective of their status or knowledge perceptions.

CHARACTERISTICS, SCOPE, AND FUNCTIONS OF MEDIA

Media offer a current awareness service, for example, instantaneous services, like reporting of current events and activities by the radio and television. Radio and television are faster means of communication than the print media such as newspapers. They are inextricably so interwoven with modern society that one cannot survive without the other. It has the following important characteristics:

- The information source in media/mass media is generally an individual (journalist, etc.) or a group of individuals (producer, writer, and director).
- Mass media channels, often known as mass vehicles, incorporate one or more facets of technology. For example, a radio uses a speaker, microphone, etc. to code/decode sound waves.
- Audiences are self-selected in mass media.
- Mass media audience is heterogeneous.
- In mass media, feedback is negligible and genuine give and take is almost impossible. Typically, a message flows from the sender to the receiver in one direction only.

Mass media performs four basic functions. These include:

Surveillance: It is a term that pertains to the mass media's news and information function. This section can be separated into warning surveillance (information about floods, attacks, wars, etc.) and instrumental surveillance (entertainment, marketprice, sports, etc.).

Interpretation: It is a function of mass media that places new information in perspective and also gives comments on its importance and meaning.

Socialization: In this function, mass media transmits values in the society, most notably through modelling of appropriate behaviour and attitude. The idea is that mass media gives a representation of society for viewers to learn and embrace.

Entertainment: It is yet another function of mass media in which it distracts society from the real world by means of entertainment. It is done by means of audio records, video records, movies, etc.

Scope of Mass Media: Mass media, including the press, have played a vital role in delivering justice. There have been a number of examples wherein the mass media have been instrumental in creating public opinion about several criminal cases, which has led to speedy justice. Thus, media plays an important role in publicising cases which require public attention. All media are expensive and need huge organisations to collect, process, formulate and disseminate information, views, and entertainment to an enormous, scattered, and heterogeneous audiences simultaneously. They encompass almost all conceivable subjects to include everything of interest to the audiences such as news of current events and activities, art and music, language and literature, science and technology, business and industry, travels and tourism, transport and communication, computers, and telecommunication and so forth.

POSITIVE INFLUENCES OF MASS MEDIA

Information disseminated by mass media has a direct impact on society. On account of its extensive reach, particularly to urban audiences, mass media has become so central to society that it is inconceivable that without mass media today, societies can function. They inform and shape social life, particularly the younger generation, to develop into good and responsible citizens. Their impact and influence are positive if they are able to fulfill the information and entertainment needs of the people in accordance with the norms of social values and culture.

By and large, the information disseminated by the mass media and their programmes is positive. They are pro-communal harmony, anti-environmental pollution, support national integration, anti-drug addiction, advocate health care and safety, demonstrate benefits of yogic exercises for healthy life, create peace for economic prosperity, anti-terrorism, and social evils, generally educative and instructive, giving helpful guidance to children and young adults, etc. As a matter of policy and principle, information dissemination and the programmes of mass media conform to government regulations, code of ethics and legal norms.

NEGATIVE INFLUENCES OF MASS MEDIA

The foremost importance in reporting is that the information reported is collected from authentic and credible sources and nothing should ever be misinterpreted. But this principle is quite often overlooked. The very nature of mass media being persuasive, may result in the media transcending ethical codes within which they are expected to perform and may become biased, manipulative, and propagandist. It is not uncommon for a political party or an agency to manipulate reports in their favour, which would indicate political control. Biased reporting can occur to obtain a favourable result.

Unnecessary sensationalism of an event from daily life may magnify its importance creating fear and panic among the public. Wrong interpretation of news may even blow-up things out of proportion and create unrest or even violence at any time and place and pose a law and order problem.

As long as the mass media give what people need or want, they remain a potent force in society. But the moment they, with acquired power and control, give what they think people want, they become manipulative and start working towards influencing the minds of people, leading to indoctrination.

COMPONENTS OF MASS MEDIA

The components of mass media (both print and electronic) comprise predominantly the following:

- Print Media.
- Radio Broadcasting.
- Television.
- Recordings on CDs, DVDs, etc.
- Motion Films.

Print Media: Print media is one of the oldest and most basic forms of mass communication. Print media comprises newspapers, popular magazines and periodicals, trade journals, posters, leaflets, books, in particular paperbacks and other printed materials. Of these, newspapers, magazines, and periodicals are most extensively used. Two notable developments in the Indian context witnessed in the newspaper industry are the commercialisation and the introduction of information and communication technologies. Daily newspapers are the most predominant ones among the print media. They have a large audience and a wide circulation.

Scope, Coverage, and Functions of Print Media (Newspapers/ Magazines): Large newspapers/magazines have their own mechanisms to get news through their own reporters from different parts of the country and also from foreign countries, in addition to their contracts with news agencies (national and international), for the supply of news and information. Almost all newspapers/magazines have their websites to get instantaneous news round the clock. They are also accessible through the Internet.

Everyday/every month the dailies/magazines publish one or more supplements on specific topics such as education and training, economics, industry, business and trade, science and technology, sports and games, arts, entertainment, and music. There are also newspapers/magazines exclusively specialising in economics, sports and games, films, TV programmes, music, business and trade, employment, government memoranda, and orders.

Generally, the daily newspapers/magazines carry news, commentaries, and analysis on political, economic, social topics on current events, personalities, feature articles of subjects of current topical interests, general information on weather, business information, share market data and analysis, local programmes and events, sports and games, films and other topics of public interest. Editorials on current specific topics are a daily feature, except on Sundays, which have a very special value as they express views and comments in consonance with the general policy of the newspaper/magazine. For those who prefer light reading material, there is a great variety of jokes and humour, fun, crossword puzzles, quizzes, comics, and satire, including something that interests the children.

Radio Broadcasting: Electronic media, comprising radio, television, satellite TV, cable TV, motion films, recordings, etc. is distinctly different from print media, as it provides news and information instantaneously. It is essentially entertainment media but has many other features, which are both instructive and informative. It carries information across distances and to the masses that are geographically, culturally, intellectually, and emotionally separated from one another. It is the fastest media much quicker than print media. Its impact on audiences is decisively much greater than print media. It is also a valuable source of information of mass media just as much as print media.

Characteristics, Scope, and Functions of Radio Broadcasting: The radio is an oral medium. There are no visuals. It is a sightless medium. Its impact, therefore, is lesser than visual media and very much less than audio-visual media. Its success has to be achieved only through the voice of the announcers, newsreaders and performers in a play, music, and sound effects. Notwithstanding these limitations, the radio has been a success before the advent of television. As the sound and voice of participants in the various programmes of radio broadcasting are the physical oral media, persons with voices suitable for broadcasting are very carefully selected through audition tests. The language of the scripts is another important characteristic of radio programmes. The contents have to be user friendly, written by persons who have a good command over the language and written in an appealing style as required in different contexts. A radio set or a transistor is far cheaper than a TV. Radio is much quicker in reporting events. The portable quality of transistors makes it possible to listen to radio programmes anywhere, at home, at workplaces, in office premises, at a picnic spot, at the bedside, etc.

The appeal and impact are achieved through voices suitable for microphones, delivery with voice modulations, accents and emphasis on words and phrases, tonal variations, and sensible pauses. These are some of the essential skills required for good broadcasting. With good, artistic, and musical sound effects, some of the radio programmes have been hits. It performs similar functions to that of mass media.

Television: Of all the electronic media of mass communication, the most powerful and influential media having an impact on the society is the television (TV). Borrowing certain features from earlier means of communication like the theatrical stage, the film and the radio, it has amalgamated them into a new media with its own identity. For example, from the stage it has borrowed movement, from the film the camera and from the radio the microphone, integrating all these into a unique medium, quite different from the other media, thoroughly telegenic, i.e. most suitably attractive to be displayed on the screen. In nature, in idiom of expression and receptivity, arithmetic communication, it is distinctly different from the other media.

Characteristic Features of TV: Television occupies a dominant position in our lives with its multi-dimensional attractive features. Despite its dominant position in our lives, it is still young, fast growing and developing with the rapidly advancing information and communication technology. The TV's sweeping dimensions can be gauged by the lively pictures it brings with the camera, such as a man walking on the moon, visuals of planets, telecasts of living creatures under the sea or in the ocean and magnificent stars in the sky. We are able to see the live telecast of the Gulf War, natural disasters like earthquake or tsunami, terrorists' attacks all over the world, world cup soccer or cricket played in any part of the globe and other events and activities almost instantaneously. Eminent persons of the world, their public performances and speeches are heard daily by the ordinary folks of villages. Thus, the TV impacts its audiences so strongly that it has led to many societal changes both desirable and undesirable.

Many of the TV programmes are highly informative, instructive, expands our perceptions and knowledge and are indeed very educative. These positive features could be used effectively to change the entire mode of learning, making people more knowledgeable and contribute to better living conditions. TV entertainment features are numerous, and people are glued to the TV to view soap operas, serials with various social and cultural themes, music, both classical and light music, various types of dances, quiz programmes for young persons and many others.

To stay well informed of current events and activities, there are round the clock news bulletins, news analysis, interviews, panel discussions on political, economic, and social issues and live telecasts of various tournaments of games and sports. Thus, these kinds of programmes are endless, covering practically every subject of human interest. Like newspapers and radio broadcasting, the TV functions to inform, educate, instruct, motivate, influence, persuade, entertain, etc. with a much greater force of impact on the society than either newspapers or radio.

Recordings on Tapes/Discs such as CD, DVD, etc.: Recordings here refer to audio, video and audio-visual reproductions on magnetic tapes or discs as well as on laser tapes. They are all part of the home entertainment environment which gives consumers direct control over what, where, when they view or listen to them. Among the many recorded media of mass communication are the video cassettes, CD-ROMs, and DVDs (Digital Versatile/ Video Discs) that are most influential. They are highly user friendly and closely linked with individual and group use. Most of these audio-visual media are designed with great care and the audio support enhances their value to a very great extent. The production of multimedia CD-ROMs and DVDs is a complex and intricate affair. Different types of specialists are necessary to produce a good video programme either for entertainment, news commentaries or analysis, learning kits, course materials for distance education and many others.

CD-ROMs and DVDs are extremely valuable for archival purposes and as sources of information. They occupy very little space. Reference materials like encyclopaedias and other types of reference works are preserved in these media and stocked in libraries. There are also private or commercial video libraries that supply CDs and DVDs on hire, especially films. It is said that the media is changing rapidly and will be more powerful in the future than it has been in the past, mainly because it puts control and time in the hands of the consumer.

Motion Films

Motion films are an important medium of popular entertainment because of their wide mass appeal and influence in the society. Combined with the TV, films constitute the most powerful media that impacts every section of the audience in all possible ways. In India, with all its cultural and linguistic diversities and the problems of illiteracy, films are the most powerful of all media, cutting across the linguistic and cultural diversities with a universal emotional language. Commercial cinema is all charming, romantic, and fanciful. The usual ingredients are songs, group dances, crime, fights, melodrama, and comedy, all bordering on imagination and unreality. The idea of the film makers, in general, is to prepare a show for popular entertainment to ensure financial success and a box office hit.

Characteristic Features of Motion Films: Although every mass media is a team effort, a film is the most collaborative medium of a much bigger magnitude than any other media. The huge financial investment, the number of persons involved, time required for shooting a film, complexity in production and distribution make it totally different from other media. Hundreds of persons collaborate to make a film in its production process. The group includes a producer, director, story writer, dialogue writer, actors both male and female, specialist persons in various aspects such as art, music, dance, fights, illumination, sound, costumes, make-up, scene set up, cameras, etc. in making a film.

Thus, a motion film is a product of the interactions between both technical and artistic persons. It uses many devices like cameras with several lenses, microphones, dubbing machines, editing or cutting machines, projectors, mixers, sound tracks, trolleys to mount cameras, celluloid, laboratory equipment, etc.

Apart from the entertainment value of films, it has also become a medium of art today, just as painting, sculpture, architecture, drama, poetry and music. It has become, in fact, a discipline in its own right, in which scholars and intellectuals participate in its growth and development. Film training institutes have developed, treating film production as an academic and professional discipline.

ACCESSIBILITY AND AVAILABILITY OF MASS MEDIA

It is quite evident that mass media generates an enormous amount of information and knowledge that are invaluable and versatile sources of information for contemporary and historical studies. Newspapers carry quite a lot of ephemeral information that may not be of much value. But nearly fifty per cent of information published in newspapers is worth preserving and useful for different studies. Similarly, magazines and periodicals also carry valuable information that is worth preserving. Radio and television channels produce almost a running commentary on the life of the people in a variety of subjects. Other mass media channels like films, etc. also enrich the society with precious information.

Accessibility and availability of mass media information and knowledge are an important national responsibility. Although there is no bibliographical control at the national level on the mass of information generated, many libraries and archives stock these materials and service them to scholars, researchers, and students. Newspapers are preserved in microforms or digital forms in national libraries, university libraries and research libraries. Considering their value as records of contemporary human life, many countries have legal regulations for depositing books and newspapers and also motion films. The Indian

Delivery of Books and Newspapers Act has the provision for depositing books, periodicals, and newspapers in the National Library, in Kolkata and three other libraries, namely the Central Library, in Mumbai, the Connemara Public Library, in Chennai and the Delhi Public Library.

Advertisements: "Advertising" is defined as a paid dissemination of information through a variety of mass communication media to motivate a desired action. Advertisements are not free. They are to be paid for. Space is bought in newspapers, magazines, and periodicals in the print media or in recordings like CDs or DVDs, or time is bought in radio, TV and on the Internet. Through this payment for the space or the time, information is disseminated. This is not for communicating information but for the process of selling or helping to sell commodities and services or gaining acceptance to ideas that may set people to think or act in a desired manner. Modern advertising has emerged as the handmaid of the industry. It is an outgrowth of mass production, mass market, mass distribution and mass communication.

Public Relations: "Public Relations" is the deliberate planned and sustained effort to establish and maintain mutual understanding between an organisation and its public. It is necessary for the organisation concerned to understand the public and relate the organisation's activities to public interest. Public Relation (PR) professionals build an image for the organisation and sustain it. In this process public relations personnel will have to maintain the best of relations with the media. These involve media meetings at the appropriate time, press releases of various types, preparation of special brochures and programmes, for TV and broadcasting, interviews with VIPs, design production of documentaries and so on. While advertisements promote marketing of goods and services, PR persons prepare the ground for such activities. Obviously, PR activities are vital and necessary for mass media.

Indian Scenario in Mass Media: In the Indian scenario, all the different mass media are functioning and operating quite well, generating valuable information and knowledge sources for contemporary and historical studies. All the characteristics and attributes described in the earlier sections and the sub-sections of this unit on mass media are relevant in the Indian scenario without any exception.

ICT AND MASS MEDIA

Research and innovation in information and communication technologies (ICTs) and mass media grow in tandem to one another. Advances in ICTs give unlimited scope for expansion in mass media in terms of round-the-clock programmes, innovation in design and development of new programmes, world-wide dissemination, and transmission, etc. In short, ICTs have facilitated a number of developments with far-reaching implications for mass media. Every component of mass media, such as the print, broadcasting, TV and recording media use it with great effect and advantage. The main focus today is on the Internet as a new social sphere, facilitating new forms of economic, political, and cultural exchange. It is multi-functional and cross-sectoral. It incorporates the World Wide Web and the e-mail. It involves market, government, education, media, and every societal sector. It is multimedia integrating visual, audio, and textual material. It enables advances in distant learning, through a new pattern of flexibility, contributing to reshaping the knowledge environment and issues of access within it.

Traditional media has shown resilience in adapting to a changing environment and in utilising new technologies. For mass consumers the result is a greater variety and expanding choice in the ways they access information and entertainment. The expansion and varied means of delivery have a stimulated demand for content development for new media.

Media Persons as Sources of Information: The usefulness of media specialists as vital resource persons in the areas of their specialisation is proven by the following points:

Mass media persons operate in a highly commercial and competitive environment which resonates in quality assurance on the products and services created/generated by mass media;

Newspapers, periodicals, TV, and radio programmes and many other media products have to operate within a strict time frame, which improves the efficiency of the media persons;

The time element necessitates the media persons to keep their information ready for use at a short notice;

Media work is a teamwork and every participant in them should fit into the team at the right place, as the output is a common objective;

Media persons' expertise, experience and knowledge never get properly recorded and hence are not easily available; and

Many groups of specialists are functioning in the mass media, both print and electronic. The institutions managing and operating these media may have to be contacted to get the assistance of media specialists as resource persons for any service.

EXERCISES: UNIT 20 – UNIT 22

1. Define "human as a source of information".
2. Define "human as a resource".
3. How would you differentiate between an information compiler and an information processor?
4. Differentiate between information generators and information gatherers.
5. What do you know about informaticians?
6. Define "information condensation".
7. Explain how common masses act as a source of information.
8. Illustrate how an institution can act as a source of information.
9. Discuss different institutions acting as information sources.
10. Discuss how the media acts as a source of information.
11. Discuss the characteristics, scope, and functions of the media.
12. Define "mass media".

13. Discuss the positive as well as negative influence of mass media.
14. What are the characteristics, scope, and functions of radio broadcasting?
15. What are the main components of the mass media?
16. Discuss the characteristic features of the TV.
17. Discuss how media persons act as sources of information.

Unit 22

Information Services: An Overview

Data: "Data" is defined as facts or figures, or information or sets of unrelated information and as such are of no use until they are properly evaluated. Upon evaluation, there arises a significant relation between the data and they show some relevance, then they are converted into information.

Information: Data presented in a readily comprehensible form to which meaning has been attributed within the context of its use. In a more dynamic sense, information is a message conveyed by the use of a medium of communication or expression. Whether a specific message is information or not depends partly on the subjective perception of the person receiving it. More accurately, all the facts, conclusions, ideas and creative works of human intellect and imagination, that have been communicated formally or informally, in any form is information. Thus, information represents processed data.

Knowledge: It is the information that has been comprehended and evaluated in the light of experience and incorporated into the knower's intellectual understanding of a subject. In other words, knowledge is the information, that one has acquired through learning or experience.

Communication: "Communication" is the process of transferring information from one entity to another. Communication is commonly defined as the interchange of thoughts, opinions or information by speech, writing or signs. Communication can be perceived as a two-way process in which there is an exchange of thoughts, feelings or ideas towards mutually accepted goals or directions (en.wikipedia.org).

Telecommunication: The transfer of information from one physical location to another by electronic means is called so. The term telecommunication refers to both analogue and digital communication, including voice and video. Data communication refers only to digital communication.

NEED FOR INFORMATION

Information is crucial for all our activities. We need it for education, research, employment, entertainment, healthcare, problem solving and lifelong learning. Information is a vital resource for the socio-economic development of a country. Accessibility of the latest scientific, technical, developmental, and commercial information gives a country economic, technological, and political advantage over other countries. Everybody needs information for some purpose or another. Students need information to supplement their textbooks, studies and for project work, teachers need information for teaching and research, professionals (doctors, engineers, lawyers, consultants, etc.) need information to pursue their careers efficiently and planners and policy makers need information to frame policies and plans as well as to take correct decisions. Researchers (scientists, technologists, social scientists, etc.) need information to stay up-to-date in their area of research, to find out new areas of research, to avoid the duplication of research efforts and to solve any problem they encounter while carrying out research. Researchers are the most extensive users of information and knowledge. As a matter of fact, most of the earlier library and information services were designed keeping in view their information requirements.

TYPES OF INFORMATION NEEDS

Information needs vary from person to person and a particular person may have different needs at different points in time, depending upon her/his nature of work, place of work, etc. However, these information needs can be broadly categorised into four types: current information needs, exhaustive information needs, everyday information needs and catching-up information needs. These are discussed here:

Current Information Needs: When users need information to keep themselves up-to-date with the latest developments in their area of interest on a regular basis, the need is known as current information need. Here, users do not need specific information, but need to regularly keep themselves abreast of information not only in their own area of interest but also of developments that may affect their work.

Exhaustive Information Needs: When a user wants to have information on a particular subject as exhaustive as possible, the need is known as an exhaustive information need. This need is an occasional one and is expected mainly from the researchers. A researcher, before starting research on a particular topic, surveys the literature published in that area as comprehensively as possible, with a view to select a new area for her/his research as well as to avoid duplication of research efforts.

Everyday Information Needs: This need is for a specific piece of information which users require, generally in their day-to-day work-related activities. For instance, a scientist working on an experiment wants to know the melting or boiling point of a particular compound. This need is basically for factual information which may range from how to spell a word or find the telephone number of an industry, etc.

Catching-up Information Needs: This need arises when a user, who is not conversant with a particular subject field, requires an account of overall development of that subject in a short and most comprehensible form. This type of need is grouped under the category of catching-up information needs. It arises when a scientist or technologist conducts research on a multidisciplinary project. S/he may be an expert in one of the disciplines, but to catch-up with other disciplines, which fall within the purview of the current project, s/he requires a brief overview of those disciplines in a simple and understandable form.

LIBRARY AND INFORMATION SERVICES

Libraries build their collections tailored to the needs and goals of the organisation they serve. Viewed historically, the library's role of making materials available ranks among the most important contributions ever made to human culture and technology. Libraries have long stored materials that enable ideas, knowledge, and experiences to be passed on from generation to generation. Without this line of communication, cultural and technological developments would not be as advanced as they are today. In day-to-day life, the library materials serve as important resources in education, work and recreation of millions of people. To the students, the library is a place where they can find information that help them carry out their school or college work. It is also a place where they can pursue knowledge outside their classrooms and beyond their textbooks. Professionals rely on materials in special libraries for information that they need for their work. They provide information related services to all known professions. Present-day libraries have extended their library services far beyond making materials available. They offer many forms of assistance to library users, which can broadly be grouped as reference and information services. These services promote the use of library materials, connect the users with the library resources and meet the information requirements of the users. These services can be broadly divided into two groups: Responsive information services and anticipatory information services.

RESPONSIVE INFORMATION SERVICES

Responsive information services (also known as passive information services) are provided in response to a request from the users. The request may come from the user in-person, over the telephone, through correspondence or via e-mail. The requests may be for finding general information about the library, its layout, how to become a member, how to use a catalogue or for finding the answer to a particular question or getting a particular document from the library. These services can be broadly categorised as follows:

(1) **Provision of general information:** General information is sought by a user, who visits the library for the first time. Such readers need directional guidance in the use of the library such as the general layout of the library, where current issues of periodicals are displayed or the location of reference and

textbooks section of the library or where is the computer terminal for searching information on OPAC (Online Public Access Catalogue) of the library if there is one, etc. Libraries normally offer a 'user orientation' or 'user education' programmes for the new entrants for general information.

(2) **Reference service:** According to Ranganathan, "Reference service is the process of establishing contact between a reader and his documents in a personal way". It is also considered as a personal service which is provided in response to the request from the users. Reference service can be either,

(i) Ready reference service (concerned with providing answers to fact finding questions, such as what, where, who, when, and how);

(ii) Long range reference service (provided to a specialist who is seeking information for research work or to solve a particular problem).

(3) **Literature search and compiling a subject bibliography:** Another very important responsive service offered by a library is to compile subject bibliographies on request. Sometimes such bibliographies are compiled on a regular basis or in anticipation of the user's needs. At times bibliographies are compiled on special occasions, such as during seminars and workshops, to provide the latest literature on the subject. Long-range reference service, literature search and bibliographies meet the current as well as exhaustive information needs of the users.

(4) **Assistance in the use of library collection and library tools:** Assistance in the use of library collection and library tools (such as catalogues including OPAC, reference books, online databases, etc.) is provided to the user so that s/he may be able to use the library more profitably. To provide this service it is important that the reference librarian should have a positive attitude towards the profession.

(5) **Document delivery service:** Document Delivery Service (DDS) is concerned with the supply of document(s) to the users on demand, either in original or its copy in print or non-print form. Most of the information services such as current awareness service, Selective Dissemination of Information

(SDI) service, indexing and abstracting service, literature search service, etc. are aimed at guiding the user to the document where the required information is available. On the other hand, DDS actually locates the required document and delivers it to the user.

(6) **Referral service:** When users are referred to the sources where the required information is available, the service is called a "referral service". Referral services do not provide users with the document or information needed by them but direct them to the sources of information where the required information will be available. The source may be either a document, an organisation or an individual.

ANTICIPATORY INFORMATION SERVICES

Anticipatory information services are provided to library users in anticipation of their demands for such services. These services are also called active information services. The need for such services was felt mainly due to:

(i) Exponential growth of published literature, particularly in the field of science and technology;

(ii) Interdisciplinary nature of frontline areas of research, resulting in the scattering of information in different disciplines; and

(iii) Publications of research results in different types of sources (like primary research periodicals, research reports, conference proceedings, dissertations, etc.), languages as well as in different formats (like print or electronic).

As a consequence of the growth in volume, diversity, and complexity of information sources, scientists, technologists, researchers, and managers faced problems in accessing information and in keeping themselves abreast of the latest developments in their fields of interest. To solve this problem, the libraries, particularly, scientific, and technical libraries started providing information services to the users, mainly to the researchers. Now, not only S&T libraries, but all kinds of libraries and information/documentation centres, are offering some form of anticipatory information service, depending upon the needs of their clients. To provide these services, the user's information needs are assessed and then services are designed accordingly. Generally, the following types of anticipatory services are offered:

(1) **Current Awareness Type:** To keep the users abreast of the current developments in their respective fields of interest current awareness types of services are offered to the users. This involves scanning the newly available documents in print as well as in non-print form, selecting items relevant to the needs of an individual or a group of users, recording them and disseminating to the users on a regular basis. Current awareness type of services meet the current information needs of the users. The types of services provided under this category are accession list, current awareness list, documentation bulletin, title announcement service, contents-by-journal-service, selective dissemination of information, research-in-progress bulletin and newspaper clipping service.

(2) **Condensation Type:** In this type of service, contents of the documents are condensed or summarised along with bibliographical details of the document. This enables the user to identify the basic contents of the document quickly and determine its relevance to their interest. At times, a well-prepared abstract serves as a substitute for the document. The types of services under this category are indexing services, abstracting services, digest services and other value-added services. The basic process involved in indexing and abstracting service is the 'analysis of information'. In indexing service, it is the 'analysis of the subject' and in abstracting service it is 'analysis of the contents.' In digest service, information is collected from various sources, is properly evaluated, analysed and consolidated to prepare a digest. The analysis and consolidation of information is done keeping in view the specialised requirements of the users.

(3) **Readers Advisory Service:** This service deals with providing reading guidance to individuals. The aim of this service is to motivate the readers to use the library and inculcate good reading habits in them. School children require this kind

of service very much. Such a service is more often offered in schools and public libraries. This service helps the readers to select the right books for educational and recreational purposes. This type of service meets the general reading needs of the users and helps in the personal development of the users.

(4) **Information Literacy Training:** Information literacy training has been known by many different names such as library orientation, user assistance, bibliographic instruction, user education and information skills training. Library orientation is concerned with acquainting new users to the library, such as objectives of the library and its organisation, collection of the library and its location, general rules and procedures of the library and reference and information services of the library. User assistance refers to helping an individual rather than a group. Bibliographic instructions concentrate on the mechanics of using a particular resource. User education or information skills training connotes an educational activity, which is concerned with motivating the user and developing a skill in the user to find and search for information independently for a study, research, and recreational purposes. Information literacy skills concentrate on cognitive and transferable skills such as problem solving, evaluation and communication skills.

WEB-BASED OR INTERNET-BASED INFORMATION SERVICES

The Internet and the World Wide Web (WWW) have introduced new and powerful ways of finding and sharing information. Many people use the terms Internet and WWW interchangeably, but in fact the two terms are not synonymous. The Internet and the web are two separate but related terms. The former is a collection of interlinked computer networks which when accessed from individual computers, gives users the ability to find information located on any computer linked to one of the networks. The Internet connects millions of computers together globally, forming a network in which any computer can communicate with any other computer as long as they are connected over the Internet. The information that travels over the Internet does so via a variety of languages called protocols.

The WWW or simply the web is a way of accessing information over the medium of the Internet. The web uses HTTP (Hyper Text Transfer Protocol) to transmit data. The web also utilises browsers such as Internet Explorer or Netscape Navigator to access web documents. The Internet and the web technology have changed the way people communicate, interact, acquire and share knowledge. A growing number of people rely on the Internet for the information that they need. With further advancements in the Internet and communication technology Web 2.0 has also evolved which provide a dynamic, interactive and collaborative platform for the users to exchange information and knowledge. In Web 1.0 environment, users read what others wrote. However, now Web 2.0 facilitates users to express their views and publish them online through services like blogs and wikis. In other words, migration from Web 1.0 to Web 2.0 is essentially characterised by the movement from 'read-only' to 'read-and-write' web.

The users of today, particularly young people, are relying on and accessing information very differently. They lead lives saturated by the media and use the Internet more than the libraries. They use portable devices and access information from their homes, from the workplace, from restaurants, indeed from anywhere. They think they can find all knowledge via Google or Yahoo. The Wikipedia provides free knowledge on every topic. Earlier users built their workflow around libraries. Now, libraries should build services around user workflow if they want to survive. Many libraries have taken up initiatives and are using available technologies to offer improved, customer driven services to their users. The types of services offered are:

Library Website: A web presence is very important for the library to reach its users. With the library's website on the Internet, users can search library sources using OPAC (Online Public Access Catalogue) from anywhere and at any time. They need not visit or wait for the opening and closing hours of the library. Users can reserve a particular publication, make suggestions for the purchase of a particular publication, renew the borrowed books online and do many more without visiting the library. Many libraries are offering reference services in an online mode.

Access to Databases: An increasing number of bibliographic, numeric, and full-text databases are available on the Internet. Indexing and abstracting databases like Chemical Abstracts, Biological Abstracts, Index Medicus, COMPENDEX and INSPEC, etc. are all available on the web with added functionality and features.

Access to e-Journals: Electronic journals or e-journals are those journals which are prepared and distributed electronically. Several traditional journals are now being published both in print as well as on the web. Libraries are joining e-journal consortia to provide access to full-text e-journals to their clients.

Access to Courseware: There is a wide variety of interactive multimedia courseware resources available on the Internet for learning as well for developing multimedia for teaching purposes. Depending upon the needs of its users, library may provide access to some of these coursewares. Some examples of the courseware available on the Internet from India are, e-Gyankosh, National Programme on Technology Enhanced Learning (NPTEL), Nation Science Digital Library (NSDL), etc.

Unit 23

Types of Services: Reference Service, CAS, etc.

REFERENCE SERVICE: MEANING AND DEFINITION

According to the American Library Association's Glossary of Library Terms, "Reference service is that phase of library work which is directly concerned with assistance to readers seeking information and in using the resources of library in study and research." According to Margaret Hutchins, "Reference work include the direct personal aid within the library to persons in search of information for whatever purpose, and also various other library activities especially aimed at making information as easily available as possible. Selecting and organizing materials with this end in view is an important part of reference work as their interpretation to the individual reader." Ranganathan defines it as "Personal service to each reader in helping him to find documents, answering his interest most pin-pointedly, exhaustively and expeditiously." He further says, "To provide the right book to the right reader, in the right personal way." According to William Katz, the reference service, defined by function can be divided into two categories: Direct and Indirect.

Direct category includes:

(a) Reference and information services that include personal assistance to the user in pursuit of information.

(b) Formal and informal instructions in the use of library and information centres and their resources.

Indirect category includes:

(a) Selection of materials needed for reference service.

(b) Reference administration, i.e. organisation and administration of reference services.

(c) Inter-library loans.

(d) Evaluation of reference section.

REFERENCE SERVICE: ORIGIN, GROWTH AND DEVELOPMENT

Though informal help to the users in the use of libraries has been provided by the libraries since long, the concept of organised reference service can be traced back to the end of 19th century in public libraries in the USA. The public libraries were the first ones to initiate reference services in an organised manner. The main driving force behind this initiative was the justification of the public funds utilised by the public libraries. The public libraries financed by public funds had to justify its existence to those who supported it. The librarians therefore had real incentives to look for new ways to demonstrate the utility of their libraries to the authorities. These values they appraised in terms of library use and the services they offered. In 1876, at the first conference of the American Library Association, Samuel S. Green, Librarian of Worcester, Massachusetts, Free Public Library presented a paper titled "Personal Relations between Librarians and Readers". He emphasised that furnishing readers with catalogues and reference tools were not sufficient and insisted that "interpreting these instruments to public by personal guidance must follow".

By the end of the 19th century and early 20th century, the concept of reference services was gradually accepted and implemented by American libraries. The leading advocates of this concept along with Samuel S. Green were Poole, Winsor and Melvil Dewey. In 1883, the first full time reference position was established at Boston Public Library and in 1891 the term "reference work" appeared for the first time in the index to the Library Journal. In the years that followed, the libraries, public as well as academic, slowly set up reference departments, established a reference collection, designated one or more library staff to fulfil reference functions which included assisting users in the use of library collection, providing answers to fact finding questions and helping readers to make the best selection from the recorded knowledge. In India, the credit for setting up full-fledged reference service goes to S.R. Ranganathan in Madras University Library in 1930.

The emergence of reference services changed the role of a library from a mere storehouse of knowledge to that of an educational institution and the role of a librarian from a mere custodian of recorded knowledge to that of a facilitator and promoter of the use of knowledge for the benefit of the library users. The growth and subsequent development of reference service was based mainly on four objectives, namely

(i) to assist the library users,

(ii) to develop the role of a library as an educational institution,

(iii) to help users make the best selection from the universe of recorded knowledge, and

(iv) to justify the existence of the library by demonstrating its use to the authorities who provided financial support.

INFORMATION SERVICE: ORIGIN, GROWTH AND DEVELOPMENT

An increase in R&D activities during the twentieth century resulted in an exponential growth of recorded knowledge. The advent of computers and communication technologies, though helped in the organisation, storage, retrieval, and dissemination of information, but increased the complexity of information sources. Scientists and technologists, due to the sheer amount of information and complexity of information sources, found it difficult to keep track of published knowledge in their respective fields. To solve this problem, libraries, particularly scientific and technical libraries, expanded the scope of reference services. These libraries not only provided reference services on demand but started collecting and organising the latest published knowledge on the users' field of specialisation in anticipation, and bringing to their notice on a regular basis. This service is known as information service. The aim of the service is to keep users well informed and up-to-date in their field of specialisation. To begin with, the service was provided by one of the scientists of the research team of the laboratory, since s/he knew the research area and had the same subject background. Later, the library personnel started providing the service. Subsequently, particularly in special libraries, reference services broadened its scope from offering mere assistance in the location of books and journals and the provision of simple factual information from limited collection of reference books to analysis, evaluation, reorganisation and repackaging of information drawn from a variety of sources in order to present it in a form which would be most useful to their users. The professionals in a special library and information centres attached to R&D organisations had the same subject background as well as the expertise in information searching. They started providing value-added services to their users. The availability of online bibliographic databases like MEDLARS/MEDLINE, Chemical Abstracts, Biological Abstracts, INSPEC and many more in almost all disciplines of knowledge, made it possible for them to search these databases online and provide in-depth services to their users. The information services which were provided covered current awareness services, abstracting services, value-added services like technical digests, etc. Most of the services provided under this category were anticipatory in nature.

Difference between Reference Service and Information Service

In literature, the terms reference service and information service are used synonymously. However, some experts refer to them as two different kinds of services on the basis of certain differences which are enumerated below:

S.No.	Reference Service	Information Service
1	It is a traditional service.	It is a non-traditional service.
2	Emphasis to provide documents.	Emphasis to provide information.

S.No.	Reference Service	Information Service
3	User is given the material or directed to locate the material.	Attempt is made to provide exact information.
4	Aim is to instruct the user.	Less concerned towards instructing the user.
5	Service provided on demand.	Service provided in anticipation.
6	Passive service: library staff waits for the user to approach and make demand.	Active service: library staff does not wait for the user to come but provides service to keep the user well informed.

Thus, information services are an amplification of reference services and are concerned with providing information, rather than documents, to the users. Information services were developed mainly to meet the information needs of research scientists and technologists. Reference services are concerned with direct, personal assistance to the library users seeking information, whereas information services are provided in anticipation of various needs of the users of library and information centres.

TYPES OF REFERENCE SERVICES

The reference and information services that libraries offer can be broadly categorised into two groups:

(a) Responsive Information Services: The service that is provided in response to a specific request by the user.

(b) Anticipatory Information Services: The service that is provided in anticipation of some need.

Responsive Information Services: "Responsive information services" (also known as passive information services) are provided in response to the requests from the users. The request may come from the users in person, over the telephone, through correspondence or via e-mail. The technology now allows users to submit their requests to the library at any time from any place in the world. In an effort to reach the users accessing the library via their computers, many libraries and library consortia are extending their reference services to include virtual references.

Virtual Reference Service: "Virtual reference service" is a reference service initiated electronically, often in real-time, when users employ computers or other Internet-based technology to communicate with the reference staff, without being present physically. Communication channels used frequently in virtual reference are chat, videoconferencing, voice over IP, co-browsing, e-mail or instant messaging. Virtual reference service is also referred to as digital reference, e-reference, online reference, and remote access reference. While telephonic reference service has long been accepted and practiced in the libraries to respond to remote users' requests, virtual reference service has been relatively a recent phenomenon.

Advantages of Virtual Reference Services:

- Quick;
- No communication barrier;
- One-on-one attention;
- Physical access to a library not required; and
- Real time updation.

Limitations of Virtual Reference Service:

- The cost of the software is high;
- Require trained staff;
- More time required to answer than face-to-face interactions; and
- The queries that rely on in-depth consultations from a variety of sources prove difficult for the librarian to communicate effectively through virtual reference service.

Based upon the type of requests or queries, the responsive information services offered in the library can be broadly categorised as follows:

- Provision of general information.
- Reference Service (i) Ready Reference Service, and (ii) Long Range Reference Service.

- Assistance in searching and locating documents.
- Literature search and compiling a bibliography.
- Assistance in the use of library tools such as catalogue including OPAC, reference books, online databases, etc.
- Document Delivery Service.
- Referral Services.

All of these services have been defined in the previous unit of this book. You can use those definitions here. In this unit, only reference services (ready reference service and long-range reference service) will be deliberated.

Reference Service

"Reference service" is a personal service which is provided in response to the requests from the users. Requests may be for directional guidance, locating answers to fact-finding questions, literature search for solving a research problem or for general help. To provide the service, the librarian may utilise the resources available in the library as well as those available outside the library. The basic aim is to make the information available to the user as early as possible. Depending upon the requirement, the librarian may give the information itself or the documents containing the information. It can be divided into two categories:

(i) Ready Reference Service or Short-range Reference Service:

This service is concerned with providing answers to fact-finding questions, such as what, where, who, when, and how. The requested information can be easily located in standard reference books like dictionaries, encyclopaedias, yearbooks, almanacs, directories, etc. The time taken to answer these queries is very short ranging from a few minutes to half an hour. That is why this service is known as ready reference service or short-range reference service. Ninety per cent of these queries are simple to handle. Only five to ten per cent of the queries may take hours of search to find the answer.

Use of the Internet as a Reference Tool in Ready Reference Service

Though standard reference books maintained by the reference department in the library provide answers to most of the ready reference types of queries but, the most enticing and omnipresent reference tool that has emerged in the twentieth century is the Internet. The usage of the Internet was limited till the advent of the World Wide Web or the web in the 1990s. The emergence of the web and Internet service providers, offering Internet services to the masses, resulted in the phenomenal increase in the Internet usage in the world. Most of the print reference sources are available online on the Internet. Online sources provide updated contents, more advanced search options, download and print options. Many reference sources provide free access to their contents on the Internet. Most of the publishers of reference books also offer online access to their publications on the web to the libraries who purchase their publications. Online access charges differ from publisher to publisher.

Advantages of using the Internet as a reference tool are as follows:

Easy access: The number of answers the Internet provides in the fraction of a second is amazing. In a normal search to get so many answers from diverse sources would take hours of effort. The Internet provides access to a universe of information anytime from anywhere.

Currency: The Internet resources are more up-to-date than their print versions. The print version of *Statesman's Yearbook* is published annually, while its online version updates its news column daily.

Multimedia: Apart from textual information, the Internet offers audio, visual and video information. Kids' online resources provide access to the complete Merriam-Webster collegiate dictionary and thesaurus free and searchable with definitions and audio pronunciations. In some areas of research audio/ visual information adds to the process of learning.

Interactive: The Internet has the capability to be interactive. Discussion groups, e-mail, newsletters and on-going comments on pages are made possible so that information dialogue can be created. Q&A NJ in New Jersey, Ask a Librarian in Florida and Ask Now in California are examples of interactive references on the Internet.

Multiple users: Information through the net is accessible to multiple users at the same time whereas print sources can be used only by a single user at a time.

Limitations of using the Internet as a as a reference tool:

Despite the above-listed advantages, the Internet is still not considered a full-fledged reference source because of its inherent limitations which are as follows:

Lack of quality control: Anyone can write anything, from anywhere in the world and leave it for any amount of time for anyone to read on the Internet. In print publications on the other hand there is a built-in mechanism for quality control. For example, in scholarly journals each article is reviewed by a peer group and edited thoroughly before it is published.

Burden of evaluation: Because of the lack of quality control, the onus of evaluating websites falls on the user herself/himself. Since the user is accustomed to accept all printed materials as valid information, using the information available on the Internet without evaluation may lead to pitfalls.

Full-text information is not free: Full-text information, like full-text e-journals, is not always free for the Internet users. Quality research articles are mostly found in expensive subscription databases.

Volatility: Contents being added, modified, deleted constantly on the websites, make the websites volatile. It becomes imperative to constantly check the quality of websites and its contents before using it for research purposes. At times some websites disappear suddenly or change their domain name making it difficult to trace them. This does not happen with print publications. Their contents remain static and publication can be safely cited.

(ii) Long-range Reference Service

Long-range reference service is generally provided to a specialist who is seeking information for research, for delivering a lecture or for solving a particular problem. Information sought may be too specialised in nature, it may be too recent, it may be related to another period or it may be in particular language. The request may come from a professor, a business executive, a government official, a decision maker or R&D personnel. Depending upon the query, information may be searched in several sources including printed as well as electronic sources. At times, organisational and informal sources are also tapped into to provide the desired information. Since, to provide this type of service, a wide range of sources are consulted, the time taken to provide the service is much longer than the ready reference service. That is why this service is known as long-range reference service.

To handle such long range and at times, intricate reference questions, there are a certain set of procedures and practices which are generally followed so that the search for the query is in the right direction and collected information is acceptable to the user. The foremost and the most important step here is to have a personal dialogue with the user. Personal interaction with the user is known as "reference interview".

Anticipatory Information Services

Anticipatory information services are provided to library users in anticipation of demand for such services. These services are also called active information services. The need for such services was felt mainly due to:

(i) exponential growth of published literature, particularly in the field of science and technology;

(ii) interdisciplinary nature of frontline areas of research, resulting in the scattering of information in different disciplines; and

(iii) publication of research results in different types of sources as well as in different formats.

As a consequence of the growth in volume, diversity and complexity of the information sources, scientists, technologists, researchers, and managers faced problems in accessing information and in keeping themselves abreast of the latest developments in their areas of interest. To solve this problem, the libraries, particularly scientific and technical libraries, started providing information services to the users, particularly to the researchers. Now, not only S&T libraries, but all kinds of libraries and information/documentation centres, are offering some form of anticipatory information service, depending upon the needs of their clients.

To provide these services, user's information needs are assessed and then services are designed accordingly. Initially, the service is provided on trial basis and when response is satisfactory then service is regularised. The following types of services are offered:

- Current Awareness Type.
- Condensation Type.
- Readers Advisory Service.
- Information Literacy.
- Web-based or Internet-based services.

CURRENT AWARENESS TYPE ANTICIPATORY INFORMATION SERVICES

Current awareness type of services is provided to keep the users abreast of current developments in their respective field of interest. This involves scanning newly available documents in print as well as in non-print form, selecting items relevant to the needs of individuals or groups of users, recording, and disseminating them to the users on a regular basis. Current Awareness Service (CAS) is an ongoing service that enables one to monitor new information on regular basis. Current awareness type of services meets the current information needs of the users.

Characteristics of Current Awareness Service

- The purpose of this service is to alert the user about recent developments in her/his area of interest as early as possible.
- Since time is the major factor in the preparation of this type of publication, it generally contains a list of journal articles, book titles, etc. with no annotations or abstracts.
- The presentation of items of information is such that it facilitates scanning.
- It has a newspaper type of approach; hence, the entire list is meant for scanning.
- The service is not confined to a very specific narrow subject area but covers a broad area in a particular subject/discipline.

Types of Services in CAS

Accession List/Current Awareness List/Documentation Bulletin: These types of current awareness services are most commonly offered by libraries. An accession list basically covers latest books acquired by the library. Apart from displaying the latest publication in the library, accession list is brought out regularly (fortnightly or monthly) to inform the users about the latest additions to the library.

Title Announcement Service/Contents-by-Journal Service: In Title Announcement Service articles of required journals are selected and arranged under broad subject headings or classified with full bibliographical details and disseminated to the users periodically as print publication or e-publication. This helps the user to know what latest articles have been published in her/his subject area of interest.

Research-in-Progress: Research-in-Progress type of publication is another type of CAS that provides information on the current R&D (research and development) activities in various research institutions in a country or in the world.

Newspaper Clipping Service: Newspapers carry useful information for everyone, from housewives to the top officials of corporate houses as well as government organisations. This service ensures that researchers are dispensed with the latest happenings around them in different fields.

Disadvantages of CAS

(i) Contents-by-Journal service has certain disadvantages. In this service, the user generally browses the contents pages of journals of her/his interests only, so s/he misses out on other articles which may be useful to her/him but are present in other journals. This is not the case with the title announcement service, where articles of the same subject from different journals are brought together under a common subject heading or classification scheme.

(ii) The user has to scan the entire list to find articles that may be useful to her/him, as the service is based on the broad subject area.

(iii) Since this type of service is based on only the titles of the articles without an annotation or an abstract, it is at times difficult to determine the relevance of the article.

These disadvantages of CAS are solved by services like the Selective Dissemination of Information (SDI) service, electronic CASs and other condensation services provided by the present-day libraries.

SELECTIVE DISSEMINATION OF INFORMATION (SDI)

The SDI service is based on the concept of personal service. It is directed towards individuals or a research group working on the same research project in an organisation. It is a personalised current awareness service, where newly received items of information are matched with the user's interest profile, those items are selected which match the user's profile and then are notified to the user on a regular basis. The concept of SDI service was put forth by a computer scientist, H.P. Luhn in 1961. According to him, "SDI service is that service within an organization which concerns itself with machine-assisted channeling of new items of information from various sources to those points within the organization where the probability of usefulness in connection with current work of interest is high."

SDI service started when computers were used for handling information in the mid-1960s. Indexing and abstracting services first used computers to print their paper products. They created computerised files on magnetic tapes that were interpreted by computers and printed their products. These computerised files could be read by computers for other purposes also. Companies and government agencies developed computer software that could manipulate information on these tapes in new ways. This software allowed searching the computerised files called databases for indexed terms or group of terms on the computer and retrieve articles bearing these terms. Libraries started using these databases to provide different services to their users including SDI service.

SDI system comprises six components, viz. user profile, document database, matching mechanism, notification, feedback mechanism and modification of the profiles:

(i) **User Profile:** To provide SDI service first the user's profile is created. The expression of user interest as a combination of subject and non-subject terms is called a user profile. Here, the user is asked to specify her/his subject interest, names of persons and organisations whose work relate to her/his field of interest and details of some articles s/he found most useful in her/his current area of research.

(ii) **Document Database:** It is a computerised file containing recent documents with complete bibliographical details along with the terms representing the subject content of the documents.

(iii) **Matching Mechanism:** At fixed intervals, which may be weekly or fortnightly, the user profile and document profile are compared by a software system. As per the instructions, whenever a close match is observed between the user profile and the document record, the details of both records are noted by the system.

(iv) **Notification:** Each individual user is sent a notification from the system whenever a close match is observed between her/his profile and document record. The notification is sent to alert the user about the recent items of her/his research interest added to the document database.

(v) **Feedback Mechanism:** The most important feature of the SDI system is its feedback mechanism. Here, the user assesses the relevance and usefulness of the items received by her/him through the system and provides regular feedback.

(vi) **Modification of Profiles:** Feedback from the users is analysed and if required the user profile is modified or readjusted.

Electronic CASs: In this type of CAS, libraries make use of electronic resources like UGC-INFONET Digital Library Consortium, CSIR-E-journal Consortium, INDEST-AICTE Consortium and MCIT Library Consortium.

CONDENSATION TYPE ANTICIPATORY INFORMATION SERVICES

In this type of service, the contents of the current literature on a required subject field are condensed or summarised along with full bibliographical details of the document. This enables the user to identify the basic contents of the document quickly and determine its relevance to her/his research area of interest. At times, a well-prepared summary or abstract serves as a substitute for the document. This saves time for a busy user. Types of services under this category are:

Abstracting service: This service is concerned with providing abstracts of recently published journal articles, research reports, papers of conference proceedings, patents, standards, and dissertations along with full bibliographical details of each item. The service sometimes covers current as well as earlier published literature depending on the needs of the users. Since the abstract provides a concise summary of the entire contents of the document, it enables the user to determine its relevance and helps her/him to decide whether to read the whole document or not.

Digest service: This service is generally provided by the libraries of industries, corporate houses, and commercial organisations. The latest scientific, technical, marketing, and commercial information is essential for the growth of industries. The people in an industry, corporate houses and commercial organisations require information on new products, machinery, manufacturing processes, management techniques, etc. to keep themselves abreast of the latest developments in their areas of interest. However, the exponential growth and proliferation of new information in a wide range of sources and in diverse formats make it difficult for technical workers and executives in these enterprises to keep track of the latest developments in product design, manufacturing processes, management techniques and market trends. To meet these information requirements, a digest service is provided. The digest service is an information service that selects, evaluates, and condenses information gathered from different sources, arranges it systematically under headings and subheadings to facilitate quick reference and disseminates it to the personnel of an enterprise.

Other value-added information services: Some information centres, particularly in science and technology, provide highly specialised services or so-called value-added services which involve analysis, synthesis, and evaluation of information for the users. This evaluated information is condensed and repackaged in an appropriate form for a well-defined user group. Such information centres came to be known as information analysis centres and data centres.

Readers advisory service, information literacy and web-based or internet-based anticipatory information services have already been described in the previous unit of the same block.

ORGANISATION AND MANAGEMENT OF REFERENCE AND INFORMATION SERVICES

The American Management Association defines management as "The guiding of human physical resources into dynamic organization units that attain their objectives to the satisfaction of those served, and with high degree of morale and sense of attainment on the part of those rendering service". This definition explicitly focuses on a target audience. Similarly, in reference and information services division of any library and information centre that serves the users, no effort should be spared to meet the information needs of these users to their utmost satisfaction. This requires organisation and management of these services with efficiency and speed. Almost all large and middle size libraries entrust these services to a separate division. However, in small libraries there is no separate division. The librarian herself/himself provides the reference service. The management of a reference division can be achieved effectively by following the different elements of management, viz. planning, organising, staffing, directing, coordinating, reporting and budgeting (POSDCoRB).

Planning: "Planning" is a process that deals with the drawing up of a detailed working programme for an organisation or a division for meeting short-term as well as long-term goals. The basic resources of a reference division must be carefully planned and developed during the planning process.

Organising: This refers to the creation of an operational structure for the reference division. The structure is determined on the basis of the analysis of work and all the different activities of the division.

Staffing: "Staffing" refers to the type, quality and the number of persons required to perform various functions of the division. The head of the division with a good academic background and professional experience must have the competence and ability to lead the division.

Directing: Traditionally, the head of the division should give direction to the staff in every aspect of the work of the division and get the best out of them. But, due to rapid technological changes, the hierarchy is flattening out to accommodate new vibrant roles and services necessitated by the new learning style. These new roles cover electronic resource management, web management, reference marketing, virtual reference service, etc.

Co-ordinating: The reference division is connected to many other divisions of the library, such as technical services division, circulation, reading room, stacks, and maintenance and serials division. Co-ordination with all these divisions is absolutely necessary for the effective functioning of the reference division and to face the users with confidence and alertness.

Reporting: Reports on the performance of the division, its achievements, and shortfalls during a year or at shorter intervals, are essential to build the image or reputation of the division. These reports carry vital details on the various activities of the division in an analysed form.

Finance and Budget: As most of the services offered by the reference division are of a continuing nature, there should not be any paucity of finance in operating any of the services, particularly those which need financial support. Budgetary allocation should be made for each of the activities, on the basis of production and distribution for a given period, usually annually.

Unit 24
Literature Search and Database Services

USERS, THEIR INFORMATION NEEDS AND LITERATURE SEARCH

The prime objective of any library and information centre is to meet the information needs of its clients as early as possible and in the most economic and efficient manner. The user may be a layperson who needs information for self-educational purposes or for problem solving, a student who needs information to supplement her/his textbook studies or for project work, a teacher who needs information for teaching and research work, a professional who needs information to pursue her/his career efficiently, a manager who needs information for a new product line or for improving existing products or a researcher who needs information for finding out new areas for research or for problem solving. The nature and extent of the information required by each of them is different. To meet these information needs of the users, the information institutions provide a wide range of services. Literature search is one such service.

DEFINITION AND ROLE OF LITERATURE SEARCH

Literature search is an exhaustive search for published information on a subject conducted systematically using all bibliography finding tools, aimed at locating as much existing material on a topic as possible, an important initial step in any serious research project. In other words, literature search is a systematic search for published materials on a specific topic. This service is concerned with searching and locating the documents in response to a specific request from the user.

Literature search plays an important role in research activities. Any researcher, while starting any new research project needs to know in detail what has already been published on her/his area of research. Similarly, at the time of reporting the research results, a researcher needs to review the literature to compare the research results with other scholars working in the similar field. This requires an exhaustive search of previously published literature on that subject and compilation of a bibliography. Literature search is also carried out to solve any research problems and to find out how other scholars have handled the same problem. Literature search thus:

- Helps in study and research;
- Avoids duplication of research efforts;
- Helps in solving research problem(s);
- Assists in learning methods and approaches that are appropriate for a particular field of study;
- Helps to demonstrate that the researcher's contribution is new and different from others;
- Assists in finding out new areas for research; and
- To satisfy the information needs of researchers (scientists, technologists, social scientists, etc.), at times extensive literature searches are to be carried out in several sources like books, periodicals, non-book materials, etc. Sometimes to provide this service informal sources are also consulted. Thus, the literature search in these cases has to be more exhaustive, both in depth and range. Besides bibliographies, other secondary sources like abstracting, indexing, and reviewing periodicals are consulted to find information.

LITERATURE SEARCH AND COMPILATION OF SUBJECT BIBLIOGRAPHY

Subject bibliographies are compiled by libraries on requests from the users. Sometimes such bibliographies are compiled on a regular basis in anticipation of the users' needs. At times bibliographies are compiled on special occasions, such as during seminars and workshops, to provide the participants with the latest literature on the subject. University and special libraries offer this service more frequently than the public library.

For literature search, compiling a subject bibliography is very important. A researcher must know the basic steps involved in its preparation. In manual search printed sources are consulted, while in computer-based search computerised databases are used. Computer database searches are most efficient in identifying published literature on that subject. Computer searches may be supplemented with manual searches of printed sources. To search efficiently for any particular topic, it is important to understand the literature search process.

Search Process: Manual (Definition and Steps)

The search process in which printed sources are consulted to find out requisite information is referred to as manual search process. The basic steps in a manual search and compilation of a subject bibliography are as follows:

(1) **Understanding the subject:** In this step professionals should gather information on the specific subject and on related areas under study. For this, subject dictionaries and subject encyclopaedias should be consulted when in doubt. Here personal interaction with the user is also very important.

(2) **Decision on the scope, coverage and period:** In this step a decision is taken on the scope, coverage and period of subject bibliography. In scope, the decision whether bibliography should be comprehensive or selective is taken. Coverage helps you to decide on the types of documents to be covered. For example, periodical articles, conference papers, thesis, research reports, monographs, patents, standards, etc.

(3) **Formulation of search strategy:** In this step you formulate a systematic plan for conducting a search. First you write a clear and concise topic statement. Next you identify the main concepts in the topic. Then select the terminology or keywords to represent the main concepts. Here a list of subject headings

and the thesaurus in that discipline can be consulted to find the preferred terms to represent the main concepts. The next step is to check whether any bibliography already exists on this topic.

(4) **Scanning (Searching of tertiary, secondary, and primary sources):** In this step abstracting and indexing periodicals are searched to identify and retrieve relevant items for the bibliography and finally primary sources are consulted to find more recent information.

(5) **Entry making:** In this step an entry is prepared for each item that is identified as relevant. Each entry should be noted down on a card, so that later these entries can be arranged in a systematic order. Each entry should contain sufficient information to identify the document for the purpose of compiling the bibliography and the needs of the intended user. To write the bibliographical details of the document in a standard format, national or international standards like IS: 2381: 1978: and ISO: 690: 1975 should be followed.

(6) **Arrangement:** The entries thus prepared are arranged in some convenient order to facilitate browsing. The main arrangement should make it possible to use the bibliography without consulting the index. If the number of entries in the bibliography is small, the entries may be arranged alphabetically, on the basis of the author or chronologically by the year of publication. But if the number of entries is large, it is better to arrange them in a classified order or under broad subject headings.

(7) **Indexing:** In this step various indexes (title index, author index, subject index, etc.) are prepared to provide multiple means of access to the user. For a small bibliography, there is no need to provide an index. But for a large bibliography author, subject and title indexes may be prepared as deemed appropriate.

Search Process: Computer-based

Application of computers and information communication technologies (ICTs) in the bibliographical organisation of published literature and its dissemination have opened up new vistas in searching and retrieving information from the vast store of knowledge quickly and with much more efficiency.

Computer-based search can be traced back to the mid-1960s when indexing and abstracting periodicals started using computers to print their paper products. With the requisite software, the magnetic tapes on which the information was stored could be searched to retrieve information from the tapes. However, because of the slow speed, the computers required much time in processing and producing the results. During the late 1960s and early 1970s, computer power, speed and memory increased and so did the ability to communicate with remote computers over the existing telephone lines. These developments paved the way for online searching. The first major online dial-up service was MEDLINE, the online version of MEDLARS (Medical Literature Analysis and Retrieval System). This was followed by other commercial online services from DIALOG (Lockheed) and ORBIT (SDC) (Walker and James) by the early 1970s. At that time, online searches were very expensive and one had to take the help of intermediaries to conduct an effective and efficient search. By the 1990s, further developments in ICTs and coming up of the World Wide Web providing graphic user interface on the Internet with tutorial facilities, online searching became easy even for the novice users.

At present all major primary, secondary and tertiary publications are available in machine-readable form. Most of the national and international abstracting and indexing periodicals are available in four different formats as follows:

(1) On CD-ROM Disc.

(2) On the web through the publisher.

(3) On the Internet via an online host/vendor.

(4) In print.

The print version of these periodicals can be searched manually using various indexes provided by the publication. The other three versions are available in electronic database form and can be searched using computers.

Basic Steps for Computer-based Searching

Each database system has its own custom-built interface that allows specific type of search with specific search operators and specific search commands. As a result, steps involved in searching electronic databases vary from database to database. With the introduction of web-based graphical user interface online search has become quite easy. However, there are some basic steps for conducting computer-based search for general searching as well as for compiling a bibliography on a specific topic. These steps are as follows:

(1) **Understanding the subject:** Same as defined in manual searching.

(2) **Decision on scope, coverage, and period:** Same as defined in manual searching.

(3) **Internet access to online search service arranged:** To search electronic databases online you require an Internet connection. To get an Internet connection you have to register with the Internet Service Providers (ISPs).

(4) **Log on to search service provider:** This is usually done through the web interface of the online search service provider. At this stage one should know the web address of the search service provider (for example, for Emerald it is http://www.emeraldinsight.com/).

(5) **Select the appropriate database:** Next step is to select the appropriate database to search. Most search service providers allow users to browse through their database categories to select the appropriate database(s).

(6) **Formulate the search expression:** This requires selection of appropriate terms or phrases for searching the database. This is normally done before the search begins. In computer-based search, the user is asked to fill a form in which the search question is stated. All this information helps to know the exact requirement of the user and selection of the suitable keyword(s) for searching the database. Then make a list of the

keywords and synonyms required for searching the database.

(7) **Select the appropriate format to display the retrieved records:** When search terms are entered into the system the database starts displaying the records that match the search expression. Here you can specify whether you want to browse the full record or brief record for selection. Most of the databases offer this option.

(8) **Reformulate the query, if desired:** If one finds the search results not satisfactory, he/she can reformulate the search statement. Online search is usually a repetitive process, where the user conducts several searches, compares the results and modifies the search statement or conducts a new search in order to get the best results.

(9) **Select the mode of delivery:** Users can download all the selected records online on his/her local computer or select an offline print out by e-mail.

Advantages of Computer-based Searching over Manual Searching

Computer-based searching has the following advantages over manual searching:

(1) **Speed:** Searching electronic databases is much faster than their print counterparts. These databases offer current as well as retrospective searching. Sitting at the computer terminal one can retrieve current as well as retrospective records speedily at the same time, whereas this is not possible in manual searching.

(2) **More Search Options:** Search options provided by electronic databases are also far more than their print counterparts. In printed sources, the searching is limited to the indexes (such as author, subject, keyword indexes, etc.) provided by the print publication. In electronic databases, there are more search options such as search by field, year of publication or journal title apart from author, keywords and subject terms.

(3) **More Services:** Computer-based searching offer more services than manual searching.

(4) **More Efficient:** It gives more efficient results than manual searching.

(5) **Real Time Process:** It gives results on a real time basis.

ELECTRONIC DATABASES

Electronic databases are organised collections of data or information that are stored in computer-readable form and can be easily accessed, modified, and updated. The database can either be publicly available or private. Private databases can be accessed only by employees of the organisations that maintain the databases. Public databases are designed for access by the public. The databases contain data in a structured form. For example, in a bibliographic database the data pertaining to the name of the author, title of the book, its edition, publishers' name and address, date of publication, price, etc. are recorded in a storage medium in a structured form for accessing these individual data elements. The range of public databases has grown to the extent that it is now possible to find data almost on any subject.

TYPES OF DATABASES

Databases are organised and maintained in different ways for different types of data or information. Data in a database may be predominantly:

Word-oriented Databases: Word-oriented databases contain words, phrases, paragraphs or text as their principal data. Bibliographic databases, full-text databases and factual databases come under this category.

Numeric Databases: The principal data in numeric databases, often called "databanks", consists of numbers and symbols that represent statistical data, demographical data, time series data, etc.

Image Databases: Pictorial databases (both fixed images and moving images), many of which are for scientific and engineering purposes, may contain representations of virtually any multidimensional structures, nuclear particles, graphs, architectural maps, etc.

Sound Databases: Audio databases contain sounds and can represent music, voice and sounds of nature or anything that can be heard. For example, the recording of a sound of a tornado or an explosion.

DATABASE SERVICES

Most databases used in the libraries are bibliographic databases (such as catalogues, periodical indexes, and abstracting services) and full-text databases (such as e-journals and reference sources). These databases are leased annually to the libraries under a license agreement by the database producers. The database content is created by a database producer, who usually publishes a print version and converts the content into machine-readable form to provide access to data on CD-ROM or online via the Internet using propriety search software. The database producer provides online access to its databases through its own website or leases the content to one or more database vendors (such as EBSCO and ProQuest), who in turn provide access to these databases to registered library staff and users. A variety of database services are currently offered by primary and secondary journal publishers, online database vendors, aggregators, digital libraries, institutional repositories, search engines, etc. on the Internet. These services are illustrated in this section:

Services Offered by Publishers of Secondary Periodicals

Publishers of secondary periodicals bring together recently published literature in specific disciplines scattered over a wide range of primary sources like journal articles, research reports, conference proceedings, dissertations, patents, monographs, etc. for public use. These publishers systematically scan the primary sources, index, and arrange each item in a helpful sequence with full bibliographical details and bring out a publication at regular intervals. These publications, known as secondary periodicals, contain bibliographical references of each item with or without abstracts. A secondary periodical with abstracts is an abstracting periodical and without an abstract it is an indexing periodical. Some of the database services from publishers of indexing and abstracting periodicals are:

1. Links from references to electronic journals and patent documents. It provides links to cited references dating back to the late 19th century.
2. CAS (Chemical Abstracts Service) Databases: CAS is a Division of the American Chemical Society, indexes and abstracts of the world's chemistry-related literature published in over 10,000 major scientific journals world over in fifty languages.
3. CAplus Database: Contains bibliographic information and abstracts for over thirty-four million records from 1800 AD to the present. The database is updated daily adding 3,000 records per day.
4. MEDLINE/PubMed Database: MEDLINE (Medical Literature Analysis and Retrieval System Online) is a premier bibliographic database of the US National Library of Medicine (NLM). MEDLINE contains over twenty-one million references to journal articles in life sciences with a concentration on biomedicine.
5. STN is an online database service that provides global access to published research, journal articles, patents, structures, sequence properties and other data.
6. Other fee-based services provided are CAS Client Services like confirmation, identification or assignment of CAS Registry number and document delivery service.

Services Offered by Publishers of Primary Periodicals

Primary research periodicals are published by learned societies, R&D institutions, government organisations, R&D units of industrial organisations, academic institutions, and commercial publishers. Ulrich's Periodical Directory lists over 2,70,000 active serial titles of which 70,000 titles represent academic and scholarly journals. The first scholarly electronic journal was the "Online Journal of Current Clinical Trials" published by the American Association of Advancement of Science (AAAS) in 1992. At present most of the scholarly peer-reviewed journals are available in print as well in electronic form. The services provided by some of the major e-journal publishers are:

1. Elsevier: It is the world's leading publisher of science and health information (http://www.elseveir.com/), publishes over 2,380 primary scholarly journals in print as well in electronic form. The publisher offers online searching of over 2,500 e-journals, twenty-six bibliographical databases and 20,379 books in science and technology.
2. ScienceDirect (http://www.sciencedirect.com): Elsevier provides access to full-text e-journals and book chapters via ScienceDirect. It is a full-text database offering online access to articles from more than 2,500 peer-reviewed e-journals and chapters from more than 11,000 books in science and technology.
3. Science Alert: It runs a saved search automatically and delivers an e-mail notification with link to the new search results.
4. Journal Issue Alert: It sends an e-mail notification when a new issue of a specific journal is made available on ScienceDirect.
5. Citation Alert: It sends an e-mail notification when a document that cites a specific article of interest is added to ScienceDirect.
6. Topic Alerts: It notifies the subscribers by e-mail when a predefined topic-related search retrieves new results.
7. ScienceDirect Top 25 Hottest Articles: An e-mail is sent every three months to subscribers, listing the twenty-five most frequently downloaded journal articles from any selected journal among more than 2,000 titles.

Services Offered by Aggregators

E-journal publishers, in addition to providing full-text access to their publications from their own websites, are also making their e-resources available through vendors and other third-party mediators for exploitation under license agreements. Third-party mediators, known as aggregators, provide online access to a large number of journals from different publishers on a single platform and customise information for individual libraries based on the needs of each library. This type of arrangement is beneficial for both the libraries and the publisher. Libraries can enter into agreements with a single service provider instead of dealing a large number of publishers. There are large numbers of aggregators providing e-journal services on the Internet. Some of them are EBSCO, ProQuest, J-Gate, etc. The services offered by them include:

1. EBSCO: EBSCO Industries Inc. is a global corporation with divisions in twenty-three countries around the world. EBSCO Industries have diversified into forty businesses, including, electronic and print periodical subscription services, research databases and related information management services.
2. EBSCO A-to-Z service provides library users with a single comprehensive list of titles that they can access through subscription. Master A to Z titles provides links and coverage information to more than 6,00,000 unique titles from more than 4,200 databases and e-journal packages.
3. Search Alerts: Current session searches can be set up as search alerts to automatically update users with new articles published on a specific subject.
4. Journal Alerts: Sends journal alert notifications to users via e-mail when a new title is made available in a specific database.
5. Links to full-text databases: Users can link from EBSCO host citations to its full-text in another subscribed database.

6. J-Gate Portal: This service provides a table-of-contents of the latest issues of journals and a comprehensive online searchable database of over five million articles with a daily addition of over 4,000 plus articles.
7. J-Gate Customised Services: This service offers J-Gate Custom Content (JCC) and J-Gate Custom Content for Consortia (JCCC). JCC is a local intranet/Internet solution to libraries providing e-access to subscribed journals.

Services Offered by Digital Libraries

A digital library is a library in which collections are stored in digital formats (as opposed to print, microform or other media) and accessible through computers. The digital contents may be shared locally or accessed remotely via computer networks. An important advantage of a digital library is its increased accessibility to users. The users of a digital library can access the contents of the library round the clock from any location. It offers multiple search options and the user is able to use any search term such as word, phrase, title, name or subject to search the entire collection. The same sources can be used simultaneously by a number of institutions and patrons. Digital libraries can provide user-friendly interface giving clickable access to their resources. Digital libraries conserve fragile materials which may otherwise deteriorate with repeated use. While traditional libraries are limited by storage space, digital libraries have the potential to store much more information, because digital information requires very little physical space to contain them. Some examples of digital libraries are:

1. **The World Digital Library (WDL):** This library makes itself available on the Internet, free of charge, with significant primary materials from countries and cultures in a multilingual format covering seven languages. The World Digital Library is a collaborative project of the US Library of Congress, the UNESCO, and partners throughout the world. It not only provides resources for educators, scholars,

and general audiences; but also builds capacity in particular institutions to narrow the digital divide within and between countries.

2. **The Digital Library of India:** Hosted by the Regional Mega Scanning Centre, International Institute of Information Technology, Hyderabad in co-operation with IISc, CMU, ERNET and MCIT for the Government of India and twenty-one participating institutions, the Digital Library of India envisages developing a collection of one million digital books. It has ensured that cultural and social books in different languages are properly digitalised. Palm leaves journals and manuscripts are also digitised.

Services Offered by Open Access E-Journals

Open-access journals are scholarly journals that are available online to readers without financial, legal or technical barriers. Open-access literature is digital, free of charge and free of most copyright and licensing restrictions. Open-access scholarly journals permit users to read, download, copy, distribute, search or link to full-text articles. Open-access literature is available in open access journals, subject repositories, and digital archives.

Directory of Open Access Journals: The directory covers free, full-text quality controlled scientific and scholarly journals. There are 6,960 journals in the directory. Currently, 3,174 journals are searchable at the article level. The database of the directory has over 6,23,995 articles. The aim of the directory of open-access journals is to increase the visibility and ease of use of open-access scientific and scholarly journals thereby promoting their usage and impact.

Services Offered by Institutional Repositories

Institutional repositories are digital archives of the research outputs of a particular R&D institution, a central repository of a group of institutions or a subject-specific repository. These repositories archive scholarly material and offer free access to this material for scholarly and educational purposes.

Some institutions in India such as the Indian Institute of Science (IISc), Bangalore, Indian Statistical Institute (ISI), Bangalore, Indian Institute of Technology (IIT), Delhi and others have established open access institutional repositories (IRs) to disseminate the research output of their respective institution. Some institutional repositories are self-archived like the Indian Institute of Science, Bangalore. The IISc (eprints@IISc) repository collects, preserves, and disseminates in digital formats the pre-prints, post-prints and other scholarly materials created by the IISc research community. In some repositories, the administrators of the repository collect the research materials from different sources and disseminate it for public use on behalf of the person concerned. Subject-specific repositories are repositories providing access to subject-specific scholarly material.

DATABASE SERVICES: EMERGING TRENDS

The impact of ICTs has brought a spectacular change in information storage, retrieval, and dissemination-related activities. Producers of indexing and abstracting periodicals and publishers of primary periodicals, which were two separate industries earlier, are now merging or entering into a partnership. Publishers of primary journals are offering online access to full-text e-journals to the subscribers of their print publications under a license agreement. The producers of bibliographic databases are diversifying by bringing out factual statistical and multimedia databases. They are offering linkages from citations to full-text journal articles on the publisher's site. As demands for multimedia databases are growing, database producers are increasingly adding graphics, images, audio, and video to the technical contents of the databases. Apart from providing linkage services, the publishers are offering additional services to the end-users like journal issue alerts, citation alerts, topic alert services and many more. Database producers are offering customised services by bringing out different products according to the requirements of different clients. A new generation of e-journal service providers are emerging like aggregators. Aggregators like EBSCO and ProQuest, with license rights from primary publishers are providing online access to full-text online aggregated databases. They are also providing links from secondary services to full-text articles online. Many database search service providers allow search results to be sorted out by various parameters like date, author, source or relevance and save it to the user's personal account. Some allow graphical displays of the search results. Many more players have joined the database service market like digital libraries, institutional repositories, open access e-journal initiators, search engines and others.

EXERCISES: UNIT 22 – UNIT 24

1. What do you understand by the term "data"?
2. Define the term "information".
3. How is telecommunication different from communication?
4. What are the different types of information needs?
5. Describe "responsive information services".
6. Write a note on "web-based information services".
7. What do you understand by reference service? Trace its origin, growth, and development.
8. What do you understand by information service? Trace its origin, growth, and development.
9. Differentiate between "reference service" and "information service".
10. Write a note on "reference services". Explain its different types.
11. State the advantages of using the Internet as a reference tool.
12. What do you understand by the "Current Awareness Service"? State its characteristics.
13. Discuss the various types of the Current Awareness Service (CAS).
14. Discuss the SDI model in detail. Highlight and elaborate its components and working.

15. Define the "digest service" in a library.
16. Write a note on the organisation and management of reference and information services.
17. Define a "literature search". Discuss its role and importance.
18. Discuss in detail the manual and computer-based literature search.
19. Write down the basic steps in a computer-based literature search.
20. What are the advantages of an automated search over manual search?
21. Discuss the emerging trends in database service.
22. What do you understand by database service?

Unit 25

User Education and Information Literacy

USER EDUCATION

"User education" may be defined as a process or a programme through which the potential users (scientists, engineers, technologists, academics, and students) of information are made aware of the value of information and are motivated to use information resources. Mews, in her book on reader instructions, defines user education as instructions given to readers to help them make the best use of the library. Jacques Tocatline (UNESCO) defined user education to include any effort or programme which will guide and instruct existing and potential users, individually or collectively with the objectives of:

(a) recognising their own information needs;

(b) formulating these needs;

(c) using information services effectively and efficiently; and

(d) assessing these services.

COMPONENTS AND OBJECTIVES

User education is a continuous process comprising two components, namely orientation and instruction. These are illustrated below:

"Orientation" is concerned with ways of acquainting the user with the library and services available and also with the organisation, layout, and facilities of a particular library. Orientation is related to both cognitive objectives (i.e. understanding) and affective objectives (i.e. feelings and attitudes). In orientation, it is important to try and create the right kind of environment for effective communication between the user and the library staff and to present an image of the library as a pleasant and friendly institution, where help can be obtained. As a result of orientation, the users should feel confident that the library staff is competent and is always willing to help them.

The second component of user education, namely "instruction", is concerned with learning the use of various information resources available in a specific library. This aspect is also known as bibliographic instructions and is concerned with the problems of information retrieval and the techniques of utilising information sources to their maximum. Bibliographic instructions may be imparted at two stages, as an introductory course and as an advanced course, depending on the awareness level of the users.

HISTORICAL DEVELOPMENT IN USER EDUCATION

The history of development of user education has been well documented. The role of the library in higher education has been a subject of debate for long. In 1934, Louis Shores introduced the concept of the "library arts college". This concept gradually evolved into the "library college". The purpose of the library college is to increase the effectiveness of student learning, particularly through the use of library-centred independent study with the help of a bibliographically expert faculty. The systematic use of the concept of user education owes its origin to Patricia B. Knapp and her 1964 report which mainly attempted at "exploring methods of developing a more vital relationship between the library and college teaching". This project was sponsored by the Monteith College of Wayne State University.

In the process of institutionalisation of user education, the lead was taken by the Council of Library Resources and the Association of College and Research Libraries in the USA. It was the British Library Research and Development Department and the Centre for Research in User Studies which promoted and gave impetus to the development of user education programmes in the UK. This institutional patronage was mainly responsible for a number of important user education projects. The UNESCO under the UNISIST programme attempted to initiate user education programmes in less developed countries. UNISIST promulgated the UNESCO General Information Programme (PGI) in 1975. The UNISIST Information Policy objectives stress on user education.

As far as development of user education in India is concerned, the field has witnessed considerable activity. For example, the IASLIC, Calcutta organised a national conference on User Education at Waltair (Andhra Pradesh) in 1981. The INSDOC (now NISCAIR), New Delhi and the DRTC-Bangalore, have been organising seminars and workshops for the promotion of user education.

Objectives of User Education

The concept of user education has caught the imagination of librarians and information professionals all around the world. It comes with the following objectives:

- Create awareness about the sources and services available.
- Highlight all the contents (print and digital) of a library.
- Hands-on training for the use of different equipment like OPAC, KIOSKs, etc.
- Ensure the adequate use of the library and its resources.
- Give an understanding of library arrangements-physical, bibliographical, and conceptual to the users.
- Interpret one's own needs so as to frame relevant questions and resources.
- Create an awareness of search techniques including the ability to devise serviceable routines.

- Improve the skills of users in the art of evaluating resources and acquiring materials or content.

METHODS OF USER EDUCATION

Education has been defined as a process that empowers the learners. This process can be affected by a variety of factors. The four basic factors that affect learning in practical situations are motivation, activity, understanding, and feedback. These factors might be considered in relation to library user education programmes as well. The choice of teaching methods and media depends on the learning/teaching situation, the subject material, the students, and the teachers. No single method will be suitable for all situations. However, teaching methods may roughly be categorised into those which are suitable for group instructions, those suitable for individual instructions and those suitable for both. These methods include:

Lectures: Lectures are the most common method of instruction. They are used for teaching large groups of students. In lecture method of teaching both audio as well as visual sensory inputs (via blackboard or overhead projector) are made use of.

Seminars, Tutorials, and Demonstrations: These are organised for small groups of students/users. Compared to the lecture method, seminars, tutorials, and demonstrations are methods that provide the opportunities for the active involvement of users in the learning process through greater interaction between the teaching staff and the students.

The Guided Tour: This is one of the traditional approaches commonly adopted to orient new users to the use of the library. This type of orientation is often given when the students have little or no motivation to use the library. This method brings library users into the actual building where they carry out a series of practical tasks concerned with the location materials, photocopying, use of catalogues and other routines.

Audio-visual Methods: There are few areas in library user education where it is necessary to use moving images. As a result, the information can be conveyed in a series of units such as slides, transparencies or printed illustrations.

Programmed Instruction: The programmed instructions can be carried out by the use of a variety of media such as printed books, automatic projection of slides or by means of a computer-aided instruction (CAI).

Signs and Informational Graphics: Sign systems and informational graphics are two of the most basic methods available for providing an orientation about the use of the library. Librarians started to apply a systems approach in which different types of signs are used to illustrate different functions such as orientation, direction, identification, instruction, prohibition or regulation or current awareness.

Individual Instruction at the Reference Desk: It is believed that the best form of library instruction can be imparted by a personalised service at the reference desk. This is because generally a user asks a question about the use of some part of the library when s/he is interested to learn about that particular aspect.

INFORMATION TECHNOLOGY AND USER EDUCATION

Computers are increasingly being used today for information retrieval activities. This has resulted in a rapid growth of computer-based online information retrieval systems. Databases and computer stored information files are produced by many organisations such as the American Chemical Society (Chemical Abstracts) and the US National Library of Medicine (Index Medicus), etc. These databases are now widely accessible for information searching from local terminals which are linked to the central computer via a telecommunication network. Such efforts have resulted in the development of a number of online information retrieval systems. The use of these systems depends on the education of the users and the availability and functioning of this method of information retrieval. Different groups are concerned with online orientation, training, and education. They are:

(1) Database producers.

(2) System operators.

(3) Institutions such as libraries or information centres.

(4) Library schools.

(5) Intermediaries.

(6) End users.

The motivation for each of these groups is expected to vary considerably. Generally, the motivation for taking part in such training programmes might be considered partly financial and closely linked to the sale of a specific product, database or information system. For the sake of convenience, online education programmes may be divided into two components, orientation, and instruction. Orientation is concerned with enabling the user to learn about the existence of computer-based information retrieval and the services available. On the other hand, instruction is concerned with enabling the user to learn in detail how to carry out a computerised information retrieval.

EVALUATION OF A USER EDUCATION PROGRAMME

The evaluation of a User Education programme has been described and interpreted in different ways by educational researchers. It is concerned with the collection of information about the effects of an educational course or programme on users. It involves a comparison of observed effects with expectations or intentions. Therefore, it is important to consider why evaluation is carried out while trying to understand what evaluation is.

Evaluation is concerned with the collection and analysis of information about the input, in terms of educational potential, the variables affecting the educational process and the end product or output. Evaluation can be directed towards the various aspects of the educational course or programme. The basic purpose of the evaluation is to collect and analyse information that can be used for rational decision making. There are three methods that are normally used for evaluation purposes. They are:

(i) **The Psychometric Method:** Psychometric evaluation is based on the assumption that it is possible to expose experimental and control groups to different treatments, while all other variables are controlled and to measure the changes by means of psychometric tests, achievement tests or attitude scales. Thus, the experimental group may be exposed to a new type of course whereas the control group follows the traditional course, in every other respect the two groups are exactly comparable. Pre-tests and post-tests are given to both groups and the analysis is concerned with establishing significant differences in the performance of the two groups.

(ii) **The Sociological or the Management Method:** The sociological evaluation method is used in the study, of changes in the structure of an organisation. This type of evaluation makes use of interviews and questionnaires. Attention is focused on the organisation undergoing the change, rather than on comparison with any control group.

(iii) **The Illuminative or Responsive Method:** Illuminative evaluation is not limited by the initial formulation or aims, but allows the expression of unexpected results. The actual implementation of an innovation is regarded as the most important part of the study. The research is focused on what is actually happening in response to the innovation.

Need for the Evaluation of Library User Education: Evaluation and the feedback received in the process allow administrators to know the successfulness of the programmes and will lead to the improvement of such programmes.

INFORMATION LITERACY

"Information literacy" is the ability of a person to recognise his/her information need and have the ability to locate, evaluate and effectively use the needed information. One of the earliest definitions of information literacy was given in 1989 by the ALA Presidential Committee on Information Literacy. It stated that "to be IL, a person must be able to recognise when information is needed and have the ability to locate, evaluate and use effectively the needed information." The concept of information literacy was first conceived by Paul Zurkowski in 1974, the then President of the Information Industry Association. He observed that information literates are trained in the application of information resources to their work. It enables them to make more intelligent decisions at work, research and study as compared to those who are not information literate.

NEED FOR INFORMATION USE STUDY

Information is the basic ingredient of our day-to-day working, learning, teaching, research, administration, etc. Information is available all around us. Those who utilise it effectively and efficiently are called "information literates". Information literacy thus becomes important as without IL it is not easy to utilise the available information because:

- It is increasing exponentially, thereby making it difficult to ascertain whether we have access to all information that currently exists;
- Anyone can publish on the Internet, thus making it difficult for the user to verify the authenticity and validity of information;
- Sources of information are many, therefore, making its control difficult;
- Information is available in different formats which a user should be adept in handling to be able to use the information; and
- Using the information for some work requires skills of analysis and synthesis.

HISTORICAL BACKGROUND

The exponential information boom and increasing dependence of society on information gave birth to information literacy in 1974. The introduction of personal computers in the 1980s saw a further rise in the information generation. Related developments in telecommunication technology brought people closer which resulted in information exchange. Developed countries also saw the rise of the phenomena of an 'information society' during the 1980s where information occupied central importance. They realised its importance and started programmes to prepare their citizens to make use of the varied information resources. The American Library Association (ALA) took the initiative and recommended the formation of the National Forum for Information Literacy (NFIL). The NFIL was formed in 1989 as a first step to collectively promote information literacy across all sections of society. NFIL had representation from over sixty-five different bodies related to the fields of education, industry, governance, etc. The Forum aimed at creating awareness in society towards information literacy by discussing developments in information literacy and publicising through announcements, advertisements, and seminars as well as encouraging research on it. A definition emerged, given by the Presidential Committee of the ALA on Information Literacy in 1989. It is the most comprehensive definition that has been most often quoted and also forms the basis of other definitions.

The 1990s saw the movement spreading to other countries. The Society of College, National and University Libraries (SCONUL), UK gave the "The Seven Pillars of Information Literacy" model to spread information literacy among the higher education community. Other models such as the Kulthau Information Search Model, Empowering 8 IL Model, Big Skills IL Model and the Pitts/Stripling Research Model were proposed simultaneously by other organisations and individuals. The year 2000 saw another important contribution to information literacy by the Association of College and Research Libraries as it outlined the standards for assessing information literacy of students. The Prague Declaration is an important event in the history of information literacy which is the result of an international conference on information literacy held jointly by the UNESCO, NFIL and the National Commission on Libraries and Information Science in 2003. It described information literacy as a basic human right in lifelong learning and as a necessary ingredient for the social, economic, and cultural development of individuals, communities, nations and society as a whole. IFLA has a blog and a list on information literacy. Professionals in India also realised the importance of information literacy and actively participated in discussions. Thus, information literacy became the topic of discussion in many seminars, conferences, and workshops.

INFORMATION LITERACY MODELS

Information literacy models are useful for LIS professionals and faculties in designing information literacy programmes. They provide a framework to develop an information literacy programme based on information seeking and writing and evaluating the information product. These models assure learning is an active and creative process that enhances critical thinking. They have also been used for designing and evaluating information literacy curricula.

The Society of College, National and University Libraries (SCONUL) developed a model of information literacy in 1999 known as the Information Skills Model. The seven skills recommended in the model are also called "The Seven Pillars of Information Literacy". The skills include the ability to:

(1) Recognise the need for information;

(2) Distinguish ways in which the information gap may be addressed;

(3) Construct strategies for locating information;

(4) Locate and access information;

(5) Compare and evaluate information obtained from different sources;

(6) Organise, apply, and communicate information in ways appropriate to the situation; and

(7) Synthesise and build upon existing information, contributing to the creation of new knowledge.

Kulthau is credited for conducting a series of studies concerning user's information behaviour. She observed student reactions while using different methods like interviews, case studies and assessing them in writing assignments, etc. Based on their responses, she proposed the Information Search Process. She proposed three models to impart library skills, viz. the source or library as the focus, the pathfinder or search strategy approach and the process model approach. The first two models have the library or the information resource as the focus, helping the user to reach and search the source whereas the last model stresses the process of information search and use and is user-centred in contrast to the other two models that are resource and information centred. The process model helps empower the user in information search and use. It inculcates critical thinking and problem-solving skills so as to strategise information use according to the situation.

INFORMATION LITERACY STANDARDS

The Association of College and Research Libraries (ACRL), 2000 formulated standards of information literacy for higher education that help in developing an information literacy curriculum for an educational institution. The standards also provide Performance Indicators (PI) and the outcomes for each standard have been presented briefly below.

Standards of Information Literacy

The information literate student:

(1) Determines the nature and extent of information needed.

(2) Accesses the needed information effectively and efficiently.

(3) Evaluates information and its sources critically and incorporate selected information into her or his knowledge base and value system.

(4) Individually or as a member of a group, she/he uses information effectively to accomplish a specific purpose.

(5) Understands many of the economic, legal, and social issues surrounding the use of information and access and uses the information ethically and legally.

Performance Indicator and Outcome of Standard 1 (Determines the nature and extent of information needed)

Performance Indicator

The information literate student:

(a) Defines and articulates the need for information.

(b) Identifies a variety of types and formats of potential sources of information.

(c) Considers the costs and benefits of acquiring the needed information.

(d) Re-evaluates the nature and extent of information needed.

(e) Refines the search strategy if necessary.

Outcomes

(a) Discusses with peers in class to identify information needs or identify a research topic.

(b) Explores information sources to gain familiarity with the topic and modifies the need to be more focused.

(c) Identifies key concepts that identify the need.

(d) Knows how information is produced, organised and disseminated. Recognises the difference between the sources in different formats.

(e) Differentiates between primary, secondary, and tertiary sources.

Performance Indicator and Outcome of Standard 2 (The information-literate student accesses the needed information effectively and efficiently).

Performance Indicator

The information literate student:

(a) Selects the most appropriate IR (information retrieval) system for accessing the needed information.

(b) Constructs and implements effectively designed search strategies.

(c) Retrieves information online or in person using a variety of methods.

(d) Refines the search strategy if necessary.

(e) Extracts, records and manages the information and its sources.

Outcomes

(a) Identifies appropriate investigative methods for information search.

(b) Investigates the pros and cons of the different methods.

(c) Selects the efficient and effective methods for information search.

(d) Develops a research plan appropriate to the investigative method.

(e) Identifies keywords and related terms for information search.

(f) Selects controlled vocabulary for information retrieval.

Performance Indicator and Outcome of Standard 3 (The information literate student evaluates information and its sources critically and incorporates selected information into his or her knowledge base and value system).

Performance Indicator

The information literate student:

(a) Summarises the main ideas to be extracted from the information gathered.

(b) Articulates and applies initial criteria for evaluating both the information and its sources.

(c) Synthesises main ideas to construct new concepts.

(d) Compares new knowledge with prior knowledge to determine the value added, contradictions or other unique characteristics of the information.

(e) Determines whether the new knowledge has an impact on the individual's value system and takes steps to reconcile differences.

Outcomes

(a) Reads the text, selects main ideas, and presents them in his/her own words.

(b) Quote verbatim matter in quotes.

(c) Evaluates information regarding its reliability, accuracy, validity, timeliness, and point of view.

(d) Recognises prejudice, deception or manipulation.

(e) Recognises the relationships among concepts and combines them into useful primary statements.

Performance Indicator and Outcome of Standard 4 (The information literate student individually or as a member of a group, uses information effectively to accomplish a specific purpose).

Performance Indicator

The information literate student:

(a) Applies new and prior information to the planning and creation of a new product or performance.

(b) Revises the development process for the product or performance.

(c) Communicates the product or performance effectively to others.

Outcomes

(a) Organises the content in a manner that supports the purpose and format of the product or performance.

(b) Articulates knowledge and skills transferred from prior experiences to plan and create a new product.

(c) Maintains a log of activities related to information seeking, evaluating, and communicating.

(d) Reflects on past successes, failures, and alternative strategies.

Performance Indicator and Outcome of Standard 5 (The information literate student understands many of the economic, legal and social issues surrounding the use of information and accesses and uses the information ethically and legally).

Performance Indicator

The information literate student:

(a) Understands many of the ethical, legal and many of the socio-economic issues surrounding information and information technology.

(b) Follows the laws, regulations, institutional policies, and etiquette related to the access and use of information resources.

(c) Acknowledges the use of information sources in communicating the product or performance.

Outcomes

(a) Identifies and discusses issues related to privacy and security in print and electronic environments.

(b) Identifies and discusses issues related to free vs. fee-based access to information.

(c) Identifies issues related to censorship.

(d) Demonstrates an understanding of IPR, copyright and fair use of copyrighted material.

IMPARTING INFORMATION LITERACY

Different types of programmes help impart information literacy skills. These range from standalone programmes to course related and course integrated programmes. A simple information literacy programme could be providing details on information sources, their scope and search techniques followed by exercises in searching databases and other sources. The course-related programmes dwell on information literacy skills in different subjects and areas. The course integrated programmes are also for a particular subject/area. The difference between a course-related programme and a course integrated programme lies in the fact that the former is a separate programme on information literacy whereas the latter is integrated into the course in a way that forms an inseparable part of the programme.

Information literacy programmes may be non-credit or for-credit. There is a feeling that information literacy programmes, like other non-subject programmes, should be non-credit. ILP is spread into four parts, viz:

Undergraduate: Beginning/General: Includes an introduction to the different types of resources (primary, secondary, and tertiary), core resources in a subject, basic research process in the sciences, basic searching skills and applying the same to a database, evaluating a resource and citing a work.

Undergraduate/Advanced: Includes the role of information the process of research, in-depth introduction to the types of resources, core information resources (print and electronic), introduction and application of more sophisticated search strategies, etc.

Graduate Students: Includes a scientific research process and the sources of information at each stage, information tools of practicing scientists, scientific publication process, etc.

Professional Scientists (Post-Doctoral and Independent Researcher): Includes updates on new features of known resources and introduction to new resources, keeping up with new literature by Table of Contents (TOC) services, browsing, alerts/Selective Dissemination of Information (SDI), etc.

Information Literacy and User Education

Library instruction programmes have evolved with time and changing information environments. Different programmes have been designed to serve different user needs. Library orientation, bibliographic instructions and user education programmes have been designed to serve the different needs of library users. Information literacy emerged as a result of the explosion of information, increasing importance and the increasing digitisation of information. However, it cannot be placed in the same category as all other programmes. It has a broader scope and objectives as it is not limited to library resources and programmes. Its purpose extends beyond knowing and mastering the contents of information sources, searching, and using information from them. Information literacy aims at developing competencies in individuals to keep themselves updated in their knowledge domains by utilising relevant and appropriate information, ethically, and legally. Subsequently, they should be able to apply this knowledge to their study, research, teaching and work. To achieve this, they need to develop reasoning, critical thinking, analytical and synthesis skills. Information literacy enables one to contextualise and see things in a greater and meaningful context. Information literacy is an enabler of lifelong learning which is the focus of learning today.

Unit 26
User Studies

USER AND USER STUDIES

People who seek and use the information to meet their information needs are referred to as "library users". The user is the focal point of all information activities at all levels. In LIS literature, a number of terms have been used to signify users. For example, the words patron, client, member, reader, and customer are all used to signify the concept of a user.

User studies have revealed that there are four basic categories of users on the basis of their approach to information. They can be classified as:

- **The potential user:** One who needs information that can be provided by specific services;
- **The expected user:** One who is known to have the intention of using certain information services;
- **The actual user:** One who has actually used an information service regardless of the fact whether he derived an advantage from such a service or not; and
- **The beneficiary user:** One who derives a measurable advantage from information services.

In addition, there are three important groups of scientific and technical information system users, distinguishable according to the kind of activity in which they are engaged in. These are:

(a) researchers,

(b) practitioners and technicians engaged in the developmental and/or operational activities in the different fields of technology, and

(c) managers, planners and other decision makers who are engaged in coordinating development activities at the local, national or international levels.

USER CHARACTERISTICS

Since the main purpose of any user study is to gather information that is useful in the design, provision and evaluation of specific information products or services geared to specific users, it becomes necessary to have a full understanding of the user characteristics. User characteristics may be studied under the following four mentioned groups:

(i) **Individual characteristics:** The individual characteristics of users deal with

(a) their perception of the problem and their definition of the problem faced along with their description of the needed information.

(b) the specific ways in which they are most likely to use information and their capacity to use a particular type of information.

(ii) **Stages in the information diffusion:** This aspect relates to the amount of knowledge an individual (or a group of users) has about a specific idea or innovation. Information needs at various stages are different and therefore information products and services have to be tailored for each stage. This might be possible only when the capabilities of the user are clearly perceived.

(iii) **Environmental or social characteristics:** The factors in the social system (such as the norms, situation, reference groups, etc.) that have an important effect on the individual's behaviour and communication fall under the category of environmental or social characters pertaining to an individual (or group) of users. An awareness about these factors enables the system designer to precisely gauge the information requirements of the user.

(iv) **Communication characteristics:** The elements related to the use and diffusion of information constitute what are known as communication characteristics. Some of these include information sources, information structures, communication channels and information systems. These aspects need to be correlated with other characteristics.

User Studies

"User study" is the means for the systematic examination of the characteristics and behaviour of the users of the systems and services. The 'user study' is directly linked with the effectiveness (performance) of the library and information services provided as they aim at the satisfaction of user needs. The concept of users and their information needs found some expression at the first conference of the Royal Society held in London and became a subject of discussion at the International Conference on Scientific Information held in Washington in 1958.

NEED FOR USER STUDIES

Information need surveys or user studies are potentially useful in bridging the gap between the kind of information services needed and the kind of services in existence. Any information system would definitely require the identification of user requirements. This has led to the efforts for the development of reliable methodologies for conducting user studies and further emphasised the need for conducting user studies as a necessary requirement for the design and operation of effective and efficient information systems, services, and products.

PLANNING OF A USER STUDY

It is important to plan a user study carefully from the beginning to the very end. In this regard, it is necessary to lay down a detailed plan for each step beforehand. The various stages of work are to be spelled out along with the general objectives of the study, translation of the objectives into a set of questions or means of answering the questions, selection of the tool or appropriate technique for obtaining the answers, the selection of the sample of users to be observed and a plan for getting the necessary co-operation, the pre-testing of the technique, the full-scale study itself and analysis of data and preparation of the final report. In each stage of work certain decisions are to be taken.

Different Steps in the Plan

Any plan for conducting a user study should consist of at least the following steps:

- Surveying the previous studies and literature in general and learning about all aspects of user studies;
- Spelling out the objectives of the study;
- Determining the variables to be studied and the specific model to be followed;
- Selecting the sample population to be studied;
- Determining the method for collection of data for observation;
- Determining the method of analysis of data or observations;
- Determining the ways of presentation of data and utilisation of the results including dissemination of such results.

METHODOLOGIES/TECHNIQUES FOR USER STUDIES

The user study methodology involves three basic steps:

- the selection of a method for user study;
- data collection by a suitable technique;
- and data analysis.

These steps are described below:

1. Selection of a method for user study: Once the need for conducting user studies has been established and the relevant aspects (variables) to be studied are decided, the next logical step would be the selection of methods for conducting a user study. From a sizable literature on the subject, it is evident that most of the general surveys, for example, interviews, questionnaires, diaries, etc., have been extensively used by researchers in the field of information use study also. The methods used so far may be grouped as under:

(a) General or Conventional Methods: These include

(i) Questionnaire.

(ii) Interviews.

(iii) Diaries.

(iv) Observation by the self.

(v) Operations research study.

(b) Indirect Methods: These include

(i) analysis of library records.

(ii) citation analysis.

(c) Special and Unconventional Methods: These include

(i) computer-feedback, and

(ii) unconventional methods.

2. Data collection by a suitable technique: There are a number of methods available for data collection. Some of the commonly used methods are:

Surveying: This involves questioning the users and obtaining answers directly from them about their behaviour, attributes, values, conditions and/or preferences. This is by far the most frequently used method in user studies. It at times also leads to somewhat biased results.

Observation: It involves making direct observations on the communication behaviour of users in given situations, practices, time periods, etc.

Records analysis: This method involves obtaining written records or other transcripts of previous communications (such as papers, correspondence, statistics) and deriving inferences about users based on the records.

Experimentation: This method involves the introduction of an element in a defined group of users and observing the results or consequences, possibly also comparing the group with another where the element was not introduced.

3. Data analysis: The next step involved is identification of some of the data analysis methods. This includes:

Statistical analysis which comprises application of standard statistical techniques to summarise, compare and test for significant data which is expressed numerically.

Semantic analysis involves application of semantic techniques to summarise and compare data which is expressed verbally.

Psycho-social analysis which involves the application of psychological, sociological or anthropological techniques to classify or describe the data obtained through a user study, which is represented conceptually, logically or representatively.

Economic analysis which comprises application of macro or micro economic techniques to derive conclusions in economic terms on data expressed in all the above-mentioned ways.

USER STUDIES: LIMITATIONS AND CRITICISMS

1. Influence or bias: The moderator can lead the conversation that reflect their own thoughts or feelings through spoken language and body language. This can affect the study's result.
2. Self-identification: If the participants do not connect or identify with the moderator, they might have a hard time being open about their experiences using the product or need of information resource.
3. Participant pool: The live session is usually done during the working hours, which is often not working for every participant. This can affect the findings of the study.
4. Difficult scheduling: Scheduling for both the moderator and the participant is hard during standing working hours.
5. Time consuming process: The user study process takes a long time before decisions are reached.

Unit 27
Information Use Studies

INFORMATION USE STUDY: MEANING AND SCOPE

"Information use study" simply means the study of the use of information. This use may pertain to oral information or recorded information. Every day we use a lot of oral information. For example, a girl is asking her mother how to cook a particular food item. The mother is giving the instruction and the girl is preparing the food.

NEED FOR INFORMATION USE STUDY

Information use study is required to perform the following operations:

Procurement policy: Procurement of recorded information involves cost, often in terms of millions of rupees. If it is seen that the procured information is not being used adequately, then it may be assumed that part of the money is going to waste. The study of information use can be used to define or update the purchase/procurement policy.

Weeding or switching over to electronic media: An active library grows continuously in size as new books are added to the library every year. This generates the requirement of further space. There are two ways, either the library is expanded with the addition of new rooms or new buildings or some space is generated by weeding out unused books. It is mainly through use study we identify the unused books which may be removed from the shelves to generate space.

Constraints in information use: The use of information is greatly hindered because of various constraints. It is common that libraries in torrid summer or extreme cold are used very less where there is no air conditioning or frequent power failures. Those hindrances can be removed after taking the information use studies.

TYPES OF INFORMATION USE STUDY

Based on the sources which people consult to gather information, information use studies may be categorised as follows:

User-based information use study: In this type, studies are conducted to find out how common people, children, students, academicians, scholars, faculty members and many others use various types of information. For example, Choukhande and Kumar studied the information use pattern of faculty members and research scholars of Amravati University.

Profession-based information use study: Doctors, engineers, scientists, teachers, subject specialists, etc. are all professionals. Information use may vary from profession to profession. A scientist may prefer to use mostly primary information. On the other hand, a librarian may use primary, secondary, and tertiary information. This method analyses information use by professionals.

Subject-based information use study: This method takes subject-based studies. It is possible to study information use according to various subjects. In such studies both electronic and non-electronic sources may be covered. For examples, Biradar studied the use of information sources in an agricultural college library at Shimoga, India.

Non-electronic source-based information use study: Non-electronic sources comprise hand-written documents like manuscripts and letters, typed or mimeographed documents like theses and circulars and all printed documents like books and journals. In this case, use study is possible for information use studies with a single document, a specific type of document, a particular category of information sources or information sources in general.

Electronic source-based information use study: Such studies are conducted more often nowadays. These studies include e-resources in general, sources in CDs, online databases, web, consortia, etc. It is also possible to study the use of these sources according to the user, profession, subject, category of documents, etc. Such study is carried on with the usage of online bibliographic databases, web, consortia, ejournals, e-books, e-zines, etc. These resources may be CD-based, web-based, online databases, etc.

Oral information use study: Everyday human beings disseminate a large amount of information orally. For example, a village level worker disseminates information about a high-yielding variety of rice to the farmers of a village. This method studies the use of such information.

Unit 28

Marketing of Information Services

MARKETING

"Marketing" consists of individual and organisational activities that facilitate and expedite satisfying exchange relationships in a dynamic environment through the creation, servicing, distribution, promotion and pricing of goods, services, and ideas. Marketing is a term which has different meanings for different people. Many a time, people see marketing only as selling, advertising or promotion. However, real marketing does not involve the art of selling what you make, as much as knowing what to make. Marketing is concerned with gaining market leadership, understanding customers and their needs, creating customer values, and satisfying customers.

NEED FOR MARKETING OF INFORMATION SERVICES

Presently, the need for marketing of information services is being felt by all types of libraries. Libraries are facing competition from other information service providers. They need to make daily decisions on the form and formats for acquiring and archiving information. Librarians are striving to provide free access to information. They are struggling with space constraints, shrinking budgets, and rising cost of materials. At the same time, users' expectations are going high with the emergence of online access to information. In response to these factors, management philosophies and administrative operations of libraries have changed. Librarians are embracing marketing techniques to be more efficient managers and effective information service providers.

Thus, libraries are facing the greatest challenge that is as the financial provisions for libraries are being continuously curtailed and they are pressurised to be self-sustained. Librarians are hard pressed to mobilise financial resources. This requires an increased emphasis on marketing.

Library services are valuable services but are undervalued because of the lack of visibility among the users. Marketing efforts can help in improve the image of library and information (LIS) professionals by establishing cordial relations with the users and other patrons.

The reasons for applying marketing techniques in any organisation, particularly in libraries and information centres, is not to achieve profit in financial terms, but to achieve high level of users' satisfaction and to enhance the perceived value of their services and products.

LINKING MARKETING WITH LIBRARY AND INFORMATION SERVICES

At first sight it may appear that 'marketing' and 'libraries' belong to different worlds. Thus, much of the debate surrounds just how marketing fits into library and information services. Many a time, marketing is considered an additional burden by LIS professionals. Many feel that marketing is not a natural activity for LIS professionals. If marketing is not seen as a natural consequence of what librarians do everyday, every time, then marketing is misunderstood and misplaced. Most libraries take decisions about the location of the library, opening hours, planning a new facility or service, offering services according to users/user groups, making free or priced services, etc. From the above discussion it is clear that marketing decisions are taken in libraries in day-to-day functioning.

ANALYSING MARKETING OPPORTUNITIES

Analysing the environment for marketing opportunities is commonly done keeping in view many aspects. The tool often used to gather information about external forces and internal capabilities is SWOT (Strengths, Weaknesses, Opportunities and Threats) analysis, which involves capturing the strength and weaknesses of an organisation or service and the opportunities and threats represented by environment trends.

All organisations, public or private, small or large, profit making or non-profit making, manufacturing or service, exist within an environment that affect the work they do and how they do it. Assessing the organisational environment is necessary to offer customised information services to users. This emphasises the importance of gathering information from a wide range of sources so as to make informed decisions. The past decade has witnessed significant changes and advancements in the various aspects of human life. The directions, restrictions, and constraints that are imposed by the environment in which a library operates are not different from those in other organisations. Even a library operates in a wider context or environment forming a dynamic relationship with other organisations. This phenomenon determines the conditions, which have a direct impact on library management. The overall environment, in which a library works, can be divided into two categories namely external and internal.

External Environment: External pressures on libraries come from the changes taking place outside the library world. It may be seen in context of local, regional, and international impact on libraries and information centres. The different dimensions for example, economic, technological, and socio-political dimensions embody conditions and events that have the potential to influence the organisation in many ways.

Internal Environment: Alongside external dimensions of environmental changes, there are also internal dimensions which library and information managers need to take into account. The internal dimensions include physical resources, systems, and people.

SELECTING TARGET MARKET

Selection of an appropriate market is important for the success of marketing efforts. A market includes all the people who have some stated interest in a particular product or service or who could be expected to have one in the future. The process of market segmentation is fundamental to the whole idea of marketing as it focuses on the user, i.e. a library's present or prospective user, rather than the product, i.e. the library's collection and services. A basic tenet underlying marketing strategy is that there are distinct market segments each with its own needs, wants desires and interests. Market segmentation is the division of market into distinctive groups of buyers who may require different products or marketing mixes. It is the division of market into homogenous groups, which will respond differently to marketing mix variables, i.e. the 4Ps of product, price, promotion, and place.

Developing Marketing Mix

Marketing mix is one of the most important and fundamental developments in the area of marketing. Marketing mix is a set of controllable, tactical marketing tools that the firm (organisation) blends to produce the response it wants in the target market. It consists of everything the firm can do to influence the demand for its product. Marketing mix is commonly referred to as the four Ps of marketing—product, price, place, and promotion. This is a simple, yet effective means of considering the key elements necessary and the emphasis to be placed on each, in order to ensure an effective implementation of marketing strategies.

MARKETING MIX CONCEPT IN LIBRARY AND INFORMATION CENTRES

Libraries take decisions about the location of the library, opening hours, planning new facility or service, offering services according to users/user groups, making free or priced services, etc. These are simple examples but are marketing decisions and may be well covered in the elements of marketing mix if thought from the marketing perspective. Libraries have found various parts of marketing functions so essential that they have used them.

Library and information centres are required to choose appropriate programmes relating to the marketing mix so as to avail opportunities for the optimum use of resources and to increase user satisfaction. The marketing mix in library and information services may be:

Product: All products or services or offers, present and potential, aimed at meeting the needs of the users.

Price: All costs put in by the user to find relevant information or service or product, may be money, time, efforts.

Place: The way in which information product/service is made available to users, on campus or remote location, online or virtual.

Promotion: All methods of communicating with users one-way, two way and both.

People: People who are involved in the delivery of service.

Physical Evidence: The surroundings of the library, within and outside, through which users make use of it.

Process: The interaction of various activities by which services are created, performed, and delivered.

DEVELOPING A USER/CUSTOMER-FOCUSED APPROACH

Every library has its main drive, the principal reason for its existence, from which all aspects of its policy, procedures, and activities are derived, which determines its culture and the attitude of its staff at every level. Many libraries either are collection centred or technology centred and some are organisation centred. Those libraries that will succeed in the future seem likely to be user-driven and with a focus towards user satisfaction. User satisfaction has to be the focus of all thinking and activity for the survival of such a library. Excellent user service is the key to user-driven service strategies. There is a continual discussion on making libraries user-centred and building a successful user-service culture while managing libraries. The satisfaction that a user or customer gets in a library will help in building loyalty that is the key to promoting a library. No one can afford to lose users. Excellent user service is the basis for effective managing library services.

LIS professionals must always remember that:

- Customers/users are the most important people to be served in a library and information centre.
- They are not dependent on the library rather the library depends on them.

- They are not just outsiders but part of the library.
- They are not just statistics, but also are human beings.
- They are the people who come with certain needs and libraries and information centres are there to meet such needs.

IMPLEMENTING MARKETING IN LIBRARIES

Peter F. Drucker rightly said, "sooner or later all thinking and planning has to degenerate into work" and all marketing, thinking and planning accordingly has to be put into work. Effective implementation of marketing largely relies upon the following aspects:

- Developing a marketing culture throughout the library; everyone must realise this and work for the marketing success.
- Promoting service culture.
- Developing growth-oriented, services-oriented staff, as the staff makes marketing success in any service unit.
- Developing a clear statement of the expenditure to achieve the desired level of marketing success.
- Developing and implementing the marketing plan and actions associated with it.
- Asking for feedback, reviews, and insights to help achieve the targets more efficiently.
- Putting marketing efforts consistently over a period of time.
- Monitoring marketing efforts as to know how the outcome of marketing activities has been effective.

EXERCISES: UNIT 25 – UNIT 28

1. What do you mean by "user education"?
2. Write down the objectives and methods of user education in detail.

3. Explain how information technology has impacted user education. Trace the historical developments in user education.
4. How would you evaluate a user education programme?
5. What do you understand by information literacy?
6. Write a note on "information literacy models".
7. Discuss the standards of information literacy.
8. What are the different ways of imparting information literacy?
9. What are the different characteristics of a user?
10. Write a note on "methodologies/techniques for user studies".
11. Discuss the limitations of user study.
12. What is the significance of information use study?
13. What do you understand by information use study? Discuss its various types.
14. Define "marketing".
15. Why do you feel that there is a need to market information services?
16. How would you plan the marketing of library services?
17. What is a "marketing mix"? Explain in detail.
18. What are the different ways of implementing marketing in a library?
19. Highlight some obstacles in marketing your library services.

SAMPLE QUESTION PAPER 1

BLIS/MLIS **1st/2nd Semester**
PAPER: LIBRARY, INFORMATION AND SOCIETY **MAX: 80**
TIME ALLOWED: 02:30 HOURS **MIN: 32**

Attempt all the questions from section A & B and only two questions from section C.

SECTION A (Short Answer Type Questions) (8×3=24 Marks)

1. What do you understand by the term KBE?
2. Define a hybrid library.
3. Define "The Copyright Act, 1957".
4. What do you understand by the term "Right to Information".
5. What is a library network?
6. Write down the full form of INFLIBNET.
7. Name a few professional categories in LIS.
8. What do you mean by CILIP?

SECTION B (Medium Answer Type Questions) (4×8=32 Marks)

1. Explain the role of a research library in a modern ICT based society.
2. Trace the implementation of library legislations in India.
3. Highlight some of the characteristics of a library network.
4. Write down the objectives of IFLA.

SECTION C (Long Answer Type Questions) (2×12=24 Marks)

1. Explain different types of libraries along with their major objectives and functions.
2. Write down some of the common features of library acts/ legislations across Indian states.
3. What do you understand by INDEST? Write down its objectives and features.
4. Discuss in detail ILA. Highlight its objectives and activities.

SAMPLE QUESTION PAPER 2

BLIS/MLIS	**1st/2nd Semester**
PAPER: LIBRARY, INFORMATION AND SOCIETY	**MAX: 80**
TIME ALLOWED: 02:30 HOURS	**MIN: 32**

Attempt all the questions from section A & B and only two questions from section C.

SECTION A (Short Answer Type Questions) (8×3=24 Marks)

1. Define a hybrid library.
2. Define Information Society.
3. What do you mean by library legislation.
4. Highlight three important features of the "The Patents Act, 1970".
5. What do you understand by DELNET.
6. Define cooperative cataloguing.
7. Define professional ethics.
8. What do you understand by IASLIC.

SECTION B (Medium Answer Type Questions) (4×8=32 Marks)

1. What is a National library? Explain its objectives and functions.
2. Differentiate between "The Copyright Act, 1957" and "The Patents Act, 1970".
3. Discuss the major components of a library network.
4. Explain the objectives of IASLIC.

SECTION C (Long Answer Type Questions) (2×12=24 Marks)

1. What are the major implications of the five laws of library science?
2. Highlight the major components of library legislation.
3. Explain in detail the services offered by OCLC and NKRC.
4. Discuss DESIDOC along with its role and objectives.

SAMPLE QUESTION PAPER 3

BLIS/MLIS **1st/2nd Semester**
PAPER: INFORMATION SOURCES AND SERVICES **MAX: 80**
TIME ALLOWED: 02:30 HOURS **MIN: 32**

Attempt all the questions from section A & B and only two questions from section C.

SECTION A (Short Answer Type Questions) (8×3=24 Marks)

1. Define a documentary source.
2. What is a patent?
3. Define a 'human' as a resource.
4. What do you know about informaticians?
5. What are the different types of information needs?
6. How is telecommunication different from communication?
7. How would you evaluate a user education program?
8. What are the different characteristics of a user?

SECTION B (Medium Answer Type Questions) (4×8=32 Marks)

1. What are the features of theses and dissertations?
2. Illustrate how an institution can act as a source of information?
3. Differentiate between reference service and information service?
4. Write a note on methodologies/techniques for user studies.

SECTION C (Long Answer Type Questions) (2×12=24 Marks)

1. Highlight and discuss the different criteria for the evaluation of an information source.
2. Discuss characteristics, scope and functions of media.
3. Discuss SDI model in detail. Highlight and elaborate its components and working.
4. Discuss standards of information literacy.

SAMPLE QUESTION PAPER 4

BLIS/MLIS **1st/2nd Semester**
PAPER: INFORMATION SOURCES AND SERVICES **MAX: 80**
TIME ALLOWED: 02:30 HOURS **MIN: 32**

Attempt all the questions from section A & B and only two questions from section C.

SECTION A (Short Answer Type Questions) (8×3=24 Marks)

1. What is a reference source?
2. Name some important secondary periodicals.
3. Define mass media.
4. What are the main components of mass media?
5. State the advantages of using Internet as a reference tool.
6. Define digest service in a library.
7. Define marketing.
8. How would you plan marketing of library services?

SECTION B (Medium Answer Type Questions) (4×8=32 Marks)

1. Discuss different types of reports.
2. Discuss different institutions acting as information sources.
3. Define literature search. Discuss its role and importance.
4. What do you understand by information use study? Discuss its various types.

SECTION C (Long Answer Type Questions) (2×12=24 Marks)

1. Discuss in detail some important secondary periodicals.
2. What are the characteristics, scope and functions of radio broadcasting?
3. What do you understand by Current Awareness Service? Discuss its various types.
4. What is marketing mix? Explain in detail.

Index